UNFORCED FLOURISHING

Jaan Kaplinski at his retreat, Mutiku, in Estonia 2009.
(Photo: Alar Madisson, Estonian Literary Museum, Tartu)

Unforced Flourishing

Understanding Jaan Kaplinski

THOMAS SALUMETS

McGill-Queen's University Press
Montreal & Kingston • London • Ithaca

ISBN 978-0-7735-4371-3 (cloth)
ISBN 978-0-7735-4372-0 (paper)
ISBN 978-0-7735-9216-2 (ePDF)
ISBN 978-0-7735-9217-9 (ePUB)

Legal deposit second quarter 2014
Bibliothèque nationale du Québec

Printed in Canada on acid-free paper that is 100% ancient forest free (100% post-consumer recycled), processed chlorine free

This book has been published with the help of a grant from the Department of Central, Eastern, and Northern European Studies at the University of British Columbia.

McGill-Queen's University Press acknowledges the support of the Canada Council for the Arts for our publishing program. We also acknowledge the financial support of the Government of Canada through the Canada Book Fund for our publishing activities.

Library and Archives Canada Cataloguing in Publication

Salumets, Thomas, author
Unforced flourishing: understanding Jaan Kaplinski/Thomas Salumets.

Includes bibliographical references and index.
Issued in print and electronic formats.
ISBN 978-0-7735-4371-3 (bound). – ISBN 978-0-7735-4372-0 (pbk.). – ISBN 978-0-7735-9216-2 (ePDF). – ISBN 978-0-7735-9217-9 (ePUB)

1. Kaplinski, Jaan, 1941–. 2. Kaplinski, Jaan, 1941–. – Criticism and interpretation. 3. Poets, Estonian – 20th century – Biography. I. Title.

PH666.21.A6Z85 2014 894'.54512 C2014-901844-4
C2014-901845-2

This book was typeset by Interscript in 10.5/13 Sabon.

For Ellen

Contents

Acknowledgments ix

Preface xiii

Introduction: From Tartu to the Calgary Olympics 3

1 Troubled Sage 15

2 Don't Touch that Rock, Sisyphus 25

3 The Medium Is Not the Message 41

4 Body Signals 67

5 Desire for Dependence 87

6 Beyond Dissidence 101

7 Self-colonization 131

8 The Art of Unforced Flourishing 149

Notes 173

Bibliography 203

Index 233

Acknowledgments

Several friends and colleagues read drafts of the manuscript at various stages of completion, offered invaluable comments, and provided encouragement. Also for translations of texts not available in English I owe thanks to Riina Tamm. Among those who were especially helpful and generous with their time are Alan Matheson, Klaus Petersen, and Marketa Goetz-Stankiewicz. Many others contributed valuable information and shared their knowledge, in particular Arne Merilai and also Sirje Olesk, Trevor Carolan, Mare Lõhmus, Vallo Kepp, Sirje Kiin, Sam Hamill, Gary Snyder, Ilse Lehiste, Ain Kaalep, Küllike Kaplinski, Lauris Kaplinski, Rutt Hinrikus, Lena Karlström, Marju Lauristin, Viivi Luik, Sara Mall-Johani, Külliki Kuusk, Hando Runnel, Fiona Sampson, Anti Talur, Rein Veidemann, Aksel Tamm, Veljo Tormis, Armula and Ants Järv, Vamik Volkan, Andres Ehin, and Raphaël Gianelli-Meriano. For editorial assistance I am grateful to Julija Šukys. Warm thanks also go to Alar Madisson, Pertti Nisonen, and Marko Vainu who provided photographs, and Sara Mall-Johani for sharing her recollections about Jaan Kaplinski and her artwork, a beautiful sculpture inspired by the poet and the man. For institutional support, time, and resources I am indebted to the Social Sciences and Humanities Research Council in Canada, the University of British Columbia, the Literary Museum in Tartu, Estonian Television, the Estonian Film Archive in Tallinn, the University of California, Davis, the Uku Masing Archive in Tartu, and Washington State University. Finally, I would like to thank Jaan Kaplinski and Tiia Toomet who kindly and patiently allowed me to intrude into their lives. Needless to say, this book owes its existence to them. I am grateful for their assistance, trust, and tolerant acceptance of *Unforced Flourishing: Understanding Jaan Kaplinski.* To the anonymous readers who provided constructive criticism and valuable suggestions, and the exceptionally supportive and skillful editors at McGill-Queen's University Press also many thanks.

PERMISSIONS

For their kind permission to reprint previously published texts, including the frontispiece photograph and excerpts from unpublished material, acknowledgment is made to the following individuals and organizations. In the case of an unintentional omission or error, an appropriate acknowledgement can be placed in future editions of this book.

- Jaan Kaplinski. All unpublished and published content by Jaan Kaplinski as it appears in this book, including excerpts from letters, e-mails, diaries, interviews, prose, and poetry, including the poem "I don't take refuge in poetry."
- Tiia Toomet. All unpublished and published content by Tiia Toomet as it appears in this book, including excerpts from correspondence and interviews.
- Bloodaxe Books. Poems from *Evening Brings Everything Back* (Bloodaxe Books, 2004), and *Selected Poems* (Bloodaxe Books, 2011): "I Opened the Russian-Chinese Dictionary," "Ice and Heather," "The Washing Never Gets Done," "Silence. Dust."
- Sam Hamill. Translator (with Jaan Kaplinski and Riina Tamm) of "The Washing Never Gets Done," "Shunryu Suzuki" (with Jaan Kaplinski and Riina Tamm), and "Ashes" (with Jaan Kaplinski).
- Riina Tamm. Translator (with Jaan Kaplinski and Sam Hamill) of "Shunryu Suzuki."
- Fiona Sampson. Translator (with Jaan Kaplinski) of "This Landscape Leaves Me Wordless" ("Ice and Heather"), and "I Opened the Russian-Chinese Dictionary."
- Hildi Hawkins. Translator of "What, After All, Can I Write?" ("Silence. Dust"), and "I Have No Principles."
- Mare Lõhmus. Excerpts from correspondence and unpublished manuscript.
- Trevor Carolan. Excerpt from unpublished manuscript.

- Lena Karlström. Excerpts from unpublished interview.
- Ilse Lehiste. Excerpts from correspondence. Originals in the author's possession.
- Alar Madisson, Estonian Literary Museum (Tartu). Photograph of Jaan Kaplinski (Mutiku in Estonia, 2009), frontispiece.
- Periodical *Keel ja Kirjandus*. An abbreviated version in Estonian translation of chapter five appeared in *Keel ja Kirjandus* 1 (2010): 37–44.

Preface

> "All life is fundamentally one," you should be open to tasting this, before asking immediately, "What does this mean?"[1]
>
> Arne Naess

> It is by remaining open to an infinite number of unexpected possibilities which transcend his own imagination and capacity to plan that man really fulfills his own need for freedom.[2]
>
> Thomas Merton

For almost a half-century now, from the end of the Khrushchev era to post-Soviet independence, Jaan Kaplinski has been a towering figure in Estonia's cultural landscape. School children recite his poems. University students choose him as a subject for their essays and theses. Short-listed for the Nobel Prize in literature, the recipient of many awards and other stellar distinctions, for Estonians he is a living classic. For his peers and readers abroad, he is one of the best. Yet, little is known about the man behind the poetry, his thought-provoking outlook, his emotional life, his aspirations and struggles.

Drawing on published and unpublished sources, this book considers Kaplinski's life and work. It also provides a glimpse of the complex cultural and political context into which he was born. But the primary aim of *Unforced Flourishing* is to pave a path to Kaplinski's inner landscape. Guided by this goal, this monograph seeks to unpack the less visible dimensions of his behaviour and trace some of his most significant relationships, choices, and interests in his personal and public life. What emerges are the contours of a man and a poet who recasts deeply ingrained assumptions about identity, culture, and nature so as to realign human flourishing with the "unforced" – the undifferentiated, intuitive, non-calculative, and naturally unfolding. It is in this light that *Unforced Flourishing* examines constraints as well as opportunities, for Kaplinski and others, as they arise from his contrarian perspective. In doing so, it offers to its readers salient expressions of Kaplinski's way of seeing and fitting into the world: from his sense of "artlessness" as a desired aesthetic effect and, indeed, the foundation of creative advance, to his view of dependence as a sign of social maturity and his critique of dissidence as a meaningful response to totalitarian rule. Together, the eight chapters reveal an engaged yet inherently non-intrusive vision, one that holds the promise of a sustainable way of life and, at the same time, richer self. The less we intervene, without limiting our creative impulse, the Kaplinski evoked in this book concludes, the more we flourish.

UNFORCED FLOURISHING

INTRODUCTION

From Tartu to the Calgary Olympics

I have to build some bulwark for myself that this pain wouldn't crush me; that I'm even able to live. To some extent I have managed to do that.[1]

Jaan Kaplinski

Jaan Kaplinski was born in Tartu, Estonia, on 22 January 1941, in a time that would leave much of his native country in ruins. With roots in Estonia and Poland, his family would not be spared the winds of war that swept through Europe. In an autobiographical note Kaplinski writes about this dark period in their lives: "Young men were arrested and deported from all over my country; families were scattered. Many children became separated from their families at that time, and I was separated from my Polish-born father who died of starvation in a labour camp in Northern Russia."[2]

Jaan's father, Jerzy Bonifacy Edward Kaplinski, hailed from Warsaw. Born in 1901, he enjoyed a sheltered if not privileged childhood, and was destined for a future among Poland's cultural elite. He lived for some time in St. Petersburg and later attended primary school in the Swiss town of Vevey on the shores of Lake Geneva. During World War I the Kaplinskis temporarily relocated to Moscow and then Kiev. After completing high school, in 1920, Jerzy Kaplinski volunteered to fight in the Polish War of Independence. In addition to music at the conservatory in Poland's capital, he studied classical and Slavic languages and linguistics at the universities of Krakow and Warsaw. Two years after he had defended his PhD thesis, in 1933, he accepted an appointment as lecturer for Polish language and literature at the University of Tartu, in Estonia, which he supplemented with teaching assignments at the Military Academy as well as the Technical University in Tallinn. In Tartu, Jerzy quickly established himself in the cultural scene.

In 1937, after a first failed marriage, he met Nora Raudsepp (1906–1982), the daughter of Jaan Raudsepp (1877–1961) and Marie Raudsepp (1881–1971, née Jänes). Her family stood out. A former school teacher, more by accident than by design, Nora's father had become involved in the book trade. Rising in the business world and enjoying financial success, the Raudsepp family soon belonged to Tartu's wealthiest citizens. By the time she completed high school in Tartu, Nora knew she wanted to become a dancer. With financial support from her parents, she studied modern dance in Estonia and at the Folkwang School of Dance in Germany. She chose to continue her training in Paris at the Légate ballet school, where she sometimes gave lessons herself, and performed in Paris before returning to Estonia, in 1932. Not yet an established dancer, but already an artist of some note, she received supportive reviews in Estonia's leading newspaper. Barely in her early thirties, however, she decided against what, until then, had appeared to be her calling, and, in 1938, she married Jerzy Kaplinski. Whatever hopes they may have harboured for their future together, these were quickly dashed and – as Jerzy, unknowingly anticipating their fate, would say in a poem that he wrote for his wife after their return from Poland – reduced to "ashes," like Nora's ideals.[3]

Visiting Warsaw in 1940, the couple were caught in the turmoil of occupied Poland. They decided and indeed managed to secure passage back to Estonia. This was a fateful choice. The invasion of the Baltic States by the Red Army was looming. Only a little later, on 23 June 1941, when their son Jaan was but a few months old and Estonia was under Soviet rule, the NKVD, the Soviet secret police, arrived at the home of the Kaplinskis in Tartu. According to his interrogation record, Jerzy Kaplinski was "suspected of criminal activities" and his arrest a so-called preventive measure.[4] He stood accused of working for the German reconnaissance and for being implicated in anti-Soviet propaganda. Held in prison without a trial, he was soon deported to "Vyatlag," part of the infamous system of Soviet labour camps, near the city of Vyatka in north-eastern Russia. In his book *To Father*, Jaan Kaplinski wrote: "What would I do with the individual who interrogated you … and who had you beaten bloody to extort a confession from you that you were a German spy?"[5]

Within six months of Jerzy Kaplinski's arrest, he was granted amnesty and officially released from prison, but, in a cruel twist of fate, not set free. Indeed, bureaucratic ineptitude probably cost Jerzy Kaplinski his life. Although the details remain uncertain – and we may never really know what happened – in all likelihood, Jaan Kaplinski's father died of ill health, and possibly starvation, at the age of forty-two, while mistakenly and unlawfully imprisoned in Stalin's Gulag.

To make matters worse for the Kaplinski family, their hometown, a city of less than 100,000 inhabitants, sustained huge losses during the war. Between 1941 and 1944 more than two thousand buildings were destroyed in Tartu, and hundreds of its citizens perished at the hands of both invading forces. Many Estonians were imprisoned, deported, or summarily executed. In his book of poems entitled *Evening Brings Everything Back* (2004), Jaan Kaplinski provides a chilling if sober account of the impact the events had on his family:

> The center of Tartu had already suffered greatly in 1941, when all the bridges were blown up and the Soviet troops kept shelling the southern bank of Emajõgi from the northern bank which was still in their hands. A much more serious blow was dealt to the town in 1944 by massive bombardment by the Soviet air force. Then several historic blocks were destroyed, as well as many hotels, cafés, the former Treffner [High School], the 'Vanemuine' theater and, among others, the house where we lived. When we returned to the burned-out town, we found a temporary refuge with friends. Some china cups, plates and other smaller things had remained intact in our cellar.[6]

The life of the Raudsepps and Kaplinskis had been turned upside down. Kaplinski later described the bombardment in a letter dated 2 April 1969, to Ilse Lehiste, a linguist and fellow Estonian living in the United States; he remembers "the air alarms in Tartu ... fleeing from attacking fighter planes, surviving the front ... where one Soviet ammunition transport train exploded, soldiers in uniform, officers, one German ... a Red Army sergeant who shared his and his superior's chocolate with us children, mass military transports, passing time in train stations, bomb shelters, moving from place to place, a burned-out home and what not."[7] The vividness of Kaplinski's memories, here breathlessly recounted, speak to how deeply he was affected by the experience and to how it lingered in his mind.

But his memories are not limited to death and destruction. In his first autobiographical account, Kaplinski's childhood appears to have been, at times, an adventure of sorts. It seems to have been a thrill for him to rummage through the heaps of rubble and damaged buildings in the city center. There, in the ruins of Tartu, he would play hide-and-seek during the years immediately following the end of World War II.[8] Perhaps it is true that later in life he really felt "a bit of nostalgia for those ruins, for the melted ampoules, the microscope lenses and the helmets that one could find there."[9]

On the whole, however, his descriptions of those early years show increasing signs of dejection. Bearing titles such as "Revenge of the Russians," several of his childhood drawings, the earliest probably from November 1945, depict air raids, burning buildings, advancing tanks firing missiles, gunboats, and presumably Soviet and German fighter planes engaged in combat. Dated 1953, one picture he drew features what appear to be prisoners who are being kept or escorted away at gunpoint, a gallows, and even a severed head held high by a soldier. We may not want to read too much into such drawings, but we know with some certainty that, to this day, the wartime memories and the damage inflicted upon his family and country cast a long shadow over him. "My family lost almost everything," Kaplinski writes, and "we lived … in constant fear and distress, loathing the authorities and their behaviour, but also in despair over our inability to do anything. We were prisoners, entirely subject to the power of the authorities."[10] Nora Kaplinski did not "like to talk about the past," Jaan Kaplinski's wife Tiia Toomet noted later, "the trauma she herself and her entire family were forced to endure during and after the war was too painful."[11] Until Stalin's death in 1953, Nora kept a suitcase ready, just in case another deportation order came – this time with her and her son's names on the list.

Although unable to escape a devastating past and easily branded a pariah by the Communist authorities, Jaan Kaplinski successfully completed high school, excelling in most subjects, enrolled at Tartu University where he studied French and linguistics from 1958–1964, and eventually embarked on a career as a freelance writer. Whatever hardships he may have endured, in just a few years he would find himself among Estonia's most prominent authors. Later, he would even rise to more fame: Jaan Kaplinski would become the internationally best-known poet of his native country.

RISING STAR – FROM TARTU TO THE CALGARY OLYMPICS

His stellar ascent did not come as a surprise to his closest friends. They described Jaan Kaplinski as the quintessential if not stereotypical poet: eccentric, intensely sensitive, highly intelligent and knowledgeable, ecstatic but also prone to dark moods, a libertine of sorts with a troubled family background, often in precarious shape financially, drawn to tumultuous relationships, easily at odds with social conventions and society at large, "wise on the page," as someone said, but "unwise in life."[12] "I knew from his first poem" that he was a "good poet," Kaplinski's mentor and teacher Ain Kaalep once remarked, not without pride, in an interview remembering the precocious teenager.[13]

And indeed, already in 1965, when Kaplinski was only twenty-four years old but had been dabbling in poetry writing for about a decade – his first published poem dates back to 1956 – he received considerable attention in major Estonian publications hailing him as one of the new and promising young writers. His debut collection of poetry – *Jäljed allikal* (Tracks at the Wellspring) (1964) – was reviewed, for the most part favourably, in Estonian newspapers such as *Edasi*, *Looming*, and *Sirp ja Vasar*, as well as in the literary periodical *Keel ja Kirjandus*. "Intelligent," "deep," "noteworthy," and "philosophical" were some of the recurring accolades used to describe his early work, and within only a few years he had established a reputation of being among the most promising young Estonian poets in recent memory.[14]

By 1967 he had published two additional volumes of poetry: *Kalad punuvad pesi* (Fish Weave their Nest) (1966), a slender booklet of which only 15 copies were printed, and *Tolmust ja värvidest* (Of Dust and Colors) (1967). The latter has stood the test of time and has remained his most popular book of verse in Estonia. The title poem of this collection has become a classic of twentieth-century Estonian literature, and for it, amidst some controversy, Kaplinski was awarded the prestigious Juhan Liiv poetry prize. According to an article published in a Soviet Estonian newspaper, what made Kaplinski a controversial choice was his relatively young age.[15] He had turned twenty-seven only a few months earlier. Veiled behind this criticism lay political considerations. The unusual complexity of the form of *Tolmust ja värvidest* raised eyebrows, as did its surrealist imagery, its religious allusions, and its use of distant places, people, and events. The latter in particular challenged ideological purists among Communist Party officials. They wanted to see a closer engagement with local Soviet life and an adherence to Socialist Realist doctrine, which defined cultural products as instruments of the Communist Party. For them, among the main purposes of literature was Marxist-Leninist indoctrination, especially of the younger generation. The absence of such top-down political engagement was considered harmful to the Soviet people and did not reflect the interests of the state.

Kaplinski had written under the watchful eyes of the KGB since the late 1950s. The fact that he was the son of a deportee, associated with people considered suspect by officials, was relatively outspoken, had a huge following especially among the younger generation, and had contacts in the West – all this made the choice to award him this prize controversial. At the same time, the Party did not want to drive underground a promising and popular author and young intellectual such as Kaplinski.[16]

As he rose to prominence during Estonia's so-called Golden Sixties, people in the West, at first primarily Estonians in exile in Sweden, Canada, and the United States, also began to take note of Kaplinski. In 1968, Ivar Ivask, the editor of the distinguished American international journal *World Literature Today* (then, *Books Abroad*), wrote: "With his second collection [*Tolmust ja värvidest*], Jaan Kaplinski has clearly established himself as the most original and exciting young poet … writing in Soviet Estonia today. His interesting poetry would no doubt evoke a wide international echo if translated into one of the major Western languages."[17]

With praise from critics and especially his peers spurring him on, several other verse collections soon followed. *Valge joon Võrumaa kohale: 54 luuletust 1967–1968* (A White Line over Võrumaa: 54 poems 1967–1968), whose provisional title had been "Concrete Landscapes," appeared in 1972. In step with his growing interest in classical Chinese and Japanese poetry, he called it his first "Eastern" collection.[18] In its much more compact, indeed, minimalist form, this publication differed markedly from his previous work. Written in a less associative manner, it is decidedly more focused on the simple, concrete, everyday reality of the here and now.

Kaplinski's next major publications fall into his Tallinn period. In 1973, soon after his wife had been accepted into the Institute of Fine Arts in Tallinn, the couple decided to move to Estonia's capital, Tiia Toomet's hometown. Maarja, Kaplinski's physically handicapped daughter from his first marriage, stayed in Tartu with her grandmother. Nora Kaplinski was her granddaughter's primary caregiver until the girl turned fifteen. Both sons, Ott-Siim (born 1970) and Lauris (born 1971), accompanied the couple to Tallinn. There, a frustrated Kaplinski became the self-described "writer-nanny," writing and looking after the children while Tiia Toomet studied at the Art Institute.[19] To supplement their income, he also worked in the Botanical Garden and published essays and other prose, including children's books and two poetry collections: *Ma vaatasin päikese aknasse: Luuletused 1958–72* (I Looked into the Sun's Window: Poetry 1958–72) and, a year later, in 1977, *Uute kivide kasvamine: Luuletused 1956–74* (New Stones Growing: Poetry 1956–74) – a volume inspired by the poetry of Lithuanian writer Jonas Mekas.[20]

By this time, the manuscript of his *Hinge tagasitulek* (Soul's Returning) was also ready for publication. In *Soul's Returning*, according to Kaplinski, several themes come together: among them a shamanistic journey to find a lost soul, a private crisis associated with Kaplinski's move to Tallinn, an affair that almost ended his marriage, the specter of Estonia's colonial history, and the desire to escape into solitude.[21] Composed between 1972 and 1975, it was not published until 1990 because Kaplinski refused to comply with censors' demands to remove religious references.

Kaplinski himself considers *Õhtu toob tagasi kõik* (Evening Brings Everything Back) (1985) to be the pinnacle of his poetic output.[22] A kind of diary in poetic form, it contains translations of poems by Li Bo, Bo Carpelan, and Sappho, as well as texts of ancient Estonian folksongs.[23] With *Evening Brings Everything Back* he continued to write in a more pronounced minimalist and increasingly non-metaphorical style, something that became a characteristic tendency of his later poems as well.[24]

Evening Brings Everything Back was preceded by *Raske on kergeks saada* (It Is Difficult to Become Light) (1982), which he called "very personal," and *Tule tagasi helmemänd* (Come Back Amber-Pine) (1984).[25] From January 1983 to November 1988 Kaplinski worked for Tartu University as the Chair of Foreign

Literature, lecturing on the history of European civilization. In that period he published the 1986 collection of poems entitled *Käoraamat* (The Cuckoo's Book). It provides a selection of poems written over a span of about 25 years, from 1956 to 1980.

Around the same time, in the early 1980s, the years of wider international recognition began for Kaplinski, first in Northern Europe, then North America and elsewhere. In Finland, two translations appeared: in 1982, there was *Olemisen avara hiljaisuus: Esseitä ihmisestä, luonnosta, runoudesta* (Spacious Silence of Being: Essays about Human Beings, Nature, Poetry), a selection of previously unpublished essays; then, in 1984, a book of poetry, *Sama meri kaikissa meissä* (The Same Sea in Us All). It was above all Kaplinski's interest in nature and Chinese and Japanese poetry, as well as his critical attitude toward the established cultural centers of Western Europe, that attracted Finnish writers to his work and paved the way for his popularity in neighbouring Finland.[26] In 1982, Kaplinski wrote to one of his long-time contacts in the United States: "I have somehow spread worldwide – a book is about to appear in Sweden, another in Finland, a third one in Czechoslovakia."[27]

When, on 30 December 1984, Kaplinski received a copy of his first English-language collection of poetry, *The Same Sea in Us All*, he told his co-translator Sam Hamill: "A bit un-American, neat and full of dignity. I mean the visual side of it. Only the big Finnish edition of my poems is a better book. When I finally [held] the book in my hand I felt a deep satisfaction. I was happy."[28] *The Bloomsbury Review* noted of *The Same Sea in Us All,* which includes poems from five different original publications covering the years 1967 to 1982: "Every page contains a surprise, a brilliant view of ordinary life in the world, a world we all share."[29] In *The Small Press,* Doris Grumbach commented: "It is a volume to cherish, to read again and again as the simple yet subtle poems work themselves under your skin."[30]

In 1986, Kaplinski was invited to a poetry evening in Oulu, Finland. For the first time in his life he was allowed to travel beyond the borders of the Soviet Union and the Warsaw Pact countries – previously, in the mid-1970s, he had been only in Poland and Czechoslovakia. Numerous trips followed, mostly to poetry readings; he went, in 1988, to the Hanseatic Days in Cologne, Germany, and then to many other countries he had yearned to see, among them Norway, Sweden, England, Greece, France, and even China.

Under somewhat ironic circumstances, his first trip across the Atlantic also came about in 1988, a year after the first open mass demonstration against Soviet rule in Estonia. The coordinator of the festival for the literary arts of the 1988 Olympic Winter Games in Calgary, Canadian writer Trevor Carolan, was the driving force behind an invitation extended to Jaan Kaplinski. He wanted him to represent the Soviet Union. In some measure, it was a controversial decision. Yevgeny Yevtushenko appeared the more obvious choice, but some of the younger members of the advisory group rallied around Carolan. Not having heard back from Kaplinski, Carolan even sent a letter directly to Gorbachev, the then General Secretary of the Communist Party in the Kremlin. But the Canadian organizers for whom Carolan worked feared that inviting Kaplinski might jeopardize relations with the Soviet Union and wanted to abort the initiative. It was too late. On 19 March 1987, a telegram arrived: "Can come to Calgary Arts Festival – Jaan Kaplinski."

At the Olympics Kaplinski garnered much public acceptance. As Trevor Carolan wrote, "Jaan ... became a festival favourite. People came from as far afield as New York and San Francisco to hear him and meet him ... After spiriting him off to Vancouver in rather unofficial mode, by car, at night, with sympathetic poets and Estonians, he gave a reading at a well-known bohemian jazz club .... The club was packed to overflowing with fans waiting to hear him. By now, of course, his story had been written up in papers coast to coast. The dark streets in Vancouver's Gastown were crowded outside and [loud]speakers had to be hung to broadcast Kaplinski's voice as he read his poetry."[31]

When he returned home, Estonians were discussing the possibility of declaring independence from the Soviet Union, something that became a reality in 1991. Kaplinski was elected a Member of the Estonian Parliament (Riigikogu), and served in this capacity from 1992–1995.

Being short-listed for the Nobel Prize in literature in 1996 – nominated by none other than the Polish laureate Czesław Miłosz – is but one measure of the international renown he achieved. Kaplinski was a guest lecturer at the University of British Columbia in Vancouver when the Nobel foundation invited him to attend the ceremonies in Stockholm. He was among the finalists for the coveted prize, which was awarded to fellow Polish poet and essayist Wisława Szymborska. The year before, he had just published his latest poetry collection

Mitu suve ja kevadet: luulet ja märkmeid (Several Summers and Springs: Poetry and Notes) (1995).

As Kaplinski became ever more established as a writer of international stature, Romanian-born writer and Nobel Peace Prize laureate (1986) Elie Wiesel co-opted him into the prestigious, but now defunct, Academie Universelle des Cultures. Its members – among them Salman Rushdie, Margaret Atwood, Umberto Eco, Julia Kristeva, and Toni Morrison – used to meet at the Musée du Louvre in Paris "to suggest ways," as the Academy's website announced, "of acting against intolerance, xenophobia, racism, anti-Semitism, discrimination against women, and of fighting against poverty, ignorance and the deliberate degradation of certain forms of life." Kaplinski belonged to the illustrious and highly regarded Academy until 1993.

After Estonia regained independence in 1991, journalists from abroad sought out Estonia's "Voltaire," as a French reporter had called him, asking for his opinion on a variety of issues concerning Estonian history, politics, and culture.[32] Over the years, he has received many awards and distinctions, national and international. Among them are the Honorary Award of the Jenny and Antti Wihuri Foundation (Finland 1995) and the Literature Prize of the Baltic Assembly, which was awarded to him in 1997 both for his collection of poems *Several Summers and Springs* and for *Ice and the Titantic* (1995), an essayistic reflection on our hubris and anthropocentric vision of the world. At the 2001 Vilenica Literature Festival in Ljubljana he was awarded the Vilenica International Literary prize; and for his collection of poetry in French translation, entitled *Le désir de la poussière,* he received the Prix Max Jacob in 2003. In the same year he became honorary citizen of his hometown Tartu. In 2004, he was honoured with the Finnish Leijonan ritarikunnan 1. luokan ritarimerkki – the highest order of merit bestowed upon foreigners by Estonia's northern neighbour. In 2012, forty-four years after receiving the Juhan Liiv prize, Estonia's most prestigious award for poetry, he became its recipient for an unprecedented second time.

Although no longer traveling as much as he did in the 1990s, Kaplinski is still a regular participant at high-profile European cultural events and has been invited to many writers' festivals and book fairs in countries such as Germany, Sweden, Great Britain, Finland, the United States, and Canada. He has been a guest lecturer at various universities across the globe – most notably perhaps the University of Tampere, Finland, and the University of British

Columbia in Vancouver, Canada. He has also served as writer-in-residence at institutions like the University of Aberystwyth in Wales. In September 2003, a photo exhibition of portraits of Kaplinski was opened in Helsinki.

Several collections of his work have appeared in English translation – *The Same Sea in Us All* (1985/1990), *The Wandering Border* (1987/1992), *I Am the Spring in Tartu* (1991), *Through the Forest* (1996), and *Evening Brings Everything Back* (2004). His poetry is available in numerous other languages, among them Icelandic, Dutch, Russian, Swedish, Czech, and, more recently, Lithuanian, Japanese, French, Hungarian, and Spanish.

In addition to a number of autobiographical texts, libretti, and anthologies of verse – most recently *Sõnad sõnatusse* (Words for the Wordless) (2005), *Vaikus saab värvideks* (Silence Turns into Colors) (2006), and *Teiselpool järve* (On the Other Side of the Lake) (2008) – he has also published several popular children's books. The first, *Kuhu need värvid jäävad* (Where are the Colors), appeared in 1975. Others include *Kes mida sööb, kes keda sööb* (Who Eats What, Who Eats Whom) (1977), *Udujutt* (Fogstory) (1977), *Jänes* (Hare 1980), *Jalgrataste talveuni* (Hibernation of the Bicycles) (1987), *Kaks päikest* (Two Suns) (2005), *Põhjatuul ja lõunatuul* (The Northwind and the Southwind) (2006), and *Õhtu on õunapuu* (The Evening is an Appletree) (2007).

The *Estonian Literary Magazine* wrote about Kaplinski's collection of poetry published in 2000 and entitled *Kirjutatud. Valitud luuletused* (What is Written: Selected Poems): "Jaan Kaplinski has been shaping Estonian poetry for about forty years. This collection, which appeared shortly before the poet's 60th birthday, contains almost all of his poems ... more than 700 texts."[33]

Kaplinski is also a prolific essayist. The essays published in the 2004 collection *Kõik on ime* (Everything is a Miracle) bear witness to his importance as a prose writer and his broad range of interests. It extends from ancient indigenous habits of thought and action to globalization and ecological concerns, from religious and intellectual traditions to consumerism, and from Eastern modes of perceiving the world to colonialism and the culture out of which he writes. The collection contains forty-five texts covering a period spanning more than thirty years, 1968 to 2002. But *Kõik on ime* comprises only a small part of Kaplinski's work. In addition to numerous translations and many other smaller contributions in the arts and elsewhere,

Kaplinski has penned hundreds of articles for newspapers, mostly Estonian, Finnish, and Swedish, but also on occasion for German and British publications. He has written about topics such as the relationship between politics and mysticism, simplified assessments of Estonia's colonial past as a history of victim and victimizer, globalization as an eliminating and monopolizing process, art as an instrument of ideology, linguistic signs as means of domination, and music as an art form that transcends the limits of language.

To date Kaplinski is the author of more than thirty books, including three autobiographical texts: *Kust tuli öö* (Where the Night Came From) (1990), which focuses on his childhood in postwar Tartu; *Isale* (To Father) (2003), a memoir of his father; and *Seesama jõgi* (The Same River) (2007), a fictionalized account of his relationship with his arguably most influential teacher, Uku Masing. The latter appeared in English translation in 2009. Reflecting his longstanding interest in the sciences, indeed, his "seemingly insatiable intellectual curiosity,"[34] he recently even published an introductory book on the history of astronomy (*Teispool sinist taevast*, On the Other Side of the Blue Sky, 2009).

But his celebrated career as a writer, which now spans nearly half a century, rests above all on his poetry. It seems only fitting, then, that in 2011, the year of his seventieth birthday, a volume of *Selected Poems* would appear (Bloodaxe Books). It includes texts previously not available in English translation and a selection from *The Same Sea in Us All* (1985), *The Wandering Border* (1987), *Through the Forest* (1991), and *Evening Brings Everything Back* (2004).

I

Troubled Sage

Ashes
of one world
crumble
upon the colors
of another one

the sunflower
lost
its crown

hoarfrost
on the scythe
grasshoppers
silent

three sheep
in the fog
the rowan tree
stripped
of leaves
and berries

to write
write
something
something
else[1]

Jaan Kaplinski

I believe that now I am at peace.[2]

Jaan Kaplinski

There is no God, / there is no director, / there is no conductor. / The world makes itself happen, / the play plays itself, / the orchestra plays itself.[3]

Jaan Kaplinski

It is easy, for those attracted to people who exude calm, to identify with Jaan Kaplinski and his poetry – at least on the surface. To the public eye, the Estonian writer's life exhibits hardly any trace of the pain he has suffered. As his success and the tenor of his poems have driven his troubles largely underground, the poet's popular image easily points in the opposite direction, revealing little of his inner tensions and struggles. Rather than being at odds with the world around him, or experiencing turmoil within, he appears at peace with himself, seemingly as calm as a sage.

"What does he look like?" the prominent Finnish-Swedish writer, Bo Carpelan, apparently asked in a 1985 Finnish radio feature about Jaan Kaplinski. The answer: "Like a saint."[4] "He is essentially a poet of epiphanies," wrote Dennis O'Driscoll in the *Times Literary Supplement* of 18 October 1996, "but epiphanies cannot be faked or induced, and his truest poems are those which resist any temptation to do so. At such times, he is the reincarnation of a classical Chinese poet who lives close to nature and writes tranquil poems of crystalline beauty."[5]

In Estonia, Kaplinski's anthologized poems and the commentaries about him and his work that frequently appear in schoolbooks perpetuate this popular image. It has a long history, reaching as far back as the early 1960s and his public performances in the University Café in Tartu – then a trendy gathering spot for Estonian students, writers, and intellectuals – or at the Wednesday-night literary get-togethers where young and upcoming authors would read from their works. Kaplinski's second wife, Tiia Toomet, recalls: "Kaplinski's poems, or at least some of them, had a downright magical effect on me. I hadn't come across poetry before that would have resonated so well with my own elusive feelings and longings for far away times and worlds … I remember his recitative-chanting manner of reading and uncanny somewhat ironic smile."[6] His mentor Ain Kaalep described him in an article published in 1967 by using the word "vates," which means healer or spiritualist.[7] It is this image, and his ambition "to heal the cleft between the self and the world, private and public being," that earned the young Kaplinski "almost rock-star celebrity among his generation."[8]

Ever since the '60s, he has been variously called a meditative intellectual, a mystic, a pagan, a preacher, a prophet, a shaman, a romantic, and a mediator between cultures – to name but a few of the more prevalent labels. When, for example, other Estonian writers turned to irony and satire as a response to Communist repression, Kaplinski's poetry, observed Ivar Ivask, provided a compelling refuge of inner calm.[9] Indeed, his aim was, as Kaplinski himself explained in a lecture given in Tartu in January of 1983, to turn away from pessimism. Many of his fellow writers dwelled on the dark side of life in the Soviet Union, but Kaplinski seemed determined to recover what he called the lost sense of the sacred. It is essential, he insisted, "to believe that something" is "sacred" and "certain." "And if that is not out there then ... it has to be inside of us."[10] Public performances such as this one in Tartu, others on Estonian television, and appearances elsewhere in the world after 1986 – when he was finally permitted to travel abroad – add to the saintly aura. In the *Globe and Mail*, the widely read and respected Canadian daily, Stephen Godfrey called him a "reluctant prophet." He wrote about Kaplinski when the poet was representing the former Soviet Union at the 1988 Olympic Arts Festival in Calgary: "Kaplinski's white hair and pallid complexion make him look older than his 46 years. He speaks soft and precise English, and his manner vacillates from calm and placid to simply world-weary ... He emerges as a man determined to find a peace far removed from political extremes."[11] Kaplinski's first public performance in Toronto prompted a similar response, this time from an Estonian in exile: "I personally went to see and admire him ... He spoke quietly and effectively, looked like an ancient prophet, and indeed is a prophet of peace."[12] A teacher from England wrote in a letter to Kaplinski: "Your poems are like messages from the place where things and people simply are instead of talking about it."[13] The Finnish author and journalist Maarit Niiniluoto has spoken of "Kaplinski's calm European approach" when he steps in front of an audience.[14] Alan Franks of *The Times* likewise noted a "solid, tranquil presence" during his interview with Kaplinski before his poetry reading on 12 April 1990, at the Institute of Contemporary Arts in London.[15] It is the liminal and serene quality of his poetry, the wisdom that speaks from them, their clarity, and the way his poems weave the physical world and his meditative stance into one that many of his readers have come to value in his publications. "I know that what drew me to his work," wrote the American poet Sam Hamill, "was the way he combines subtle social-political observations within the Zen-like personal voice and vision."[16]

The more widely published photographs of him also suggest a strong contemplative, centered presence. The photograph of Kaplinski on the back cover of the 1987 edition of *The Wandering Border*, his second collection of poetry in English translation, illustrates this tendency. Also used for his first English-language poetry collection, *The Same Sea in Us All* (1985), the photograph shows Kaplinski with his hands raised to his chin and folded as if in prayer or deep thought. His eyes appear to be almost closed, his facial expression is serene. The publisher chose this photograph over another one that portrays a more casual, light-hearted Kaplinski. A similar photograph depicting Kaplinski in a meditative pose was taken almost twenty years later by the Finnish photographer Pertti Nisonen and, in 2003, exhibited in Helsinki.

When Kaplinski served as member of the Riigikogu (1992–95), the Estonian parliament, the then secretary of the Free Democrats, Mare Lõhmus, remembers him as someone who always made "a very calm and collected impression in front of his colleagues. He never raised his voice; he could be obviously disgusted with things but never angry ... When you listened to him you got the feeling that he stood slightly [above] the rest of the world. Not because of his ego, but more because he just took the world for what it was."[17]

In the introduction to *The Same Sea in Us All*, the editor writes: "Through his Buddhist training, Kaplinski has moved away from the dualistic vision and into a 'middle way' based upon balance and self-discipline, a practice that permits a freedom concerned not with achieving residence in some distant Paradise, but rather in realization of the Paradise that is within."[18] Similarly, the editor of *World Literature Today*, Ivar Ivask, has observed of Kaplinski's poetry that, standing in "the tradition of Whitman, Claudel and Saint-John Perse," it is "perhaps at its most memorable and effective in such long rolling lines of free verse that express a prophet-shaman's concerns."[19] Elsewhere, too, Ivask detects in Kaplinski's poems "visions of luminous serenity and inner peace."[20]

Does Kaplinski see himself in this way? His shared sensibility with, for example, the American poet, philosopher of ecology, and activist Gary Snyder offers us insight into his self-image during the late '60s and early '70s. For all their differences – one spent much of his life on the West Coast of the United States and in Japan, the other was forced to remain behind the Iron Curtain in Soviet Estonia – they were in many ways remarkably close in terms of what engaged their curiosity and informed their sentiments. This affinity, most visible in their deep relationship with nature, also often shines through in their poetics. It mirrors "the 'ecological consciousness' which the poetry proposes," to borrow a critic's apt assessment of Snyder's work.[21] Unsurprisingly, then, at the very beginning of their correspondence, in 1969, Kaplinski revealed to Snyder: "we have written nearly the same words and created the same utopias."[22] Snyder remembers their "parallel interests" clearly: both were drawn to "Buddhism, nature, shamanism," and "indigenous cultures."[23] In a letter to Snyder dated 27 January 1971, Kaplinski wrote: "I'm one of your little tribe of neo-Shamans," a mediator between present and past, people and the nonhuman world.[24] As late as 1981 his poetry revealed a debt to shamanism and yet he saw himself increasingly pulled away from poetic incantations and, instead, moved "towards the concrete, towards simplicity and inner peace."[25] Snyder, too, tended to "sheer away from abstractions," rhethoric and rhyme, and approach ordinary speech in his poems.[26] Kaplinski called the same sense of "artlessness," which his own later poetry often evokes, "a fairly natural course of events"; it aligned with his lived experience and inner development.[27] As if to suggest that divisions have dissolved and a soothing unity arisen in their place, he writes in one of his poems:

ALL IN ONE
one in all
mind in body
body in mind
the strange in the ordinary
the ordinary in the strange[28]

The Kaplinski System (2012), a documentary film about the Estonian writer produced decades later, in large measure coincides with this image. Predominantly set at his country retreat, it is a poetic, and at times idyllic, portrayal of a man very much at ease with himself and with his social, environmental, and intellectual surroundings – a true image, but only in part.

DEPRESSION AND DESPAIR – SHATTERING THE IMAGE

Below the surface of Kaplinski's serene persona we find a man hovering at the edge of a downward spiral of depression and despair. The discrepancy often frustrates him, and he tries to correct his image, sometimes even with the help of a poem such as the following one from the collection *Evening Brings Everything Back*: "I've been a poet, I know/ more about myself than those people / who understand only my poems of youth / ... / and in whose imagination I was turning / into a Poet, a Jaan-on-a-pedestal. / In reality I've broken all ten commandments, / many written and unwritten laws, / rules of grammar and rules of poetry."[29] We also know from Kaplinski himself that many of his poems, especially the ones in the collection *Raske on kergeks saada*, were "not written by a joyful self."[30]

That he is a much more complex figure than his international public image suggests becomes abundantly clear in his other publications, including his newspaper articles. Since Estonia's regaining its independence in 1991, he has been a frequent contributor and syndicated author, known for his wit, sharp tongue, and often aggressive and occasionally hostile but always outspoken commentary. In Estonia he has also been subject to considerable criticism, most notably after 1981, when, due in part to the pressure exerted by the KGB and in part to complex personal reasons and convictions, Kaplinski publicly responded to an open letter he had initiated and signed together with other prominent Estonians – the so-called Letter of 40. His reputation never fully recovered from what appeared to be a "recantation." More recently, he has alienated many Estonians with his refusal to write in Estonian. This decision represents a protest against what, in Kaplinski's view, is a misguided zeal to regulate the Estonian language rather than allow it to evolve on its own.

His autobiographical confessional self-examination *To Father* (2003), in particular, goes a long way towards dislodging the Zen-like image his poetry suggests and that his persona as a poet projects. In addition to his novel *The Same River* (2009), which is set in the Soviet Estonia of the early 1960s, *To Father* provides the most comprehensive, honest, and public account of his life to date – with many of his regrets, unfulfilled dreams, embarrassments, humiliations, and disappointments laid bare for the reader. He presents his sorrows and most private thoughts, yet, surprisingly, appears calm. In 2002 and 2003, as he takes stock of his life when writing *To Father* at his country retreat near his hometown Tartu, Kaplinski seems content. He not only publicly acknowledges his life as it is; rather (in words borrowed from the poem "Sisyphus" by Sam Hamill – one of Kaplinski's North American editors and publishers), it is as if Kaplinski has finally arrived at a point of "real comfort / in saying, So this is / what I've become, this is / the man I am."

While working on *To Father*, he discovered solace in soul mates, including to some extent his father, Jerzy Kaplinski. With the support of people close to him, and through his own writing, he was able to come to terms with himself, and appeared firmly convinced that he had indeed succeeded.[31] "I believe," concluded the then sixty-two-year-old Jaan Kaplinski on the last page of *To Father*, "that now I am at peace."[32]

Less than a year after the publication of *To Father*, however, Kaplinski attempted suicide, and not for the first time. Perhaps the following passage from an e-mail conveys at least a measure and an inkling of his despair. In this intensely private correspondence, originally written in Estonian, Kaplinski recalled two events, far apart in time but intimately connected in content: one takes place around Christmas 2004 and the other four decades earlier, in 1962 – when he was a student at Estonia's Tartu University, 21 years old and renting a room in Elva, a small town nearby. The e-mail begins with a short description of Kaplinski's situation at the time of writing the letter, 1 June 2005:

> Thanks to the new prescription I am slowly recovering and I am not especially thinking about suicide any longer. But I am clearly prone to it ... I suffer from a bipolar (manic-depressive) impairment, euphoria coupled with inspiration alternates with deep depression, which under the influence of some external factors may become dangerous, even destructive. This is also when suicidal thoughts come, which around this past New Year were changing to an obsession and also already to a compulsion so that I felt that I couldn't handle things any longer and I sought professional help. I have attempted suicide twice in my life. One time was in Elva during my student years when

> I tried to cut my wrists, fortunately very clumsily and incompetently. The second time was now, around Christmas, when I tried to kill myself.[33]

The sentiment of contentment that he expressed in *To Father* clearly owed more to wishful thinking and an emotional surge than reality. The truth, we now know, was rather different.

"The brightness in him is too bright," his wife Tiia Toomet has explained, "and the darkness too dark, the clash does not let him live in peace."[34] She has understood him better than anyone else: that he is a man who craves the kind of human closeness few, if any, can provide; that, although a writer himself, he is drawn towards wordless communication in a world of words, signs, and symbols; that he yearns for the sacred in secular times; that, unlike most, he detects more richness in nature than in human imagination; that he is attracted to his homeland's more "exotic" side – its "mystical connections with Asia, Siberia, forests, swamps and shamans" – at a time when it is more firmly aligned than ever with values and modes of thought vastly different from his.[35]

Unsurprisingly, then, in the cultural, political, and social context to which he belongs, Kaplinski has often felt "like a monk whose monastery and even religion are located somewhere else."[36] The alienation has sometimes left him vulnerable, and an inner volatility has taken hold of him. "Ecstasies" alternated with "depressions," as he revealed to an acquaintance in 1982.[37] Two decades later, he still suffered from such inner tensions. As it turned out, they probably were also symptoms of a more serious problem that had plagued him throughout much of his adult life: "I now have read a bit about depression and bipolar disorder ... OCD, and have come to realize that I have suffered from such disorders since my twenties."[38] "My downs have been quite terrible," he wrote to a friend in 2005. "Sometimes even the antidepressants seem not to help. But I hope to find some stability."[39] Since 2006 he has been receiving cognitive psychotherapy and remained on medication for depression. Appearing tired of writing, although not necessarily less capable of it, he has developed a keen interest in astronomy and photography. Thoughts of suicide occasionally resurface, however – perhaps merely cries for help triggered by unhappy love affairs, but signs of deep despair nonetheless.[40]

Behind his serene poetry, the conciliatory tone of *To Father*, his sage-like demeanour, and his apparent sense of inner balance, then, emerges a conflicted man, impulsive, easily agitated, prone to dark moods, and at times lingering on the edge of self-destruction. Very much like the young poet in Kaplinski's semi-autobiographical novel *The Same River*, he too finds himself caught in a "seesaw between ecstasy and depression."[41]

THE HEART OF THE MATTER – LOGIC WITHOUT HINGE

A prolific writer, Jaan Kaplinski has published widely and to considerable acclaim, but what really lies at the heart of his troubles and guides him in his thought appears destined to remain elusive or misunderstood. The terrain he covers is too vast, multifaceted, and disparate, it seems, to reveal its particular shape. Conflicting affinities, a traumatic past, and heightened private intensities, together with the unsedimented quality of his thought and fragile emotional state, add to the mystery of Estonia's controversial poet laureate, essayist, and philosopher. It is as if Jaan Kaplinski defies understanding.

For many who share this sentiment, including those who know him well, he embodies the eternal intellectual nomad, a restless, conflicted soul, always on his way, searching. Although they greatly admire his independent thought and achievements, in their eyes he has remained a "stranger," both to himself and others.[42] Indeed, what at times rings through in their voices is an unspoken though deep sense of unease.[43]

But this perceived lack, to which Kaplinski's unsettled and unsettling mentality easily gives rise, is not necessarily a weakness at all. Indeed, in complicated ways the source of his troubles is also his signature strength. What forms its core and makes his innovative impulse difficult to detect comes to light when we consider the matter more fully, and by examining unpublished sources, such as his diaries, correspondence, interviews, other archival materials, and statements by those close to him. These allow us to probe deeper and, when read together with his publications, see with increasing clarity what previously stayed in the shadows. We discover a profound coherence at work – but, reaching beyond standard views, one without a hinge on which everything might turn. "Unforced flourishing," a term that serves as the title for this book, is meant to convey both the contrarian perspective and the sense of awareness that anchor Kaplinski's experience and guide him in the philosophical dimensions of his thought.

Once we have designated the principal conceptual framework for this study, we find that "unforced flourishing" unites the two sides of a timeless pursuit: gaining an answer to human fulfillment and transforming it into lived experience. But, as it is conceived in this book, "unforced flourishing" also constitutes a challenge to firmly entrenched and reified core conceptions. Among these, perhaps the most prominent presumption holds that human fulfillment depends predominantly on assertive, goal-bound initiative. Built on a distinctly different foundation, "unforced flourishing" calls for diminished intervention in favour of an engaged responsiveness without agenda.[44] This shift in perspective means more fully embracing the fact that we are inherently "wild"[45] and, as such, not at odds with ourselves and the larger "self-managing and self-organizing" world to which we belong.[46]

The aim of the following chapters is to provide a glimpse into this world as it illuminates Jaan Kaplinski's inner landscape. Offering a unifying view, unburdened by a preconceived "centre" that imposes order, unforced flourishing promises to unite even the most incongruous and controversial elements that operate in Kaplinski's mentality and behaviour: from his passionate but unrequited way of loving (chapter 4) to his understanding of dependence as a sign of social maturity (chapter 5); from his rejection of dissent as a meaningful response to totalitarian rule (chapter 6) to his thinking about cultural shaping as a colonizing and self-colonizing practice (chapters 3 and 7); and, finally, to his sense of "artlessness" as a desired aesthetic effect and, indeed, the foundation of creative advance (chapter 8). At its very richest, and least contentious, however, it is Kaplinski's deep and unqualified identification with the nonhuman world that invokes and engages with "unforced flourishing" (chapter 2).

2

Don't Touch that Rock, Sisyphus

I have no principles.
In my depths are no thoughts.
In the depths is clear water that flows
in the dimness over stones, a few shells or caddis fly,
minnows
and roach,
water-moss and speedwells
that tremble in the current
like the strings of an instrument, only unheard.
At the bottom of the stream are no thoughts,
only flowing, only the current's
categorical imperative
which bends and bows with it
the mosses and speedwells, the fish and caddis flies,
teaching some to cling to the stones on the bottom,
others to the flowing water itself,
which is called swimming.[1]

Jaan Kaplinski

Estonian people banished their souls banished them and let pastors and priests exorcise them cut down the sacred trees and broke the stones with fire in order to get a strip of land to cultivate what else could he do the poor boor who hoped that now finally he could buy freedom that he could buy himself free with money with hard work with business with cheating with writing with singing with making music with staging plays ...[2]

Jaan Kaplinski

Seen through Kaplinski's eyes, the Estonian verb "looma" represents the essence of unforced flourishing. Etymologically linked to the word for "nature" ("loodus") and "animal" ("loom"), it means both to "bring" and to "come" about.[3] It is a fusion of intention with chance, one might say, reminiscent of a sentiment Kaplinski in part shares with other intellectuals and artists, some in many ways very different from him, famously among them contemporary German painter Gerhard Richter. In Richter's pictorial aesthetics and artistic practice, it has been said, the act of painting is "simultaneously in the hands of the painter and out of the painter's control";[4] "chance encounters of materials and structures" merge with a "subject's residual intentionality."[5] The artwork thus takes shape in a process of purposefully responding to what lies "outside of any preordained formal, social, political, or aesthetic order."[6] In this sense, the unrehearsed resembles the unforced and holds a central place for Richter, as it does for Kaplinski.

Put differently, unforced flourishing conceives of two otherwise separate and contradictory processes as one: it conveys engagement and attentiveness, but our involvement is directed towards bringing to fruition what happens of its own accord. Expressing a complex matter all too simply, one might say that Kaplinski's intention is to "invent nothing" and thus "receive everything," to borrow Gerhard Richter's words about his kindred existential perspective and sense of diminished authorship which informs his unique approach to abstract painting.[7]

One essential underlying assumption implicit in this inverted point of view, it bears repeating, is that we are born altruists at home in a self-organizing world rather than egoists fundamentally at loggerheads with nature and others.[8] Vital to Kaplinski's thought and intuition, this assumption betrays a propensity for the "undifferentiated," the trusting awareness that more exists than is "signified within human culture."[9] Together with Norwegian philosopher and ecologist Arne Naess, Kaplinski knows that we do "construct concepts of things," and that "every conception of nature" is indeed "made within society"; but for Kaplinski and Naess there is no sensible "way from this to declaring nature to be socially created."[10]

Kaplinski's embrace of a world extending beyond human design also recalls his affinity to Swedish poet Tomas Tranströmer, whose poetry he has translated and whom he championed for the coveted Neustadt International Prize for Literature. Among the "recurrent themes in his poetry," Kaplinski detected "the presence of something strange, great, and mysterious." He cited Tranströmer's poem "Carillon" as an example of this "religious attitude toward the world" and "feeling of awe and wonder" that he shares with him and that his own poetry and way of life mirrors: "I lie on the bed with my arms outstretched. / I am an anchor that has dug itself down and holds steady / the huge shadow floating up there, / the great unknown which I am a part of and which is certainly more important than me."[11]

Rather than disregarding what lies outside the reach of language – indeed, beyond all of our constructs and goals – the undifferentiated, then, emerges as a primary guiding value for Kaplinski. Everything is embedded within it, the human and nonhuman. This gives rise to intriguing questions: What happens to someone compelled to transform this seemingly diminished sense of themselves and increased confidence in a self-organizing world into a way of life? What kind of traces would it leave in one's behaviour and significant relationships? How would it influence choices and shape interests, personal and public?

Nowhere are the effects of Kaplinski's inherently non-intrusive but attentive and receptive vision more visible than in his relationship with nature. Surpassing the limitations of human imagination, one might say that the nonhuman world embodies unforced flourishing – not in words, images, or symbols but as lived experience. For Kaplinski, then, human fulfillment is not merely a matter of social well-being, essential though it is. He claims equal if not higher status for the nonhuman world: in his eyes, balanced individuals are mindful of both community and nature. But, perhaps even more importantly, they also accept "nature's influence" upon them, as he noted in a letter addressed to the psychological anthropologist Francis L.K. Hsu.[12] In fact, it is this receptive sentiment towards nature that has carried Kaplinski along throughout much of his life and excited his imagination like little else.[13] Arne Naess has said about nature that it is "overwhelmingly rich and good and does not impose anything upon us," something that is also true for Kaplinski.[14]

As we shall see, woven into the fabric of Kaplinski's sense of nature is not only a sedimented and uncommonly strong intuitive attachment to the nonhuman world, but also an ethos of equality that easily accords as much respect to nature as it does to people, and, ultimately, a spiritual dimension without which he can't imagine human life as meaningful. "Biophilia," "biocentric equality," and the sanctity of nature: together these concepts form a pattern that promises human fulfillment and guides much of Kaplinski's work, his thinking, as well as his behaviour. It is this convergence that integrates well with unforced flourishing: the diminishing of agenda-bound human intervention in favour of an attentive responsiveness towards the nonhuman world and what occurs naturally. In Kaplinski's own words, rather than giving prominence to a fixed, preconceived design and segregation, which human shaping necessarily entails, he invites us to remain open to a world unburdened of differences between human beings, gods, and animals, a world where "one creature could be all three all at once."[15]

BIOPHILIA – HALLMARK OF KAPLINSKI'S POETRY

Kaplinski grew up in a small town but in many ways personifies the consummate cosmopolitan, well-traveled, at home in many languages and cultures across the globe, attracted to the multicultural and intellectual spirit of metropolitan centers, such as New York, in particular, but also Vancouver, London, Paris, Stockholm, and, more recently, Berlin and Moscow.[16] However, those close to him know that for Kaplinski the urban environment is no match for the solitude and ecological wealth that rural Estonia offers. Although he "would like to dwell for a couple of months a year in a real city," his love for nature appears to be so deeply ingrained into his personality that everything else – urban, social, cultural – almost always pales in comparison.[17]

Kaplinski's intimacy with nature, and the contentment this relationship brings into his life, reflects what the evolutionary biologist Edward Wilson has called "biophilia" – a profound, possibly innate, often largely subconscious, and also easily undervalued affective bond with all living things. Our "existence depends on this propensity," Wilson wrote in 1984, "our spirit is woven from it, hope rises on its currents."[18] Observed from this point of view, one might say that biophilia is the hallmark of Kaplinski's poetry and one of the principal themes uniting the body of poetry he has published over the past fifty years. The range of perspectives to which his poems grant access extends from issues regarding conservation – in his first poetry collection, which appeared in 1965, he asked: "Is every book worth the forest, that died as paper, / without coming to life in printed words?" – to expressions of identity with the nonhuman world.[19] In *Evening Brings Everything Back*, for instance, originally published in 1985, he wrote:

> In fact trees and shrubs are part of us, they are simply at a greater distance from our body than hands or feet, so it is possible to think that they don't feel pain, that chopping away our branches and trunks doesn't cause us serious injury. But we cannot live without trees. The fewer trees there are, the less we live. In reality we are chopping up and cutting down parts from our own body, we are burning and poisoning ourselves. Instead of the forest new human beings can be born, but they are disabled people, people without branches, without roots, without trees, without Amazonia, without Borneo, without Ruwenzori.[20]

With similar directness, "Peace conquers everything," a poem from 1991, connects poetry to the human and the nonhuman world. It ends with these lines: "Poetry is an extension of the heart, / an extension of its beating / into trees, bushes, / apple blossom, scarlet grosbeaks, / spider's thread, clotheslines."[21]

It is hardly surprising, then, that early on critics took note of Kaplinski's capacity to teach readers of his poetry to "see nature again"[22] and regard human–nature relations as a measure of maturity.[23] His poetry even drew the attention of a member of the Committee for Nature Conservation of the Estonian Academy of Sciences who, in 1968, identified preservation and protection of "all manifestations of life" as the dominant theme of Kaplinski's poetry.[24] A few years later Kaplinski was called a "poet of ecology" who writes in "defence of life and its ecosystems" and against a "levelling civilization."[25] Ain Kaalep, the prominent Estonian intellectual (and a mentor to Kaplinski), once observed of Kaplinski's poetry that it encourages us to view ourselves as a part of the biosphere,[26] and, moreover, that perceiving the human and nonhuman world as one constituted the core of his poetry in the 1970s.[27] Kaplinski's poetry of the early 1980s conveys essentially the same message. In Kaplinski's lyric work, some see nature depicted as a pathway to our inner well-being.[28] Poet and prominent academic Jüri Talvet, for instance, detects in Kaplinski's poetry a "biocentric individualism" and a critique of "anthropocentric alienation from nature."[29] Informed by an ethics anchored in the nonhuman world,[30] from the "very beginning Kaplinski's poetry has been characterized by his devotion to … ecological motifs," wrote a reviewer of the 1,000-page collection of poems that appeared shortly before the poet's 60th birthday.[31] The book bears witness to a sense of "oneness with nature," which has "deepened over the years," wrote a Finnish writer and translator who also knows Kaplinski's work well.[32] Although it cannot and does not pretend to be "the thing itself," the "natural environment is not background, stage setting, or capework" in his poetry.[33] It is often the focal point:

Thaw weather. Silence.
Fog turning into drizzle
making your glasses hazy. Trees
little by little getting rid of their burden of snow.
Rocks at the roadside breathing out
the cold of past days.
Rocks white with frost.
Some cars far off on the other side of the hill
close to the other lake.
Some chickadees in the treetops
above us above the silence.[34]

MUTIKU – KAPLINSKI'S WALDEN

As did his teacher Uku Masing and his spiritual ally Albert Schweitzer, Kaplinski knows nature not only through the lens of images and words.[35] With an unusual unadorned directness, matched in the West perhaps only in the poetry of Tomas Tranströmer and Gary Snyder, nature constitutes the centre of attention in many of his poems. He also lives in nature. What Walden was for Thoreau and Tvergastein for Arne Naess, Mutiku is for Kaplinski: a place in nature evoking a rich and intimate sense of belonging.

Approximately thirty kilometers from his hometown, tucked away in the countryside is Mutiku, or Vana-Mutiku, as the former manor is called today. A little-used narrow dirt road meanders through meadows, past small farmsteads, and eventually leads down a gently sloped hill right to Kaplinski's house and property in the country. It is a quiet place dotted with a few timber-framed buildings, ponds, a vegetable garden, berry patches, and apple trees, all surrounded by a multitude of various deciduous trees and brushwood extending towards a birch and alder grove, acres of coniferous forest, and, in the distance, a bog. Along a partially overgrown pathway stretches a meadow, home to a variety of wildflowers, nettles, and ferns. This is Mutiku. The name "Mutiku" means gnat or mosquito in Estonian, but for Kaplinski it means home.[36]

Before Kaplinski's children reached school age, they spent all of their summers at Mutiku. Most of the time they would arrive in late April and stay until well into fall. Frequently, Jaan would visit there during winter as well and "enjoy the solitude."[37] On 29 December 1995, he noted in his diary: "Am by myself in the sauna at Mutiku. Heated both the sauna and the house: outside it is bitterly cold, -16 ... In the sauna the temperature is already above 0. Read some ancient Chinese poetry." Mutiku is also where the extended family would gather. In the 1970s, Kaplinski's mother and Tiia Toomet's parents would join them there, as would friends and, later, their grandchildren and their own children's partners and spouses. While the Kaplinskis changed apartments more than a half-dozen times in the city, they would always return to their country home, during the summer months, for school breaks, and for special occasions and celebrations, including Christmas and New Year's Eve.

In 1970, shortly after their first son was born, Jaan Kaplinski and his wife, Tiia Toomet, purchased Mutiku, or "old Mutiku farm," as it was officially known. For several years, Kaplinski had looked for a suitable place in the country, ideally near a lake and forest, with clean water and away from any industrial sites, somewhere in Estonia's south-east. Shabby, bare, and neglected, the property needed a lot of work. All of the dwellings were in ill-repair, the foundation, floors, and much else sadly neglected. But this paled in comparison to what Kaplinski felt he had gained in return: Mutiku was his escape from the crowded city apartment and, in some ways, represented a return to the life he had lost to the ravages of war. Although he was a toddler in 1943, he nonetheless remembers his grandfather's bee hives and big garden surrounded by a fir grove on the outskirts of Tartu, which was still countryside in those days. "Thinking back, I realize that I have always longed to return there," Kaplinski wrote in 1973.[38] It was his "paradise" – until the family property was seized by the occupying German army, and the family was relocated from the country to downtown Tartu.[39]

Another important role in Kaplinski's awakening interest in nature was played by an old farmstead in southern Estonia near the village of Pindi in Võru county. From the late '40s on, for about ten years, Kaplinski would spend his summers at Tammiku, as the place was called.[40] It was the home of his grandmother's elder sister and her husband, both of whom were schoolteachers. There Kaplinski discovered all kinds of books, periodicals, and magazines. The "library" included an eclectic variety of fiction, as well as publications on farming, health, and religion. Copies of prewar Estonian literary periodicals, such as the highly regarded *Looming*, were also part of the collection. It was, as Kaplinski wrote, "his window into the world."[41] Although he also enjoyed exploring the surrounding fields, river, lake, and forests, he spent much of his time in the attic reading. Growing up on a heap of books, as it were, this is how he first learned about prewar Estonian, English, and French literature, in addition to life on a farm in the countryside. Recalling the summers at Tammiku, Kaplinski emphasizes the freedom he enjoyed there to follow his inclinations and roam around barefoot. Although his "first summers at Tammiku coincided with perhaps the darkest period in Estonian history,"[42] the Stalinist purges and deportations, to him it was a home away from home, in many ways carefree – and in the midst of nature.[43]

By the time he had acquired Mutiku, he had also gained a deep familiarity with nature. But attending to his retreat he understood with increasing clarity "that our life is nothing other than … repairing and mending: an attempt to keep in order an aging body, declining memory, clothes wearing out and a home going to ruin," as he would write looking back at nineteen years of living in the countryside.[44] Especially at the beginning, the Kaplinskis spent much of their time with emergency repairs and making the place liveable, building a new well, replacing the stove, and demolishing what could not be restored.

Even in the early years at Mutiku, though, Jaan was preoccupied with the surrounding landscape. "At last he had a place," his wife wrote recalling their first years at Mutiku, "where he could apply his botanical interest."[45] Although the previous owner of Mutiku, a farmer, had kept some apple trees and berry bushes and even a few willows in the marshland further away, on the whole, the main area in the immediate vicinity of the buildings was rather barren, mostly fields and pasture with hardly any trees or other greenery, except for some lilacs and ash trees. It was intensively cultivated farmland and, as was typical of rural land-use at the time, much of its biodiversity had been lost. Kaplinski was determined to change that. In fact, he was soon able to write to one of his like-minded friends to say that he was growing some of his food himself at Mutiku – peas, lettuce, potatoes – and hoped "to plant some dozen new apple trees and buy some bee hives."[46] In years to come, he would do much more than that. He would add cherry trees, raspberry and currant bushes, and fill "every single ever so slightly bare spot with tiny tree and bush seedlings."[47] Kaplinski did not exaggerate when he told a French filmmaker that he himself had planted almost everything that grew at Mutiku.[48] The region's fertile soil helped turn into success his efforts to regenerate the vegetation and reintegrate biodiversity. He even wrote about it in his poetry. In "Ice and Heather," an autobiographical prose-poem first published in 1989, we read: "The fastest-growing are the larches ... and the birches, oaks and pines are also tall enough for the children to climb. I've planted some exotic trees too. A few have grown well, for example the Lodgepole Pine, *Pinus contorta*, that comes from North America."[49]

But, more remarkably, as Tiia Toomet observed, he treated his refuge "almost as if it were a living being for whom he is responsible and who needs constant care."[50] In his autobiographical book about his father, Kaplinski called Mutiku a "small nature reserve" and himself a caretaker of the habitat he had recreated[51] "where every tree has a character of its own, where there are so many other plants ... so much bug life and birdlife ... nature in its real complexity."[52] Expressive of a sense of "civilization that wildness can endure,"[53] he considered Mutiku the result of teamwork – between himself and nature, symbiotic rather than parasitic.[54]

Raphaël Gianelli-Meriano's documentary about Jaan Kaplinski, "The Kaplinski System" (2012), visually captures the importance that nature and his country retreat hold for him. Shot almost entirely at Mutiku, the images evoke a deep sense of comfort, calm, and belonging. We see Kaplinski walking in the forest, chopping firewood, making hay, and swimming in his pond behind the sauna. At Mutiku, he wrote to Ilse Lehiste in 1976, he felt "more like a human being,"[55] a sentiment that would grow only stronger over the years.[56]

NATURE UNDER SIEGE – HOW TO RESTORE LOST BALANCE?

Even as a young man Kaplinski knew that this "refuge of the spirit," as Edward Wilson referred to nature, "richer even than human imagination," was at risk.[57] Sounding the now perhaps all-too-familiar but no less urgent alarm, Wilson wrote that if it is reversible at all, the damage inflicted upon the natural world would take "millions of years to correct ... the loss of genetic and species diversity by the destruction of natural habitats."[58] Kaplinski was deeply attuned to this sentiment, lamenting in an article first published in 1997 that we often "don't find closeness anymore with tree and forest, stone and river."[59] Although "the memory of this closeness and the desire for it" is still "very powerfully alive in us,"[60] in his view the world is dominated by replicas, representations, and largely guided not by nature but a "consumerist fundamentalism."[61] Worse still, it is as if nature itself has become a product. Obviously, "we can buy new clothes, a new car, plant a new garden," but "nature can't be exchanged for a new one, nature can't be thrown away," he cautioned.[62]

As the ecological crisis threatens to grow into an ecological catastrophe, we need to practice "smart poverty,"[63] to learn to "want less" and think rather than create, Kaplinski argued.[64] The sooner we understand that the "smart take little,"[65] and we turn our back to a "civilization of wealth," the less impoverished we will be, he noted in 2001, thus underscoring what he had argued already in the 1970s.[66] As a matter of fact, Kaplinski wrote, we have achieved such "unprecedented command" over nature that we are less and less subject to its "regulating rules."[67] This weakens the integrity of the larger planetary ecosystem, and, unless we are able to reverse this downward spiral, we might throw "the entire world off balance."[68] The most unsettling problem, then, is that we can no longer rely on nature to act as a counterbalance. Therefore, it is now up to us to restore the lost equilibrium between people and nature.[69]

ETHOS OF BIOCENTRIC EQUALITY

In response to a world where "human considerations" have to such unprecedented extent "come into conflict with ecological considerations," and in an effort to draw attention to the ecosystem as a whole, Kaplinski has also published a number of texts, mostly essays and some autobiographical prose-poems, that explicitly address his ecological concerns and explore salient dimensions he sees at work in the environmental crisis.[70]

Largely in line with the major trends of the environmental movement, from Rachel Carson's seminal publication *Silent Spring* (1962) to perspectives articulated by Deep Ecologists and political organizations such as the Green Party, his writings consider issues ranging from indigenous practices to "speciesism" to the prefiguration of "green" thought in Buddhism to the effects of globalization on our views about nature and the nature-culture divide. Among his most important contributions are the following: "Eelarvamused ja eetika. Utooplisi mõtisklusi" (Preconceived Notions and Ethics. Utopian Reflections) (1968), "Kirves ja puu" (Hatchet and Tree) (1972), "Ökoloogia ja ökonoomika" (Ecology and Economics) (1972), "Mõtisklusi inimkultuurist ja ökosüsteemidest" (Reflections on Human Culture and Eco-Systems) (1973), "Putukad ja inimised" (Bugs and People) (1976), "Aukartus elu ees" (Reverence for Life) (1984), "Jää ja kanarbik" (Ice and Heather) (1989); "Läbi metsa" (Through the Forest) (1991), "Alistumise ja leppimise aeg" (A Time of Surrender and Reconciliation) (1998), "Roheline Buddha" (The Green Buddha) (1998), "Globaliseerumine: looduse heaks või looduse kahjuks?" (Globalization: For or Against Nature?) (2001), and "Ornitofilosoofia: Ronk Nestori märkmeid" (Ornithophilosophy: Ronk Nestor's Notes) (2004).

What, in sum, emerges most forcefully from his essays is this: in contrast to much of contemporary culture, indigenous peoples did not have a fetish for the new and did not view progress as a guiding principle. Instead, their cultures included taboos and rituals which served as ecological controls. Guided by a sense of the sacred, these safeguards remained in place, even at times of extreme need. In Kaplinski's account, this secured a sustainable way of life. Environmental decline set in, Kaplinski has argued in his essays, when, in the course of human history, material affluence became a primary value and the sense of the sacred shifted from nature and religion to human beings. Seeing themselves as the creators and sole centre of ethical considerations, humans turned producing and consuming into the "true religion and rituals of our time."[71]

What then, Kaplinski asks, if not consumerism, can give meaning to our lives, satisfy our curiosity, our thirst for knowledge and variety? In nature he detected not only a seemingly inexhaustible source of wealth to meet such fundamental needs but also the key to a healthy sense of self. The more we identify with nature, he appeared convinced, the more we grow as individuals.

Rising to the challenges posed by the environmental crisis also entails a transformation of fundamental values that Kaplinski found articulated in Albert Schweitzer's 1936 essay "The Ethics of

Reverence for Life." Bridging the divide between people and other forms of life, it described a path leading away from "speciesism" and "anthropocentrism." First available in Estonian translation in 1972 (*Loomingu Raamatukogu* 46), Schweitzer's essay was well known in Estonia already in the 1960s. Indeed, it was Jaan Kaplinski's mentor, Ain Kaalep, who had published an article on Schweitzer's essay in 1965 (*Edasi* 19). Other publications on Schweitzer followed in widely read journals, such as *Eesti Loodus* (1966) and *Looming* (1970). Kaplinski recognized himself in Schweitzer's desire to care humbly for all living beings and in the awe they inspired in him. Heightened responsiveness to the nonhuman world, and indeed a spiritual affiliation, is also what the title of Schweitzer's essay "Ehrfurcht vor dem Leben" (Reverence for Life) conveyed to Kaplinski. To be as idiomatic as possible, he translated it as "Kõik on ime" or "kõik on imelik," which means both "everything is miraculous" (*ime*) as well as "unusual" or "strange" (*imelik*). At work in Schweitzer's essay, Kaplinski noted in 1984, is an intuitive identification with the nonhuman world, which Kaplinski considered to be an "inevitable precondition" for any meaningful change in our thinking and behaviour.[72] In Kaplinski's view, Schweitzer's mentality aligned with an ethos of equality in human-nonhuman relations. Carried along by the spirit of Schweitzer's biocentric egalitarianism, which bestowed intrinsic value upon all life, Kaplinski, citing Schweitzer's essay, expressed concern about the human-nonhuman divide and rejected the anthropocentrism that reaches back into Christian views of the world.[73]

To Gary Snyder Jaan Kaplinski wrote that the Estonians had "remained fundamentally un-Christian"; "anthropocentrism" was "foreign" to them, and for this reason "Buddhism would have had much more success" in Estonia.[74] He found himself in broad agreement with Bertrand Russell's declaration in "Why I Am Not a Christian."[75] In his 1927 lecture Russell was critical of a number of presuppositions primary to Christian belief, including the "idea that things must have a beginning" and that there must be a "lawgiver"; neither coincides with Kaplinski's sense of unforced flourishing.[76] As some Protestant theologians themselves have pointed out, the ecological effects of these ideas have been disastrous, especially when Christian missionaries colonized polytheistic pagan cultures. Christian beliefs clashed, at times violently, with their cyclical and animistic world.[77]

GROWING ECOLOGICAL AWARENESS, BUT NO TANGIBLE CHANGE

Although Kaplinski and others in many countries have over the past forty years given much weight and reason to ecocentric perspectives and ecological health, most continue to hold on to the view that humans are intrinsically superior beings, including theologians who, to some extent, identify with deep ecological approaches to the environment.[78] Kaplinski has likened the prevailing speciesism to the "attempt of one group of animals to assume the position of lead animal," calling it in a fictional account entitled "Ornitofilosoofia" a form of discrimination that has become part of our "true religion" and definition of "culture."[79] Evoking his experience of the landscape of Europe's far North, and as if resigned to the impossibility of bringing about a transformative change, he asks in one of his poems in the collection *Evening Brings Everything Back*: "How can people retire into their values, fears and beliefs like snails into their shells? How can one live in this world egoistically, how is it possible to lose the sense of wonder, to live without noticing this sky, these white rocks, these crowberries, checkerberries, dwarf birch trees and diapensias? How is it possible to turn one's back on it all and build huge stone castles where there is art, music, color, aroma and spirituality, where there are just no life and no light of men, no plantain and knotgrass?"[80]

Kaplinski has had reason to be concerned. No matter how good our intentions or how sophisticated our designs, even our most promising interventions to support nature and its self-regulating capacity have largely remained unsuccessful. While the appreciation of our dependence on nature and recognition of its intrinsic value has risen to unprecedented levels, appeals from followers of prominent grassroots environmental movements in favour of a fundamental ecological reorientation of our way of life, including calls from "deep" ecologists for a biocentric egalitarianism and others advocating an "ecologization of society," have all met with considerable criticism, even from within the green movement, and have had little success in securing tangible and significant change.[81]

Kaplinski would agree that we have not been able to reverse certain basic habits of thought and patterns of behaviour that run counter to unforced flourishing: overdependence on human culture and symbolic wealth still obscure ecological perspectives. Not enough importance is accorded to mutual identification in the social world, and reciprocity in human–nature relations remains marginalized. Maturity is still largely associated with increased independence and creativity as well as a reasoning too readily tied to subjective transformations and a sense of the self as creator. Calculating behaviour continues to dominate and trump trust in instincts. Still broadly accepted is the presumption that ultimately it is human design that underlies human flourishing.

DON'T TOUCH THAT ROCK, SISYPHUS – PRESERVING THE "UNATTAINABLE"

How, then, would "true" change come about and our wants diminish to sustainable levels? In Kaplinski's own words, how can we "protect us from ourselves?"[82] Kaplinski agrees with those who believe a shift is needed from an exclusively secular and consumption-driven view of the world to a perspective that includes faith in a higher power that would compel us to sacrifice our standard of living and focus more on quality of life than on material wealth. For Kaplinski this transformation means that our understanding of sacredness has to shift from the traditional religious domain to nature.[83] This raises another fundamental question: how do conceptions such as the "sacred," the "divine," or the "spiritual" – not as a refuge but as a cornerstone of human advance – fit into our contemporary world?[84]

To better understand what Kaplinski's vision entails and what it would mean to follow his convictions, it is helpful to turn to two strong but very different voices from Europe's cultural landscape, the Norwegian philosopher and father of Deep Ecology, Arne Naess, and French existentialist Albert Camus.

Reflecting on the symbolic dimension of mountains as expressions of our desire for the unattainable and the quest of mountaineers to reach the summit, Naess arrived at a striking conclusion: rather than blindly following the urge to conquer a mountain, we need to embrace both the struggle as well as the "unreachability of all we long for" and accept that we are "always on the way." "In recognition of this," Naess argued, "the few unclimbed, old, majestic mountains, which for thousands of years in many cultures have been supreme symbols of the unreachable, should be left unclimbed."[85] In other words, they should be treated as sacred.

In Kaplinski's view there is a profound difference between those who regard something as sacred and those who don't: the former believe in a value greater than themselves, a perspective he considers essential for our survival. Owing to a dominant egocentric perspective, Kaplinski wrote in 1973, the latter, by contrast, mistakenly think of themselves as sacred.[86] Echoing the sentiment expressed by Naess, Kaplinski added to his blog in 2010: there "are things I avoid describing and speaking about. I cannot and don't want to say anything about the redwood trees I saw on the coast of Oregon and northern California. I don't want to tell anything about what I felt and thought looking at them and walking under their shade. [There] are things we should not try to describe, things that should remain nameless, indescribable, ineffable. In the past such things were considered sacred."[87] But can such a sense of sanctity again become a key value? Isn't Kaplinski urging a perspective that runs counter to our secular thinking and is therefore met with suspicion or dismissed altogether as a vestige of a past tied to superstition?

Implied in his point of view is a critique of French philosopher and Nobel laureate Albert Camus who famously captured a fundamental presumption of our times when he wrote about the hero from Greek mythology, Sisyphus. The gods condemned him to repeat the same meaningless task of pushing a rock up a mountain only to see it roll down again. We need not despair over this fate, Camus concluded. While essential to the human condition, it is not a form of punishment. On the contrary, it "is enough to fill a man's heart."[88] Instead of imagining Sisyphus happy, as Camus insists we must, or perhaps even dreaming of achieving the impossible and seeing the rock come to rest on top of the mountain, Kaplinski's path towards human fulfillment points in a decidedly different direction. To borrow from American poet Sam Hamill, he looks at "the great stone of Sisyphus ... from the hill's other side" and acknowledges the necessity of his struggle – but, and this is the crucial point Kaplinski makes, also imagines Sisyphus happy whenever he finds the inner strength and wisdom to let the rock be.

In other words, it bears repeating, Kaplinski places his trust in nature, the self-regulating. He knows that when this trust is lost, human well-being suffers and we become strangers, to others and to ourselves. But he also knows that reason alone can't dislodge Sisyphean habits of thought. What remains is a leap of faith – this, at a time when prejudice against religious sentiment runs deep. Our secular age and age of ecological collapse, with nothing remaining untouchable, leaves Kaplinski unsettled. In his own words, his "desperate need for Nature" makes him a member of a "small and powerless minority" for whom "a forest, a beach, the cloudy or starry sky" mean more than anything human-made. In his perception, nature remains a source of endless wonder and possibility – extending beyond our imagination, unbound and unforced.[89]

3

The Medium Is Not the Message

This landscape leaves me wordless, nameless and without desires. I'm a man without qualities, nearly nothing, a pair of eyes and the longing to stay here, to decrease, to grow smaller, closer to rock and soil, to change into a low plant, a crowberry, a bearberry, lichen, an inscription on rock, an inscription I still can't read, that is both a greeting and a farewell. Like the Saami *joik*, the song without words, without a beginning and an end, born here on the open hills under an open sky.[1]

Jaan Kaplinski

I am not attracted to the arts... It's difficult and sometimes almost impossible to explain, that the essential part of what I do doesn't interest me, or rather, only its edge interests me.[2]

Jaan Kaplinski

In his *Parallels and Parallelisms*, Kaplinski offers a revealing perspective that helps to illuminate the complexities and subtleties of unforced flourishing.[3] The most important claim he made in this book of 2009 is that human fulfillment is closely tied to either a primarily "communicative" or a "meditative" mode of being. Those drawn towards the communicative mode look at "reality" as if it were a text. For them, Kaplinski argues in an article entitled "philosophy and silence,"[4] nothing exists unless it can be put into words. That is to say, they have learned to place their trust in mediated experience and hope to realize fulfillment through symbols that resonate with such an intensity and richness that they leave us in awe.

Those, on the other hand, who are, like Kaplinski, drawn towards the meditative do not attach such a high value to language and the artistry we have learned to perform with words and other modes of communication. At its extreme, they do not believe that human flourishing is best served by signs, silence by sounds, nature by culture, the "unspeakable" by words, as one might say – no matter how rich and sophisticated the means we deploy. They don't necessarily question the worth of symbol-making as such; it is a need of social life and physical survival. More importantly, they are aware of its capacity to draw attention to its limitations. What they seek is a new sense of balance, one tilted away from human intervention towards the spontaneously unfolding.

Still, some see the communicative stance as being intimately connected to a form of second-hand living with profoundly deforming and alienating consequences. For them, our symbolic universe is at the root of what has been called "the pathology of civilization."[5] "We seem to have experienced a fall into representation," the "anarcho-primitivist" philosopher John Zerzan has observed. "In a fundamental sort of falsification, symbols at first mediated reality and then replaced it. At present, we live within symbols to a greater degree than we do within our bodily selves or directly with each other," he claims.[6] "To represent or be represented is a degradation." Culture, Zerzan concludes, "must be met by a resolute autonomy and refusal that looks at the whole span of human presence and rejects all dimensions of captivity and destruction."[7] Although it is hard to know how he looked at the world as a young man, there are indications that in the early 1960s Kaplinski shared this "anarchist" spirit of human flourishing. Still in the 1970s, he wrote that we live in "a world of words, symbols, concepts… a very illusory world which, paradoxically swallows things more real than itself – trees, animals, landscapes, men," leaving us with "nothing, only symbols, only shadows."[8]

It was a very different Jaan Kaplinski, seemingly unburdened by the lack of immediacy he would experience later in life, who found himself mesmerized by the power of words when the world of "culture" opened up to him in a way he had not known before. True, it would turn out to be a false start, taking him on a path leading from nature, to culture, and, finally, to culture transformed into second nature. But when he first discovered poetry, this more common path, which later in life he, as a writer and as a man, would struggle to move away from, provided young Kaplinski with an imaginary refuge from his troubles – the turmoils of adolescence and the changing, yet in many ways still intolerably oppressive, political climate that characterized post-Stalinist Estonia. All of this gained a particular urgency for him in 1956 when fateful events were unfolding in

Eastern Europe with aftershocks felt as far away as Kaplinski's own home country. It was the year of the Hungarian uprising.

BUDAPEST 1956 – WHAT NOW?

For the fifteen-year-old Kaplinski, 1956 ushered in the end of his childhood. Listening to Radio Free Europe and the BBC, he learned that demonstrators in Hungary had taken to the streets. They demanded secession from the Warsaw Pact. The pro-democracy demonstrations quickly grew into a mass uprising that brought Hungary's capital to a standstill and, for a short time, left the Kremlin unsure of how to react.[9] What occurred in Hungary led to public declarations of solidarity in Estonia. Even anti-Soviet graffiti appeared, a rare occurrence in the former Soviet Union. Some went further and encouraged armed resistance against the Soviet presence in Estonia.[10]

The widespread public support the Hungarian uprising enjoyed in the Warsaw Pact countries and throughout the territories occupied by the Soviet Union caught officials in Moscow by surprise. Countermeasures were hastily put into place: the KGB intensified its efforts to identify and silence political activists. The Communist Party increased its political activity, and more systematic attempts were introduced to further mould public opinion and muzzle dissenting voices.

In Estonia the Communist Party-controlled media outlets were utilized to mount a propaganda campaign to discredit the demands of the Hungarians for self-determination. Using official stereotypical Communist terminology, the Estonian newspapers labeled the mass uprising in Budapest an "adventure" directed against the people[11] and referred to the Hungarian demonstrators as "bandits" and criminals who put "democracy" and "freedom" at risk.[12] According to the propaganda spread by the Soviet print and broadcast media, the aim of the Hungarians was to diminish the power of the workers and exploit the masses.[13]

As he would later attest, Kaplinski was devastated when he heard the news that the Soviet military had launched a massive military offensive against the Hungarians. On 9 November 1956, Soviet troops had moved into Budapest and brought the uprising to a violent end. Not only did Moscow deny Hungarians the right to self-determination but two years later, following a secret trial, the Communist authorities also had Hungary's Prime Minister Imre Nagy and other members of his government executed for treason.

This was particularly upsetting for the then seventeen-year-old Kaplinski. "Budapest was a significant turning point for me," he later on would write. The uprising "marked the end of my childhood and the beginning of adolescence. It was a challenge, one of the important challenges to which I tried to find an answer in my imagination."[14] He would find a response, at first, in the imaginary world of literature, and of poetry in particular – it could "amalgamate anything with everything," he felt.[15]

The Communist Party's response to the uprising left little doubt in Kaplinski's mind that Soviet-style socialism was a farce. It also dashed all hopes that the West would come to the rescue of the people behind the Iron Curtain, a scenario Kaplinski often overheard his grandparents and their friends mention in their discussions. In his fictionalized autobiography *The Same River*, Kaplinski wrote: "Europe, with America's help had built a protective wall against Communism, just as the Romans did against the German Goths ... Communism had to be allowed to fry in its own fat, die a natural death."[16]

By all accounts, the fate the Hungarians had suffered in 1956 also made abundantly clear that the Communist regime would not listen to the will of the people, that the system could not be reformed and, despite its bankrupt social politics, was not going to collapse any time soon. Budapest drove home a lesson most Estonians would heed for a long time to come: it was pointless to ask for the withdrawal of Soviet troops, to demand free elections, a multiparty system, or independence. None of this would be tolerated by Moscow, even after Stalin's death. Young Kaplinski came to understand ever more clearly that this was the reality of the so-called Thaw under Khrushchev.

With the evaporation of any hope for decisive political change, a more pragmatic attitude towards the Soviet occupation gradually replaced direct opposition against the foreign rulers, especially among the younger generation of Estonians, those who had not experienced the war as adults. With few exceptions, armed underground resistance came to an end. Increasingly, Estonians began to see it as an advantage to work for their own interests – but within the confines of the political reality, rather than trying to sidestep or overtly resist the system.

Despite the events in Hungary, many were nevertheless hopeful that the shift away from the previous era of repression under Stalin would lead to more political and cultural autonomy for Estonians. Uppermost on many Estonians' minds at the time were the deportees who had been banished to prisons and labour camps far away from their homes in Estonia. Would the survivors still be allowed to return from Siberia as Khrushchev's amnesty promised, or did Budapest put an end to this, too?

As complicated and unpredictable as the political situation still was, cautious optimism increasingly characterized the general mood under Khrushchev. This shift was largely grounded in tangible differences between pre- and post-Stalinist life but not any radical political transformation. For example, the policy of forced immigration to Estonia of foreign workers from other areas of the Soviet Union was all but halted. This gave way to some relaxation of cultural politics. Much that had receded from public discourse or had been banned altogether began to surface again. While the hierarchical central Communist structure remained in full force, censors, for example, did permit the publication of books that thematized the 1941 deportations of Estonians to Siberia or noted the Estonian resistance, topics that had been taboo under Stalin and whose mention was even subject to prosecution.

The most important difference for many was the fact that the threat of being deported to Siberia had diminished. Until Stalin's death in 1953, Nora Kaplinski still had to be fearful that she, together with her son, might be sent to Siberia. Not only had they escaped this fate, which some considered astonishing, but now deportees also began to return from the Gulag. In 1956, a wave of political prisoners arrived in Estonia and for the first time many people heard directly from them and in their own words about their plight in what Solzhenitsyn would come to call the "Gulag Archipelago," the vast system of prison and labour camps scattered mostly throughout the eastern and northern expanses of the Soviet Union where millions perished.

Kaplinski remembers the homecoming of Kalle, the eldest of three sons of a family linked to the "Forest Brothers," members of the Estonian armed resistance to Soviet occupation: Kalle had been sixteen when he was sentenced to ten years at the Vorkuta prison camp in Russia's far north. He was among those who returned after Stalin's death in the mid-1950s. Witnessing such a homecoming and listening to the stories Kalle had to tell "was one of my so-called universities," Kaplinski recalls.[17] And meeting Kalle, of course, probably reminded Kaplinski of his own father, Jerzy Kaplinski, who had vanished.

Despite such painful memories, life after Stalin's death became more bearable for Jaan and Nora Kaplinski. In 1956, his mother was again allowed to work as a teacher, which had been impossible in the late 1940s and early 1950s when many educated Estonians were specifically targeted for reprisals by the Communist Party. Those labeled "cosmopolitan" – being associated with "Western" values – together with other members of the cultural elite, were considered untrustworthy and blocked from employment in their professions. Many of them were not only expelled from professional associations and dismissed from work – Nora "lost her job probably in 1949" – but also persecuted, even arrested and deported.[18] The last large-scale wave of arrests of so-called socially dangerous persons in Soviet Estonia occurred in 1950–1951. Nora Kaplinski was not sent to prison but lost her job at the Literary Museum in Tartu. She was also let go from her position as French teacher as a result of this witch-hunt. It did not matter enough that she probably was the most qualified French language instructor in Tartu at the time.[19] Translating became her main source of income, but as the wife of an "enemy of the people" she could not publish anything under her own name.[20]

Before Stalin's death, many institutions associated with prewar Estonia had been closed, modernist artworks removed from public places, more than 80% of prewar Estonian language publications destroyed, journals and newspapers taken out of circulation, and publishing houses shut down. From 1946 to 1952, the number of literary texts published in Soviet Estonia had declined by more than fifty percent, and the Writers' Union of Soviet Estonia, controlled by the Communist Party, waged a ruthless campaign against so called "bourgeois nationalists," allowing only a handful of writers to publish. Their work typically amounted to little more than Communist Party propaganda.[21] Erasing the memory of independent Estonia was the goal of these purges. For the Kaplinskis, and many other Estonians, it meant a life of poverty, fear, and humiliation.

To make matters worse, an acute economic downturn left the agricultural sector in ruins. Food shortages became commonplace. To illustrate the severity of the situation, Kaplinski likes to draw attention to a fictionalized account of this period: in her 1985 novel *Seitsmes Rahukevad* (*The Seventh Spring of Peace*), Estonian writer Viivi Luik evokes images of a terribly impoverished life in the Estonian countryside in the late 1940s and early 1950s, and of the disastrous effects of forced mass collectivization, mismanagement, and the waste of resources, rotting wheat, and emaciated farm animals.

By the mid-'50s conditions had improved. Although even under Khrushchev's reign Kaplinski was seen as the child from a "suspect family," and he and his mother continued to be treated as outcasts, one difference in particular made them feel less isolated and introduced a welcome change into their lives: they were able to reconnect with friends and relatives who had fled Estonia during the war. Until 1954 it was as if their loved ones had vanished.[22] For the first time, after years of silence, Kaplinski's mother received letters and parcels from friends and relatives in the West. Ilse Paris (née Saat), who had left Estonia in the 1940s, wrote from Freudenstadt in Germany. Another close friend from Switzerland sent books. Arvo Mägi, a literary historian and journalist who escaped from Estonia to Sweden in 1944, kept Kaplinski informed about the Estonian cultural scene in the West, as did others who, at times, sent typewritten poems hidden in letters. In this way he became acquainted with the most prominent Estonian writers in exile, among them Bernhard Kangro, Ilmar Laaban, and Kalju Lepik. Later, Kaplinski's network of contacts grew to include Estonians living in the United States, such as the publisher and critic Hellar Grabbi, whose correspondence with Kaplinski between 1965 and 1991 is now available in print,[23] the academics Ivar Ivask and Ilse Lehiste, as well as many others. While such contacts with the West were tolerated, they were not without risk, as Kaplinski himself learned the hard way in the late 1950s. A poem written by an exile Estonian poet was in circulation in Tartu, and when it was traced back to Kaplinski, he was called to task by the KGB. Intervention by the mother of a friend, a communist official, helped avert his expulsion from university.

THE GHOST SHIP – DISCOVERING THE POWER AND LIMITS OF POETRY

At around this time, not through contacts in the West but rather through family friends, Kaplinski came into possession of André Maurois's book *Ariel: A Shelley Romance*. The book tells the story of the English Romantic writer Percy Bysshe Shelley. He is depicted as a tender soul with a "love of books" but suffering at the hand of educators whose aim it is to "form 'hard-faced men,' all run in the same mould."[24] Shelley, however, is a boy who "displayed a sensitiveness of conscience most unusual in one of his class, as well as an incredible tendency to question the Rules of the Game."[25] In Maurois's book Kaplinski also found much that resonated with his, as he put it, "craving for beauty," his awakening sexuality, the bullying he initially suffered at school, the more liberal but still unpredictable and harsh political climate in Soviet Estonia, the crushed uprising in Hungary, the return of the deportees, his growing awareness of Estonia's and his family's history, his contact with the West, and what he felt were increasingly suffocating conditions at home.[26] All this amounted to "difficult times," Kaplinski wrote in his 2003 memoir *Isale,* when he turned his mind's eye back to the second half of the '50s.[27] Everything, good and bad, seemed to come all at once, he remembered, and was amplified by the turmoil that often accompanies adolescence. "How is it under man's control to love or not to love? But the essence of love is liberty and it withers in an atmosphere of constraint," Kaplinski would read after school in Maurois's book about Shelley.[28]

During this period, Kaplinski used every opportunity to escape the claustrophobic conditions at home – where he, his mother, and his "aunt" Mara (Marie Pael) shared one of two rooms. The second room, with access through the first room, served as the bed- and living room for three more people. There was a common kitchen and one bathroom shared by several groups in the house. "At night," he wrote in his autobiographical novel *The Same River*, "it was difficult to move about without his aunt, who slept in her own bed in another corner of the room, hearing. If he turned over more noisily, coughed or went to the toilet, his aunt was sure to ask him whether he was ill. He had trained himself to move soundlessly in the dark, suppress his coughing and turn over as little as possible, because he could not bear these kinds of questions."[29]

Occasionally, there would be drinking and singing late into the night, which Kaplinski found particularly bothersome. During the day, there was hardly any privacy and quiet either. If his mother did not work on translations or study, people would drop by for coffee, taking advantage of the central location of their flat and the hospitality of both his mother and grandmother. "Our place was always brimming with visitors," Kaplinski commented in a television production about his life.[30] Returning to the apartment in the early '70s, he remarked: "Very little has changed there: in our larger room there is a tall, white glazed tile stove, which was never heated; through the window, one can see the daily bustle of the young people on the steps of the university, which grandmother could admire for hours. The rooms are just as high-ceilinged and dim, the hallway as crooked and dark."[31] Living there meant gloom, pressure, and anxiety – "nothing but suffering."[32]

At the time he was attending the *First Middle School* in Tartu (more famously known as the *Hugo Treffner High School* dating back to 1804), where he had been a student since grade one in 1947. School was a "sad" and "grey" place, filled with "anguish and drudgery."[33] He would much rather roam the streets of Tartu or, like Shelley in Maurois's book, be on the run from his taunting schoolmates. He was a loner "at least since he had started to read poetry and write it himself."[34] Others also shunned him because he wasn't good at sports – he had trouble catching a ball – and had a Polish name. About forty years later, when one of his sons decided to name his son Jerzy Edvard, Kaplinski wrote: "I don't like this. I have myself been in trouble because of my father's name and I wouldn't want that anymore for anyone."[35]

Instead of being with his schoolmates or at home, he would sometime try to find a quiet place on the banks of Tartu's Ema River and read Maurois's account of the great Romantic poet:

> Shelley closed his book, stretched himself out upon the sunny, flower-starred grass, and meditated on the misery of man. From the school buildings behind him a confused murmur of stupid voices floated out over the exquisite landscape of wood and stream, but here at least no mocking eye could spy upon him. The boy's tears ran down, and pressing his hands together, he made this vow: ... "I swear never to become an accomplice, even by my silence, of the selfish and the powerful. I swear to dedicate my whole life to the worship of beauty."[36]

But Kaplinski's most significant early encounter with the world of *belles lettres*, as he tells us, came in the guise of a Russian Romantic writer and appears to have been rather accidental. It could have been through school that Kaplinski first became acquainted with one of Mikhail Lermontov's books. The literature curriculum was based on Russian texts. It is also possible that he found a volume of Lermontov's work at home. This much we know: although he wasn't at all interested in literature at that time, one day in the mid-1950s he stumbled upon Lermontov's poem "The Ghost Ship."

If there are turning points in one's life, then this encounter can be regarded as having changed the course of his existence. As he would later recall, as a young man he had been mesmerized by the poem and its main figure. Lermontov's 1840 adaptation of a poem by the Austrian writer Joseph Christian von Zedlitz centers on one of the icons of the heroic tradition and symbols of freedom, Napoleon Bonaparte. He personified "the quintessential man of action" and "sheer will"; his "biography held forth the possibility of self-creation through great deeds, regardless of one's starting point or past."[37] The poem speaks of past glory but also evokes Napoleon's enemies, his defeat in Russia, and his having been "robbed of his kingdom." Rising from the dead and as a ghost visiting France, he finds himself alone, without recognition, abandoned and betrayed by his followers. The poem ends in sorrow and, finally, in the last stanza, with stoical acceptance of his fate. Napoleon returns to his grave on St. Helena, but his ghost lives on.

Through the unexpected discovery of Lermontov's verse, the world of literature opened up to Kaplinski. Discovering this poem was like a "jolt," Kaplinski would tell his students at the University of Tartu some forty-five years later.[38] The poem was a revelation, he remembers. "I wept, and started my long journey in the promised land of poetry."[39] For a decade he stayed "intoxicated" by poetry, in a "daze," as he wrote in an article published in 1973.[40]

Soon after his encounter with Lermontov's poem, he began to write poetry himself and to read his own work to friends and in small cafés, something which he would come to dread later in life. One of his earliest poems, probably written in 1956, the year of the Hungarian uprising, was printed in 1960 in his school almanac (*Sulesepad*). It is a poem that speaks of new hope in the midst of winter. He published some of his earliest poems in a collection entitled *Uute Kivide Kasvamine*. They include mostly rhymed, self-absorbed poems with titles such as "Strange" (Võõras), "Restlessness" (Rahutus), and "Beyond Melancholy" (Sealpool Nukrust), and often evoke, as the titles suggest, a dark, anxiety-ridden mood. The collection also contains the poem "mu meel unus mägede taha" (I forgot my thoughts behind the mountains). Set to music, it is often performed at commemorative national events in Estonia.

But what first drew him to poetry and poets like Lermontov and Shelley would later come into conflict with his own views about art and on deeper existential questions. It has been said that, for Lermontov, "unique individual identity" constituted one of the "highest values"; it aligned with a sense of self attached to striving for independence, glorious deeds, and plans.[41] Shelley too was a poet fascinated by the idea of the singular individual.[42] While the mature Kaplinski was drawn to what in this book is conceptualized as "unforced flourishing," an unobtrusive responsiveness, the teenaged Kaplinski identified with its inverse, the heroic mode: it is characterized by a Faustian determination, as one might say, and a stoic, indeed tragic, disposition known to us from the "great men of action" of Western high culture. Like Lermontov's Napoleon, these heroes embody Promethean ideals of assertiveness and self-creation, manipulation and conquest rather than cooperation and adaptation.

Baudelaire and Rimbaud are two other writers Kaplinski often mentions in connection with his teenage years and the captivating appeal of literature he experienced. Their work presents much of what we have come to value in great art: an "imaginative re-creation of the object, an object transformed by subjectivity," evoking ideas, moods, and emotions aimed at penetrating behind the façade of ordinary life.[43] In the '50s, Kaplinski found himself drawn to the transformative power of the human imagination – and literature (with its arsenal of stylistic effects, narrative techniques, and poetic devices) as its richest and most sophisticated medium. But as he grew older, a very different sense would take hold of him. Increasingly, he began to see the artist's creations as an obstacle, more easily impoverishing than enriching our experience and understanding of ourselves and the world around us.

In his autobiographical novel *The Same River,* the unnamed student remembers two lines of a poem by Baudelaire entitled "Correspondences": "Man travels there through forests of symbols, / That all watch him with familiar looks."[44] Although still captivated by Baudelaire's poem, the young student is no longer entirely certain about his unquestioned regard for the power of words and the need to create an imagined world. Are symbols really more important than the symbolized? "Perhaps" is the student's cautious answer:

> Perhaps man really is surrounded by a forest of familiar symbols. Perhaps there are correspondences like this all over the world, correspondences between man and another, between man and place, man and tree, man and rock, man and poetry. Perhaps it is man's challenge to find his own place in this network of hidden correspondences. Perhaps life acquires thereby a more genuine content. Perhaps the correspondences that

> have been found and activated begin to chime together and produce a harmony.[45]

But when, in the early '70s, he reflected on this period in his life, Kaplinski found himself of two minds about literature and his emotional reaction to it as a teenager. While literature had opened up a new path, and he had become a successful writer himself, he could not help but think that this gain was also accompanied by a significant loss. He felt as if his "craving for beauty," which Lermontov's "The Ghost Ship" had awoken in him, lacked a deeper sense of integrity. The aesthetic domain now seemed to flatten and reduce rather than enrich his sense of self and understanding of the world: "It has been said that human beings are born old and it is their fortune if they manage to turn into a child before they die," Kaplinski wrote in 1973. "In puberty, however, humans become false." While the "power of poetry" revealed itself to him in "The Ghost Ship," as he put it, in the end this experience did not ring true. Instead, it appeared to him as if its "Bonapartism" and "romanticism" had emanated from "a false epoch."[46] His doubts grew and deepened into a sweeping rejection of the "beautiful." Calling it an "illusion," he concluded in one of his poems of the 1960s, "It is time for esthetics to die."[47] This radical shift in sentiment, that would culminate in dismissing "culture" as such, coincided with another turning point in his life: he left home, the crowded flat in Tartu, for a place of his own and away from his mother, away from a "huge deficit of tenderness."[48]

LEAVING HOME – FAILED FIRST MARRIAGE

From an early age on, Kaplinski resented how his mother's refined and disciplined form of behaviour had intruded on his life and deprived him of the emotional closeness he craved. Nora Kaplinski owed much of her poise and capacity for smooth and cultured conversation to her prewar schooling in the performing arts, philology, art history, and literature. In Kaplinski's eyes, she personified European high culture, particularly French and German, in their family.[49] Kaplinski thought that his mother's somewhat subdued and reserved manner that aligned with both her mentality and "civilized" background was probably also her way of coping with the painful wartime past that had left her life in shambles.

Colleagues and friends remembered her fondly as a woman with impeccable taste, class, and grace – not so Kaplinski. "Priggishness went on his nerves," Kaplinski's second eldest son has remarked. "He had to help guests with their coats." Even in the poverty of an overcrowded communal apartment, coupled with the misery and harsh political climate of the Stalinist and post-Stalinist years, Nora Kaplinski's circle of friends, mostly members of Tartu's prewar cultural elite, "still tried to uphold the old style of living."[50] Of his mother, Kaplinski observes: she "just was absorbed in her grief and in the ideology that one must not spoil one's child."[51] Elsewhere, he draws a parallel between what he sees as the tendency of Western civilization to destroy its own past values and his mother's attitude towards him: "Mother wanted to get rid of the past, escape, symbolically kill herself" and, "symbolically, perhaps also me because she destroyed all my things, as soon as possible, sometimes with strange excuses."[52] We don't know much about their relationship except what can be gleaned from scattered statements by Jaan Kaplinski, mostly in his publications and his diary. They point to diverging paths, emotionally and intellectually. Indeed, it is as if they represent two very different worlds: one taking pride in a cultivated habitus, the other reaching beyond it, seeking more unmediated, direct contact.

This much is certain: frustrated, Kaplinski left home, the crowded flat on University Street in the center of Tartu where he shared a single room with his mother well into his late teens, and even a bed until he turned twelve. Soon after he had found a place for himself, he met his future wife, Küllike Kolk, on the Elva-Tartu train on his commute to university. They fell in love and, having left a husband and daughter behind, she moved in with Kaplinski. Their first and only child, Maarja, was born with a defective spinal column – the result of spina bifida – which was accompanied by damage to the central nervous system and hydrocephalus, the accumulation of water on the brain.

When, in 1964, Kaplinski learned of his daughter's birth defect, his life changed forever. He wrote in *To Father*: "I stayed away from friends, literary and cultural life, but came closer to life."[53] His marriage to Küllike Kolk turned out to be a "very unhappy" union.[54] In his memory, those years were among the "saddest years" of his life and it is perhaps not surprising that he wrote the poems of his collection *Of Dust and Colors* in this period.[55] They include incantations for a better world. The title poem begins with the lines: "New butterflies are made of dust and color, but we / are planted in the ground like broken bones to replace ourselves. / Somewhere in storm and darkness, waves lap newborn islands / like the lioness licks her cubs."[56]

Kaplinski, as Küllike Kolk recalled their relationship decades later, embodied her romantic ideals of an artist. She was drawn to the intellectual atmosphere and the world of literature he represented in her eyes. As novel and exciting as he, his friends, and his family appeared to her, she soon began to feel inferior in this milieu. Although she seems to have no memory of anyone openly disapproving of her, she nevertheless recalls a sense of alienation and of being out of place.[57] Financial worries added to their stress, and Küllike's pregnancy increased the couple's dependency on Kaplinski's mother. When Küllike Kaplinski had to interrupt her studies at the University of Tartu, she became increasingly concerned about her own education. She also had trouble facing a future with a child in need of special care, and coming to terms with being separated from her other daughter. Soon she wanted to get out of the relationship with Kaplinski, start a new life, and pursue a career of her own. Eventually they seemed more and more incompatible – emotionally, sexually, and intellectually. Doubts about their life together began to loom ever larger. By 1967 their marriage had broken down.

THE ANARCHIST – "WE HAVE ART IN ORDER NOT TO DIE OF THE TRUTH" (NIETZSCHE)

Around this time, a few years after their daughter Maarja was born and Kaplinski had graduated from Tartu University (he had been enrolled in the Department of History and Linguistics as a student in Romance languages and literatures from September 1958 to July 1964), Kaplinski published a controversial poem about one of his then favourite musicians, the American free-jazz saxophonist John Coltrane. "Not even an Estonian Communist has ever written something as fanatic," Kaplinski's long-time mentor and friend, the freelance writer and prolific translator of European poetry, Ain Kaalep, exclaimed, calling his friend's text "a downright disgusting poem."[58] Kaalep took exception to Kaplinski's radically dismissive attitude toward European culture, which to Kaalep seemed, and indeed was, different from the Communist regime's contempt of Western art, literature, music, and other expressions of creative life. Until Stalin's death in 1953, any association, past or present, with Western European culture was labeled degenerate by the authorities and constituted just cause for imprisonment.

Kaplinski's protest against "culture" did not come to the fore until the '60s when he put into question the widely held and valued view that Estonia's identity was and had to remain deeply anchored in the cultures of the European West. With this critique he ran counter to the cultural renaissance of the "Golden Sixties" and the reintroduction of the in many ways Eurocentric narrative of the Young Estonia movement into the emerging mainstream Estonian discourse of the '60s. While Estonia more openly directed its focus toward the West – and became known as the "Soviet West" – Kaplinski turned his attention elsewhere and gradually discovered ways of perceiving closer to his own inclinations.

Reading, for example, the work of Benjamin Lee Whorf, he also developed a more critical attitude toward language and a keen, and even liberating, awareness of its inherent limitations: "Of course, Zen was in the air in the Sixties, but I was already somehow prepared [for] it, I had understood that words and things do not belong together. I remember that I felt great relief, and even some e[c]stasy understanding that 'a tree is not a tree.'"[59] In a further complication, his critique of "culture," paradoxically, accompanied his own ever-increasing output as a writer – essays and, in particular, poems – culminating in his ascent to star status on the cultural scene when he was barely twenty-five years old.

To better understand Kaplinski, it is useful to imagine "culture" for him as a "potential space" (Winnicott) that gives rise to symbols. They constitute phenomena subjectively transformed by the power of imagination. As has been argued, this power to create symbols and the high value placed on them derives from internalized memories of care and a trust in the ability developed during early childhood to look after oneself in the absence of such care with the help of substitutes that comprise what commonly is known as "culture." As this "potential space" together with its "transitional phenomena" came into Kaplinski's field of vision and his awareness of his own and other cultures increased, he wanted to see this territory of the imagination diminished. As if unable to trust this space, he did not measure the value of cultural expression in terms of its potential to provide fulfillment. Instead, for him, the potential of culture to point beyond itself became paramount. His was a symbol-defying attitude towards culture, an unorthodox disposition that increasingly came to characterize his thinking in the '60s, first in an undifferentiated, even anarchist, and later in a more subtle and circumspect manner.

The young Kaplinski's position initially did not merely constitute a critique of "culture" but also a radical refusal that echoed the 1919 manifesto of an "anarcho-futurist" group. In their manifesto they wrote:

> Tear down the churches and their allies the museums! Blast to smithereens the fragile idols of Civilization! Hey, you decadent architects of the sarcophagi of thought, you watchmen of the universal cemetery of books – stand aside! We have come to remove you! The old must be buried, the dusty archives burned by Vulcan's torch of creative genius. Past the flaky ashes of worldwide devastation, past the charred canvasses of bulky paintings, past the burned, fat, pot-bellied volumes of classics we march.[60]

In his "anarchist" period, as one might call this phase of his intellectual development, Kaplinski wrote so easily about "culture" that it is not always clear what he meant, although diminishing its importance as our "symbolic universe" appears to have been his aim. An American-Estonian critic, who corresponded with Kaplinski already in the '60s, wrote in the international literary quarterly *Books Abroad* (*World Literature Today*) of the young poet's "sweeping condemnations of history, culture and modern civilization" as well as his rejection of "esthetics as an alien, superfluous matter in the Great Balance of nature."[61]

It was in his little-known second collection of poems published in 1966 and entitled *Kalad punuvad pesi* (Fish Weave Their Nests) where the twenty-five-year-old Kaplinski equated culture with illness: "CULTURE IS the symbiosis of man's viruses and cats no bird song / for a long time to come no living leaves / if it runs shoot it if it stands still chop it down … / you are a carcinoma which doesn't know better but to grow at the / expense of the living tissue of nature free enterprise that / doesn't know anything but to destroy life to destroy itself."[62] The opening poem of this 1966 collection of verse ends with an equally outspoken and sweeping rejection of dominant cultures, powerful nations, violence, conquest, persecutions, and ruthless killings:

who the hell needs your history Augustus Burchard von
Dreylöwen Cromwell Hegel Heydrich Höss
Cain Columbus Mohammed
Napoleon Nero Philip Stalin Suvorov
Torquemada
Genghis Khan whom should we then remember
not a single one let us remember
that our kingdom is more than your world
with all
its history that Tecumseh is dead and that on
the last page of all great and famous
deeds there is always some eichmann who
counts the corpses
keep your history for yourself keep for yourself
your great deeds
kill your dead and destroy your cities
but let us be
and remain let us live let us remain Indians
until the end of the world.[63]

"Culture is not enough" – he noted in his diary when he recalled his Coltrane poem more than a decade after writing it – "animated, we can even negate culture altogether."[64] Expanding on his critique of "culture," in March of 1987, he gave a lecture on the Babylonian epic of Gilgamesh, presenting the hero as his own ancient predecessor. He emphasized that Gilgamesh left the ancient Mesopotamian city for the wilderness, thus following in the footsteps of the other protagonist, Enkidu, who embodies a way of life outside of culture and civilization. Enkidu lives with animals, eats and roams with them, and sets them free when he finds any of them trapped by hunters. Kaplinski noted that this masterpiece of world literature was probably not only the first to raise the question about the meaning of life, but also the first to suggest "that there might be no point in Culture and Civilization in whose name we have exerted ourselves."[65]

ERUDITE CRITIC OF CULTURE – A WALKING CONTRADICTION?

Kaplinski's critique of "culture" is riddled with paradoxes. It surfaced at a time when he himself was deeply immersed in his own largely humanist education. Although many university courses were steeped in Marxist-Leninist doctrine, there were some exceptions. Kaplinski fondly remembers several instructors who lectured at Tartu University, such as the literary historian Villem Alttoa, Arthur Robert Hone, who taught European languages and literatures, and the renowned cultural theorist and expert in semiotics, Jyri (Yuri) Lotman.

Kaplinski "knew Lotman well," but he considered himself closer to another member of the Tartu-Moscow group of semioticians, the Russian philosopher Alexander Piatigorsky.[66] Kaplinski met him in 1964 at the first Summer School of Semiotics held in Tartu where Piatigorsky gave a talk dealing with mythology and folklore, a topic of interest to Kaplinski.[67] Their real intellectual kinship becomes more apparent in Piatigorsky's assessment of cultural semiotics and of the "semiosphere" as such, a term often attributed to Yuri Lotman.[68] While Lotman's understanding of semiotics "evolved from a theory rooted in Saussurean linguistics and in mathematical procedures to a biological, organismic approach," it reminded Piatigorsky of a fundamental limitation he believed to be inherent to semiotics.[69] As he noted critically in a lecture commemorating Yuri Lotman: semiotics grew from a perspective in which "man creates culture," then explains to "himself his creations" and subsequently easily mistakes his explanations for an explanation of life as such.[70] At the core of this "ontologization of culture" lies the claim that signs, including verbal signs, are primary, a view Kaplinski does not share.[71] For him "the world is not a semiotic phenomenon."[72] His 1966 poem "Once More Spring Pulls" (Jälle kisub kevad) echoes this sentiment. Man, he writes, "is closed in himself and has invented his own reflection / and the reflection of that reflection: culture, literature, / architecture." Rather than seeing man as "a closed surface reflecting only himself, / the ancient darkness in his vaults," or being like a "ship anchored in himself, in his history, / his time, a big ship decaying on the village pond," Kaplinski in this poem evokes an alternate view: human beings "should be clear" instead, "a mirror reflecting everything: / this spring, these birds returning."[73]

Another, perhaps even more important influence on Kaplinski's edification issued from his so-called alternative university, a group of Estonian intellectuals whom the authorities did not permit to teach officially but who nonetheless had a great influence on the younger generation.[74] Ain Kaalep, the well-read and popular cultural historian, poet, and admirer of German classical literature, was one of them.[75] Since contemporary literature, not to mention foreign literature, was hardly ever taught at universities, Kaalep's knowledge of modern European culture was important to Kaplinski,[76] and it was Kaalep who introduced him to two prominent personalities: Uku Masing, one of the most enigmatic and influential counter-cultural figures of the era in Estonia, to whom Kaplinski would become closely attached, and Artur Alliksaar, a writer who arguably was the most innovative and influential Estonian poet of the time. In Tartu, Alliksaar was known as the "king of the bohemians" and "primus motor," the transformative force of post-war Estonian poetry.[77] Communist Party officials considered him suspect and frequently reprimanded those who associated with this extraordinary poet.

Kaplinski was seen to be the most erudite member of a small group of young intellectuals who in the late '50s and early '60s met to exchange ideas, talk about politics, and cultivate and deepen their knowledge of topics that were not part of the university curriculum. Kaplinski, one member of the "Salon" recalled, was the central figure of the group. He brought books that weren't available elsewhere and enjoyed sharing his thoughts, in particular about literature, cultural philosophy, and religion.[78] It was his relatives across the Baltic Sea, in Sweden, as well as friends from abroad, who supplied him with publications otherwise unavailable in Soviet Estonia.

Kaplinski's critique of "culture" also came at a time when the authorities, with a more or less hidden political agenda, actively pursued a policy that was receptive to national cultural interests whose extent Estonians had not seen during Kaplinski's lifetime. There is broad agreement among historians that the first half of the '60s led to a significant increase of Soviet Estonia's and other Soviet occupied countries' "cultural capital," which is why the so-called Golden Sixties are often regarded as an era of cultural renewal and innovation, especially with respect to literature and poetry.[79]

In addition to the literary renaissance, this period of cultural revival saw Soviet Estonia reconnect with Western European intellectual life and world literature. The local cultural scene was also enriched by the return of deportees from Siberia. Traditions driven underground by the Stalinist purges were, as a consequence of Khrushchev's amnesty in the 1950s, rediscovered by a promising new generation led by such future giants of world culture as Arvo Pärt and Veljo Tormis. As a matter of policy, the Communist regime now actively encouraged more open cultural expression and, under the auspices of the KGB and the Department of Propaganda and Agitation, also sought contact with the émigré community. Many taboos, such as mention of the Gulag, exile literature, and conditions on the collective farms, were broken and became public knowledge.

The 1962 publication of Alexander Solzhenitsyn's *One Day in the Life of Ivan Denisovich* serves as an example of the degree to which previous taboos were now allowed. The text appeared in Estonian translation a year later in the series Loomingu Raamatukogu, which, as part of the general liberalizing trend under Khrushchev, had begun publishing in 1957 and had since played an important role in broadening Estonia's cultural landscape. The introductory note referred to Solzhenitsyn's text as a witness to "those sickly phenomena which are connected to the period of the personality cult which the Party had condemned and banished."[80] Many foreign literary texts became publicly available for the first time in Estonia, including works by Franz Kafka and others who lived and wrote under very different political circumstances, such as the Czech playwright Václav Havel, the Swiss writer Friedrich Dürrenmatt, and the postwar German author Wolfgang Borchert.

In 1964, the President of Finland, Urho Kaleva Kekkonen, paid a visit to Estonia. A year later the Tallinn-Helsinki ferry line was in operation. New movie theaters opened, performers from the West were invited, exhibitions and other public events were organized – all in an effort to reach beyond the Iron Curtain. This especially changed the face of Estonia's capital, the hometown of Kaplinski's wife, Tiia Toomet. The city was brimming with "books, movies, performances, poetry," she wrote. "Never again has it been so joyfully and promisingly open."[81]

What was reduced to blatant acts of terror during the Stalinist period became a much more sophisticated game of manipulation in and of the public sphere. After Stalin's death in 1953, physical violence largely turned into more or less subtle symbolic and moral pressure as well as programmatic attempts to convert and re-educate the local population. While, deep down, many still lived in fear, in the context of Khrushchev's vision of "different roads to socialism" even dissenting voices were largely tolerated by the authorities, at least on the surface and as long as they were not explicitly anti-Soviet. Within the confines of the state monopoly over all mass communication, it was clearly a period of unprecedented intellectual and artistic freedom for postwar Soviet Estonia, and this spawned a spurt of optimism and cultural growth – until 1968. The "Thaw," named after Ilya Ehrenberg's 1954 novel, now reached an end.

Increased curtailment of local autonomy was ushered in with Brezhnev's rise to power in 1964, but until the 1968 crackdown on Czechoslovakia by Moscow-directed Warsaw Pact troops, cultural activity was not yet significantly affected. The reverberations of the crushed "Prague Spring" made themselves felt through tighter censorship and stricter control of contact with the West. Two days after the tanks moved into Prague, on Friday, 23 August 1968, the front page of Soviet Estonia's leading Communist Party newspaper, *Rahva Hääl*, carried the headline "Needed and timely help for the people of Czechoslovakia." The article left little doubt about the Kremlin's position: "No one will ever be allowed to rip out even a single link from the union of friendship between socialist countries ... The enemies of socialism should take note that all their schemes are destined to fail." A general mood of pessimism and even resignation took hold as policies of Russification and centralization rapidly weakened the autonomy of Soviet Estonia. The liberalization processes of the late '50s and '60s came to a grinding halt and, worse, went into reverse. What Václav Havel wrote about Czechoslovakia captures the sentiment shared by many well beyond the borders of his own homeland: "August 1968 did not mean just the routine replacement of a more liberal regime with a more conservative one; it was not just the usual freeze after a thaw. It was something more: it was the end of an era; the disintegration of a spiritual and social climate, a profound mental dislocation ... the whole world crumbled, a world in which we had all learned to live well and move with some ease."[82]

Kaplinski's conflicting but simultaneously bold critical attitude toward "culture," which grew out of this context, found its most prominent and sweeping early expression in his Coltrane poem, which was first published in 1968 in the literary periodical *Noorus* (Youth). Here Kaplinski declared much if not all of European high and popular culture and civilization to be superfluous, from its composers to its explorers and conquerors, from its architecture to its music and philosophical edifices:

> blow your horn John Coltrane ... blow away the solid cities, the memorial tablets, the holy / scriptures, / the national heroes, classical literature, the renaissance, epics, / romantics, Young Germans, Slavophiles, Cromwell and / Richelieu, / James Cook, Columbus, Vasco da Gama, Philip, Louis, all of / them! / Blow away their discoveries and their borders, blow away / their names, their rooms and streets, away, blow away Ludwig / van Beethoven, G.W.F. Hegel Goethe Disraeli Alexander by / the grace / of God Johann Strauss Baudelaire James Joyce, away into the / winds / of oblivion, into the hot holy black winds of oblivion, / their philosophy, their music, their pride and history, / ... blow away their culture, / their armless marble statues, away, back into the earth.[83]

In a similar vein, the twenty-two-year-old Kaplinski noted in diary entries dating from 1962 to 1964 that "the entire European culture is based on a sick overexertion." Shortly before, he wrote: "Perhaps the European will finally also understand that he is in hell and tortures himself with his wishes." Other entries assert the need to escape from all opinions, words, and philosophies, that everything is sacred, except our rational mind, and that we should look outside, not at the window.[84]

ESCAPE FROM ART – APPROACHING THE SOUNDS OF SILENCE

One of Kaplinski's fellow students and long-time acquaintances, the late Estonian poet Andres Ehin, described this consciousness and sensibility in terms of a "passion for the infinite" that is stronger than the fear of it.[85] While he referred to the Estonian poet Artur Alliksaar, who, in 1958, had returned to Estonia after having been arrested and sent to a labour camp, Ehin probably also had other Estonian poets and intellectuals in mind, such as Uku Masing, Ilmar Laaban, the prominent exile Estonian surrealist, and Jaan Kaplinski.

For Kaplinski, however, even poets like Laaban, whose surrealist texts influenced his own early work, were too focused on the arts and aesthetics.[86] Beauty, aesthetic appeal, and literariness no longer held any a special value for Kaplinski. "We are mistaken if we consider the aesthetic dimension to be more important than other" domains, such as ethics, he wrote in *Ööd valged ja mustad* (White and Black Nights), a 2003 book containing some of his correspondence with Finnish-Swedish essayist Johannes Salminen.[87] This view was not new in Kaplinski's thinking. It had emerged already in the early '70s. For example, in a letter dated 27 July 1972, to the American poet Gary Snyder, with whom he had corresponded already for several years, Kaplinski wrote:

> Some time ago [Ivar] Ivask sent me a collection of poems by British authors. I found them, in general, very learned, and nearly impossible to read, as I lack the good British college education ... In our country ... there is no such poetry as these fellows are writing and I don[']t simply know if we have to regret it. But sometimes I regret [that] our (this time Estonian) poetry is too much poetry (be it good or bad). It would be important to draw nearer to the reality, to what simply is, from moment to moment.[88]

Concerned about the predominance of representation and mediated experience, he wrote three decades later, "drifting towards an artificial world, we are losing our connection with reality. An iceberg may be hidden behind this artificial world."[89]

Kaplinski believes that culture and language also align with violence.[90] Of the "Western mind" he has said that it has a "tendency to think in words and see the world as a world of defined meanings," which, for him, "is a kind of rape."[91] This easily forgotten "dark" side of symbols and their extension of or outright complicity in aggression appears to be among the main reasons why, already in the early '60s, Kaplinski challenged the timeless and often unquestioned value attributed to literature. "At any rate, it isn't honest and sensible," he wrote in a 1968 essay entitled "About the Meaning of Literature," to see something "sacred, eternal and valuable in itself in literature."[92] He addressed the issue more bluntly in his diary in 1962. There he raised the possibility of culture being nothing but a disaster for humankind; he called writing a lie, suggested that literature could vanish all together, and coined the term "aliterature" (in Estonian "aliteratuur").[93] Decades later, in a poem first published in

1991, he exaggerates this point somewhat but nonetheless gets straight to the heart of the matter, asserting that "art seems so artistic" and that his aim had become "kirjutada end kunstist lahti, / kirjutada end endast lahti,"[94] "to write himself free of art, / write himself free of himself."[95] Kaplinski has, in fact, often expressed ambivalence towards his craft, and at times even been dismissive about his being a writer. In 2003, the sixty-two-year-old admitted in an interview at his country home near Tartu, "I am not at all interested in literature."[96] One might say that he never particularly was, at least not as an adult, as his wife Tiia Toomet confirms.[97]

Not having much in common with other writers, he often dreads their company. When he and Tiia Toomet in 1973 moved from Tartu to Tallinn, they lived in a government subsidized Writers' Residence. Kaplinski apparently disliked the apartment from the beginning. For him it was a brooding and dark period in his life that included frequent bouts with depression.[98] Located in the center of the city, and with a KGB agent downstairs, for Kaplinski their fourth-floor apartment was a noisy and ominous place. He thought it abnormal that writers would be housed together in one building.[99] "In the company of literary people I haven't known how to be relaxed or engaged," he noted in his diary in 1981.[100] "My problem has been," he wrote in an e-mail to a close friend, "that I cannot read fiction anymore." He all but hates the word "poet"[101] and can't help but feel that he wants to "escape from art, from that which is called culture to which belong all those exhibitions, presentations, discussions, forums, performances, awards, conferences, cultural capitals," and the like.[102] He has even referred to his public reading tours, provocatively but still revealingly, as the literary prostitution of a "call girl." In his book *To Father*, he offers this commentary on writers' festivals: "Voluntarily and out of interest for literature I'd never go to such places. The performances of writers are mostly deadly boring and, for me, reading poetry is a great strain, hard work ... ; probably like the work of a prostitute."[103] Expanding on this analogy, he writes: "In the past we were forbidden to make love to the rich men from the corrupt West. Now we compete for their favour and gifts. We go and sleep with them when we get a telephone call. We call girls and call boys of the Western world are the luckiest of the post-Communist prostitutes. Many of our former harem-mates envy us. We are quite busy, we have to make love to many people, life has become much more expensive and insecure."[104]

In a 1968 publication he argued that the aim of literature cannot be the survival of art:[105] "Even the life of a bee or a cat is worth more than no matter what kind of art, that could be created by destroying that life. And life has the right to defend itself against art if art begins to oppress and endanger it."[106] He maintains that life "cannot be contained in words ... cannot be explained or understood ... can only be lived."[107] To flourish, unforced, as he put it in one of his poems in the 1998 collection *Night Birds, Night Thoughts*, means not to "take refuge in poetry."[108] Otherwise writing "gets in the way of living," and of the aim "to do everything without hindrance," as he made clear in *Through the Forest*.[109] Poetry, in this view, diminishes rather than enriches our sense of fulfillment. In 1968, writing about the "Meaning of Literature," he comments: we "need writers just as we do physicians; we shouldn't think, however, that some day this need for both could not disappear and that such a condition would be bad."[110] In the same year, he explained in the Estonian literary journal *Looming*:

> For years I've followed the gradual decline of my interest in the majority of that which is published under the name of belles-lettres, and is performed on stage or screen. Only in poetry one comes across something, albeit rarely, which reaches past this ennui ...This erosion of interest doesn't spare even great figures from the past or present, neither Goethe, Kafka nor Joyce; modernism in this guise is quite tiresome with its rather foolish pretentiousness. I feel, that I no longer need any of this ... We think that we have continuously developed since the stone age, and only made gains without losing anything. In fact, we've lost a great deal.[111]

Unsurprisingly, then, Kaplinski prefers to "study things, not just invent them,"[112] and finds the idea intriguing "to live in a world where there would be no public cultural life. To live on a solitary island with your family or in some other little group of like-minded people," as he wrote to American poet Sam Hamill. "What would be the goals and values there?" Kaplinski wondered. "What kind of poems or literature would we create there if any at all?"[113]

In this account rendered so far, it has become clear that literature is not the mature Kaplinski's religion. With his criticism of literary art, and culture in general, he instead reaches for an understanding of reality anchored in a more "elementary humanism"; for this reason, he struggles to move "away from superhuman values such as history, the state, a people, class, culture," away from "all of this third."[114] The same sentiment that underlies this striving – one guided by the longing for a predominantly intuitive and correspondingly less mediated way of living – in large measure also shapes Kaplinski's private and personal life.

4

Body Signals

I don't take refuge in poetry.
My poems are refuge taking
in you morning light,
in you morning shadows,
in you morning voices,
in you morning news,
in you early passers by.[1]

Jaan Kaplinski

Why did his world have to be so erotic? Why did everything always have to remind him of sex, arouse him, take his peace of mind away?[2]

Jaan Kaplinski

Writing about quite intimate details in our lives is important, and can even help other people.[3]

Jaan Kaplinski

I have lived a strange life [but] I have learnt to … tolerate the companion I have been to myself for these seventy years.[4]

Jaan Kaplinski

In his 2007 autobiographical novel *The Same River* (*Seesama jõgi*), Kaplinski wrote about the longing to return into the ocean[5] or to "disappear, die, dissolve" into the Ema River, the Mater Acquarum in his hometown Tartu, as if to relive the relationship between mother and child in its earliest phase and "melt into everything else."[6] Echoing this earlier – one might say, mystical – longing, Kaplinski noted in a newspaper article about Lao-Tse: "We should be one with our life, not putting anything between us and our life."[7] According to his recollection, published in his first semi-autobiographical text, written in the early 1970s and entitled *Where the Night Came From* (*Kust tuli öö)*, the roots of this persistent yearning reach deeply into his childhood, a time when he thought of himself merged with his surroundings, "exactly in the center of his world which was connected to all other worlds, open in all directions."[8]

For prominent thinkers from the more distant past, such as Lao-Tse, whom Kaplinski associated with notions fundamental to unforced flourishing, it is the infant's "invisible" union which presents the ultimate mode of existence – seemingly unmediated, unaware, and unrestrained.[9] "He who is in harmony with the Dao / Is like a newborn child," the Daoist philosopher is credited with having written. How does one arrive at the Dao? Kaplinski asked in his afterword to the Daodejing. His answer: "By emptying oneself, by abandoning knowledge, striving, one's ego, even morals and ethics,"[10] by once again becoming, as it were, a child – the way we are when we fall in love, unencumbered by "boundaries," and connected to "everything."[11]

Here Kaplinski aligns with a stage in human development in which unforced flourishing, fulfilled and frustrated, finds another seminal expression, namely in the period that belongs to early infancy. It is generally acknowledged that infants initially lack awareness of themselves as bounded and differentiated from their environment. They don't have an inkling of their individuality. Instead, in their perception – as it has been construed – the environment appears to be an extension of themselves. The infant, as yet unable to distinguish between self and other, simply is. One might say, the experience of the infant is nameless. Words are superfluous. Until their individuality and their capacity for symbolization develops, and they learn to be alone, infants are also subject to the illusion that they are omnipotent. What they need, provided there is appropriate care, largely comes to them as if by magic. Resonating with the seemingly contradictory meanings of the Estonian word "looma," mentioned earlier, this strengthens the perception of infants – if one can put it in these terms – of creating as well as being one with the world around them. While this identity of involvement and evolution helps maintain the illusion of their creative powers and the sense that there is no difference between inside and outside, in reality, of course, infants are not omnipotent at all. They are, instead, subject to an aloneness that takes place "under maximum conditions of dependence."[12] Oblivious to this reality of extreme vulnerability, they experience – and this is commonly regarded as part of their normal development – the bliss of complete, unimpeded harmony.

The value frequently assigned to this phase in the maturation process brings into view the distance that separates the perspective underlying unforced flourishing from more familiar conceptions of human fulfillment. Although the desire to re-experience this kind of "mystical union" is believed to stay with us throughout our lives, in the case of adults, except in the context of theistic and non-theistic religious experiences, it is often regarded as a sign of immaturity and weakness. In extreme cases this desire may even develop, it has been argued, into a pathological condition carrying with it the threat of moving the individual "back towards less and less sanity, more and more dependency."[13] Ultimately, we are told, the "fulfillment of such a longing" for unity of experience "would be the equivalent of the loss of personal identity, that is of *psychic death*."[14]

For Kaplinski, however, the inverse holds true: lack of access to the undifferentiated world in early infancy represents and constitutes a fundamental loss. "Living like this," he writes in the novel *The Same River*, "a normal everyday life was also dying, the shell of habits, beliefs and commitments that grows around a newborn child is a coffin, a sarcophagus."[15] In other words, from the perspective of unforced flourishing, early infancy yields a sense of maturity which the development towards increased independence, and the individuality tied to it, puts at risk.

In contrast to Kaplinski's perspective, the widely accepted understanding of healthy development entails what can be regarded as a shared space and a permeable boundary between individuals and the world surrounding them: like a membrane, the boundary defines us as individuals.[16] At the same time, it allows us to connect to a common area, an intermediary or "potential space" (Winnicott). It constitutes a shared space that binds us together, in co-operation and conflict. Importantly, it is also the location of "play," for children and adults alike, which, as Winnicott pointed out, "expands into creative living and into the whole cultural life … It can be looked upon as sacred to the individual in that it is here that the individual experiences creative living."[17] In this fashion, we are told, the infant becomes ready to explore the world and begins to develop a sense of self without being traumatized by the separation this entails: "The baby's confidence in the mother's reliability, and therefore in that of other people and things, makes possible a separating-out of the not-me from the me. At the same time, however, it can be said that separation is avoided by the filling in of the potential space with creative playing, with the use of symbols."[18] As a consequence, "children become capable not only of differentiating themselves from others but of maintaining an image of an object in its absence."[19] Representing the union with the mother, such objects help "the child to support her absence" and in this way deal with the pain of separation and otherness.[20]

This, according to Winnicott, is how confidence in the world develops, how trust is placed in it; as the infant's individuality unfolds, the foundations for a healthy and mature individual – "a solid sense of self" – establish themselves, and the capacity to meet social needs, and create and savour a communicative culture grows. Indeed, this is also where the love for human-made objects, material and non-material, takes root and merges with a sense that humans, as creators of their destiny and happiness, are inherently superior to all other living beings.

On the other hand, as Winnicott understood, a very different intuition might come to characterize an individual. The toddler may not learn to hold an image of the absent mother in its memory and sooth itself with the help of such a representation. Instead of developing trust in its own ability to create such comforting symbols and fill the void, or potential space, left by the absent mother, "the infant can have no hope whatever," we are told, "of a capacity for excited relationships with objects or people in what we as observers call the real world, external or shared reality."[21] The process of individuation, ego development from dependence to relative independence, is inhibited, the capacity for self-care, symbolization, play, fantasy, and all the vitality associated with it, as well as cultural experience in general, is diminished.

If we challenge these points by pressing them further, various basic, indeed existential, questions arise. What if, contrary to Winnicott, we held on to the vision of an undifferentiated world in spite of the resistance it might provoke? What if, instead, we were compelled to call this quest "rational" and engagement with it "creative" and let it spill over, beyond the aesthetic and spiritual realms, into other domains of our lives? Considering such questions and possibilities brings us closer to understanding Jaan Kaplinski, including what governs his contrarian inner experience of social and intimate relationships.

For him, it is not enough to cultivate a shared space where the edges of our selves are allowed to fuse, creating links across divides. Instead of maximizing the potential of this intermediary space, he, in contrast, concentrates attention on minimizing it. The crucial point here is this: diminishing Winnicott's "transitional" space, for Kaplinski, does not necessarily mean diminishing the capacity for human fulfillment. Rather, its quality and focus changes, and access is granted to a different path to social and intimate relationships – one predominantly nonverbal, guided by "silent signals," and driven by the desire to stay in tune with our intuitive self.

What, then, does it mean for Kaplinski to connect to others and for relationships to flourish, unforced, following the "silent signals" we habitually tend to exclude, curtail, or push to the margins?

INSTINCTS AT WAR – AN IRREPARABLE RIFT?

A close friend of Kaplinski has said that she has "never seen anybody love being in love as much as he does."[22] Is it this unusual intensity that has put him at odds with those whose love he has sought? Or has he been "simply afraid [of] and frustrated with being in love, but unable to do something against it," as he has noted.[23] Of this, at least, Kaplinski is certain: "I am capable of falling in love completely and this complicates what follows. And I can't change this."[24] Accepting substitutes – art, music, literature, perhaps even religion – has seemed equally impossible for him, and it is easy to see why. To him, they are "the product of … unsatisfied love" – a lowly, perhaps even misguided rather than sublime stand-in.[25] Nor would he wholeheartedly accept the "fact that the people we love have their own lives to live."[26] In his eyes, this insistence on maintaining a certain distance is less a matter of acknowledging individuality, a "real other," than expressing a "terrible feeling of vulnerability to loss," a hidden fear that our secret wish for more complete togetherness might be frustrated.[27] As a consequence, it becomes more difficult to admit who we are and what we really want.

Unable either sufficiently to curtail or treat his instinctual forces lightly, for a long time these forces clashed with the spontaneous but inherently altruistic responsiveness of unforced flourishing, the heart of his sense of human fulfillment. Resolution of this conflict that pitted his sexuality against his signature sentiment appeared impossible. He was at war with himself. All this left Kaplinski chronically "love sick."[28] Astonishingly, though, he emerged convinced that love can be its own cure – if only we let it. This is to say that, in his account of love, our instincts are not as deeply conflicted as common wisdom holds. Put in Freudian terms, "renunciation of desire" is not a necessity, at least not as much as is generally thought.[29] Recalling views about sexuality and love he attributed to one of his soul mates, the writer Isaac Bashevis Singer, Kaplinski noted: "although it can be the source of much anguish, our instincts don't lie."[30] But we don't easily trust our bodily instincts. The body's signals point to a sense of human fulfillment at odds with our civilized selves.[31]

A HOSTILE WORLD – THE UNBEARABLE LIGHTNESS OF PROXIMITY

To gain better access to Jaan Kaplinski's account of love, we first need to take note of his apparently paradoxical behaviour towards others. It masks what appears to be his true aim: all he really wants, it seems, is closeness. But, as he wrote in one of his plays, he likes to be so close "that there wouldn't be anything at all in-between us, that nothing would fit between us, neither space nor time nor anxiety."[32] Kaplinski's assertion from *The Butterfly and the Mirror* resonates with the fundamental yet paradoxical desire to "rid oneself of one's essential otherness, of both body and mind" that persists, as psychoanalytic thinkers have argued, "in the heart of every human being."[33]

The trouble is that he is not comfortable around people. He shies away from them not because he dislikes companionship or fears embarrassment or being judged too harshly. On the contrary, he craves close friendship and intimacy, but to an extent that easily appears excessive to many and perhaps even threatens their sense of self. Being socially ill at ease, in Kaplinski's case, does not reflect a need for distance; rather, it merely conceals his frustrated desire for a closeness that is unburdened by the boundaries that identities require and produce. Is it, then, for this reason – a need for closeness seemingly impossible to satisfy – that he so often seeks seclusion and ends up being lonely?

We don't know whether the conundrum also leads to the true source of his art, but the fact that he refers to his work as both a poetry of "loneliness"[34] and, at the same time, a "declaration of love to the world" suggests that he is indeed caught in a double bind that bleeds into his poetry, and perhaps even lies at its heart.[35] In one of his poems that evokes conflicting images of lonesomeness, abandonment, and the wholeness of maternal care, he concludes: "Our own intellect, our own history / have brought us into this void, / step by step, as mother walks her child, / and suddenly lets it fall / from the brink of the world / we were taught to live / and to believe in."[36] In a text accompanying artwork by the Estonian artist Kaljo Põllu, he alludes to this sense of forlornness as a fact of life, part of the human condition: "Together with a human being is born his loneliness, his being alone ... When the blood tie is severed the human being cries out – the crying means loneliness."[37]

Convinced that he is not liked and certain that others are uncomfortable in his presence, Kaplinski often thinks of himself as socially clumsy and prefers to stay away from social events.[38] Even at home, with members of his own family, he has been known to seek out tasks that allow him to be on his own. As one of his sons once remarked, whenever an opportunity arose he would monopolize household chores that promised solitude, such as going into the cellar to look after the coal for the furnace or doing the laundry.[39]

At times this tendency has been embarrassingly obvious. Recalling episodes from their life together, Tiia Toomet spoke of her husband's outright antisocial behaviour.[40] As some have observed, not without dismay, Kaplinski sometimes appears ignorant of the hospitality and efforts his hosts extend towards him. He is known to leave public performances unexpectedly, express impatience with social rituals and graces, or dispense with them altogether. He finds it difficult to "discern other people's feelings,"[41] as some have noted, and can appear insensitive.[42] This is not to say that he means to offend or alienate. Rather, for Kaplinski, public performances, such as poetry readings, are marred by great emotional strain.[43] The world then appears to him like a "foreign and hostile force."[44]

Shortly after his 45th birthday, on 29 January 1986, he wrote in his diary: "Lately socializing has become difficult. Can't handle going to the library, today couldn't even get myself to go to the bookstore to ask if an order had arrived." Even almost a decade later, after years of participation in poetry bashes, arts festivals, and countless receptions with dignitaries, organizers, and fellow writers around the world, he still feels apprehensive in public places and social situations. Calling his own behaviour excessive, in his diary he recounts one instance when he "more or less fled" a public event "without collecting the travel money and without speaking to several people" with whom he should have talked.[45] In his own view, he is as timid an adult as he was a child: "Here I am, officially 54 years old, yet I still feel like the shy little boy from University Street who was afraid to go to the store."[46] Perhaps stricken again by social anxiety, just moments before he was to take the stage at a high profile public affair in Sweden, he unexpectedly, and probably to the surprise of all assembled, asked a friend to take his place, go on stage, and perform the poetry reading on his behalf.[47]

Being in public, and especially performing his poetry, has become ever more excruciating. His shyness, and indeed embarrassment, have intensified[48] and developed into a social phobia that has grown even "more serious with age."[49] Shortly before his 70th birthday, which he would spend in New Zealand to "escape" from any anniversary celebrations in Estonia, he even wondered whether he might be autistic: "I hate phone calls ... I have problems with replying to mails, difficulties with talking to [the] public ... I can tolerate talking to other people not longer than about an hour, with the exception of some people, first of all some of my family members."[50]

Preferring to stay in the background whenever possible, he retreats into the solitude of his country home. And even there he appears to be most comfortable away from the main house and everyone else, either in the sauna or behind his ponds at the edge of the forest in a small one-room converted trailer. As his desire for closeness is unusually strong and deep but rarely satisfied, he is left with few friends. Juhan Viiding, the Estonian writer and celebrated actor, was among the exceptions. When he committed suicide, Kaplinski found himself without a single close male companion.[51]

Already as a child, he appears to have suffered from a heightened sense of social unease. Perhaps it was even fear of others, which, as one of his fellow writers suggested, arose from the "despair, despondency and pain" his parents experienced in 1940–41 when he was still in his mother's womb and the world around them collapsed into the turmoil of war.[52] This much we know with some certainty: worried about his difficulty interacting with other children, his mother enrolled Jaan in school at the early age of six, which made him the youngest in a class of 49 classmates, most of whom were two years his senior. Nora Kaplinski hoped this would help young Jaan's social skills and give him something to do. But instead of making new friends, he withdrew even more. Prone to ill health, he also often missed school, Kaplinski's grade one teacher recalled.[53] Still, he did exceptionally well academically. Except for sports and music, he earned all first-class honours but remained a loner, perhaps despite or possibly because of his academic aptitude. His Polish name and fatherless state may have further contributed to his solitude.

While he continued to be a loner during adolescence, he withdrew even more in his twenties. Ever since, he has struggled with his seemingly antisocial disposition. However, it is not only that Kaplinski is socially uncomfortable, inclined to impassivity and, on occasion, even off-putting, apparently ungrateful aloofness, disinterestedness, and ignorance of basic social graces. He also lacks ease in social situations and the role playing needed to make and keep friends.[54] Warming up to another person by engaging in small talk and exploring the potential for a closer relationship without making claims does not come naturally to him. "In every way I am different from everybody," he notes in his diary, "and I have probably never succeeded in approaching women the way it is normally done."[55] In his autobiographical novel *The Same River*, he writes that the young student-poet was "too serious" and lacked the playfulness needed to develop relationships.[56] "With the girls he had to play some kind of courtship game that never worked out for him."[57] He was "too direct," and this "often annoyed people."[58] Rather than employing social rituals, Kaplinski, like his autobiographical protagonist, tends to bypass them as if unforced social flourishing were an inevitable outcome and no bridge was needed from play and mere potential to the actual, from signs that signal the desire for closeness to closeness itself. Never having learned to enjoy this kind of play, the rift between him and those whose nearness he sought widened to a gap.[59] In one diary entry Kaplinski even wonders whether his shyness was due to traumatic experiences during his youth, a remnant of Stalinism when he was counted among those considered suspect by the authorities.[60] But perhaps it was something else altogether: a lack of emotional intimacy, perceived or real, in the mother–son relationship.

TOUGH LOVE AND THE LOST ART OF SELF-SOOTHING

The narrator of Kaplinski's autobiographical novel *The Same River* writes about the unnamed protagonist and his family: "They never talked about how they felt about each other. Everyone in the family lived and died alone, separately, like snails in their shells. If someone inadvertently or in desperation stretched their soft body a little way out of the shell, they scared themselves as well as others."[61] In his autobiography *Isale*, Kaplinksi describes how he grew up in the company of women who cultivated an ironic disposition towards relationships with men and,[62] as he later noted in an e-mail, "were either old as my grandmother, widowed or single."[63] The prevailing attitude of these women towards men was one of sarcasm, he said in an interview, and sexual matters were treated as a taboo subject.[64] As he revealed, the harshest punishment he received from his mother on a couple of occasions had to do with his pubescent indiscretions of a sexual nature. At one time, for example, he was caught drawing female private parts. For that he received a strapping, in his mind undeserved and, given his sensitive disposition, possibly "fateful" for his development.[65] Together with the fact that he lived in a social environment perhaps typical of Nordic countries, where revealing one's emotions was frowned upon in general,[66] all this left him with the sense that sex was something "bad" and that one's feelings had to remain hidden.[67]

But the roots of his troubles reach deeper, he seems convinced. As his wife Tiia Toomet has remarked, it is as if he has spent his entire life escaping his childhood.[68] It bears repeating that in his childhood he may have lacked physical and emotional closeness with his mother. According to his recollection, she avoided taking him into her lap, holding and pampering him; he never received the affection from her that he craved. In later years, too, the distance between them seemed to grow, emotionally and intellectually. "It is very painful and very sad, not being able to find any contact with one's mother," he confessed in his 1981 diary,[69] adding that he can't even imagine "a warm, trusting and good relationship with her."[70] Perhaps worse than that, the already fragile bond with his mother was marred by contradictory demands, as he recalled in *Isale*. She "wants her son to be close to her," he lamented, to "listen to her, love her, do as she tells him; but when the son really comes close, trusts her, the mother pushes him away, saying something bad, insulting."[71] Some "timid attempts to get closer ... ended so badly," the forty-year-old Kaplinski admitted in his diary, that the experience left him distraught and drained of any "courage to ever try again."[72] Although we cannot be certain of Kaplinski's specific circumstances, psychoanalysts agree that the consequences of too little loving, supportive, and consistent care during early childhood reach deep into adult life. The possibility that he did not receive the necessary maternal comfort and care as an infant may very well explain why he has found it so difficult, perhaps even impossible, to successfully deal with inner conflicts later on in life.

Adults who as infants were lovingly eased into becoming increasingly independent are more likely to trust their ability to cope with separation. It is said that this capacity for self-reliance develops when there are enough reassuring early childhood memories.[73] Over time these are internalized and, in a further development, give rise to a comforting mental image representing the mother. This image is eventually replaced by substitutes, such as a blanket or a teddy bear, which, as symbols, stand in for memories of wholeness, warmth, and care. Aided by this internalized soothing maternal environment, as we know from Winnicott's work, the ability to confidently and independently deal with inner pain grows. Expressing "little or no identification with an internal caretaking mother," Kaplinski lacked the "psychic resource" necessary for relieving emotional or mental stress.[74] With his capacity to self-soothe diminished, he was compelled to look for relief elsewhere. The child within him turned to "endless compulsive pursuits that bring only temporary relief."[75]

Although judgments of this kind are perhaps too easy to make, this nevertheless is how Kaplinski may have developed such "immense expectations" linked to "erotic relations," as he put it, and become overly dependent,[76] craving that elusive "complete unison" where all differences align into a deeply felt unrehearsed "harmony" between two people.[77] Indeed, if we are to believe the almost seventy-year-old Kaplinski's own words, most of his "passionate love stories … were initiated or at least greatly helped by the women" involved.[78] While it often is less stressful for him "to communicate with women than men,"[79] his attitude toward women remains conflicted. Even as he has "desired and feared" them, "the combination of desire and fear had become a huge wall between him and the fulfillment of his desires."[80] Unsurprisingly, perhaps, he appears "incredibly ashamed and awkward when he speaks about his sexual desires."[81]

Although troubled by not knowing how to initiate a relationship and convey his thoughts and feelings in a more indirect, playful, and less intrusive way, his intuition and intellect have compelled him to nurture his sense of unforced social flourishing. In his eyes only an "artless" approach can grant access to the closeness he seeks.[82] Like the character in his novel, Kaplinski dreams of a bond that might stir others to think and experience what may at first seem impossible: a union so sensitive and giving that it is sustained by the most simple of signs, perhaps not needing any words at all.[83]

The supreme value he assigns to silence in his poetry integrates well with this desire for unmediated closeness. Indeed, everything appears to be rooted in silence: "In the beginning is no beginning. / In the beginning is silence. Silence is within you." And in the same poem, he summarizes his stance as a poet: "It is not worth being a 'poet' – writing poems, unless you cannot / do otherwise – if you can, leave them unwritten."[84] Another poem, composed in 1996, ends with these lines: "it really makes little sense / to write so many poems / on paper. / Maybe in wind, / maybe in water, / maybe with silence / without words / on the silence on the fresh snow."[85] Elsewhere, in the collection entitled *Through the Forest*, he expands on this idea: "When you write, you have died a little. / If you want to write about life / it is difficult to grasp it / and live. / You have stepped away from life: / instead of living, you write."[86] But even if his dream of wordless love were to come true, he worries that his erotic urges would intervene and strain against a way of loving that unfolds of its own accord. It is this collision that leaves him at war with himself: as the force of his desires wells up, the love he seeks is dragged down.

LOVE SICK – FROM AFFECTION TO AFFLICTION

In the vivid words of a close female friend, Kaplinski's experience of love "overwhelms his entire personality. He wants to crawl under the skin of his loved one, be the absolute center of her attention."[87] The intensity of his desire described here parallels Kaplinski's own depiction of erotic passion in his novel *The Same River*. About the main character's attraction to a woman, he writes: "leaving a thirsting lust behind; he would have liked to really take Malle, to eat and drink her."[88]

The mysteries of another person's life, especially those concerning issues of intimacy, do not easily reveal themselves. But Tiia Toomet, Kaplinski's wife since 1969, knows that his sexual impulses are his most troubling, if least understood, side. Indeed, the instinctual forces at work in him are, in her words, "unbelievable and incomprehensible," "deep" and "dark."[89] Perhaps alluding to his own inner turmoil, in *The Same River* Kaplinski speaks of a "blind, scorching desire" for a "woman's body," a desire "more important than anything else," stronger even than love.[90]

Although sexual themes are rare in Kaplinski's work, and he himself does not think of his poems as overtly sexual, traces of a preoccupation with sex can also be found in his poetry. In his collection of poems entitled *Evening Brings Everything Back*, he writes: "I like sex more than ethics and aesthetics / I like women more than high ideals."[91] Indeed, there are many indications from Kaplinski's life that this depiction of a man easily and perhaps even all-consumingly infatuated with women not only reflects his own views but also shapes his behaviour. What his poetry masks is the confused, deeply passionate, indeed, unusually irrational side of his love.[92]

During one of his engagements as a guest lecturer abroad, in Vancover, Canada, the physical beauty of a woman mesmerized him and, if we are to believe his diary, caused him to fall so irresistibly in love that he could not do anything but think of her.[93] Casting aside any scruples and thoughts about fidelity or causing offence with his amorous advances, one morning the then fifty-five-year-old Kaplinski even knocked on her office door and, when she opened it, reached for her hand, placed it on his chest, and, his heart pounding, asked whether she could feel how excited he became when he saw her.[94] Although it turned out to be a one-sided and short-lived affair, Kaplinski appears to have been so infatuated that it "didn't seem to matter" what she said. In an interview years later, the woman recalled of her encounter with Kaplinski: "He was so amazed with his feelings."[95] It wasn't so much that the possibility of rejection looked inconceivable to him, as he explained his behaviour in retrospect. Rather, plagued by selfdoubts, "shyness and clumsiness," he was "afraid of being rejected."[96] When it became clear to him that his love would indeed remain unrequited, he tried to convince her, almost in tears, that falling in love is a wonderful gift not to be wasted. Holding incompatible views of their relationship, the two quickly parted, leaving Kaplinski to wonder how much of a fool he might be in her eyes.[97] What he wrote in *The Same River* about his young protagonist's attraction to a woman in the 1960s resonates with Kaplinski's own encounter as a grown man in his fifties: The student "looked towards her and suddenly felt he desired her. The feeling was unexpected and surprisingly strong, subsuming everything else for an instant and momentarily depriving him of his power to say anything sensible."[98]

Jaan Kaplinski's inability to maintain a more moderate love relationship and settle into a less intense, all-embracing degree of closeness that nevertheless includes sexual intimacy, appears to be a trait so firmly anchored in him that it has not changed much over the years. His wife Tiia Toomet recalls two telling moments in 1968, a year before they married, that revealed to her the unusual, if not distressingly extreme, nature of his disposition. "One time when he was about to leave, as he bent over to tie his shoe laces he suddenly stopped moving and then said: 'Right now I feel so good that I'd like to die. There is no reason to continue living, whatever comes can only be worse.' Another time the then twenty-seven-year-old Kaplinski promised to row a boat into the middle of the Ema River and set himself on fire if I did not marry him."[99] Leaving Tiia Toomet stunned, this latter experience felt, as she recalled it, "like a giant thundering ocean wave that all at once descended" upon her.[100]

Almost forty years later, this overwhelming way of loving – he has referred to it as a "colossal" passion with an inescapable hold over him – has continued to chart the course of his intimate relationships.[101] Judging by some of his love letters to another woman, his feelings have at times become all-consuming, welling up to a point where everything reminds him of his loved one: "You came too close, directly into me and now I can't get away from you, anywhere. I carry you with me everywhere ... If I would fly away, you'd be with me ... You are in my stories, poems ... There is no place without you."[102] He longs for her presence and obsessively checks for missed phone calls and e-mails.[103] For more than a year, he keeps a message from her on his cell phone.[104] In long e-mails he not only professes his love for her but also raises the specter of suicide should the relationship fail and the affair come to an end. He simply can't bear the thought of being without her.[105]

SEXUAL TRAUMA – LOSING CONTROL

Most likely written in 1972 but not published until 1990, Kaplinski's autobiographical work *Where the Night Came From* includes a Brazilian legend. It tells the story of human beings who live in harmonious accord with plants and animals. Everything exists in a state of unity until the protagonist, a young man, wants to sleep with his wife. First he must separate time into day and night. But when this is achieved, he is upset because with the arrival of the night "everything in the world had gone to ruin."[106] The fulfillment of erotic longing extinguishes the union between the human and the nonhuman, separates narrow self-interest from the broader social good, and puts human beings at odds with themselves. Resonating with this story that ties sexual pleasure to the dark side of our lives, Kaplinski later remarked about himself: "My tragedy has been that I am a very sexual person."[107] But no matter how much he "hate[s] being adulterous, lying or hiding [his] feelings," he finds himself, as if addicted, unable to stop.[108]

The theme of a man's enslavement to his sensuous desires also surfaces in Kaplinski's play *The Butterfly and the Mirror*.[109] "There really isn't much left of me," one of the characters confesses, "only this love that thinks for me, decides and talks."[110] In *Isale* (To Father), as well, Kaplinski admits that sex has caused him more pain than pleasure.[111] And in his book *Kevad kahel rannikul* (Spring on Two Shores), he acknowledges that he is no stranger to former US president Bill Clinton's "sexual addiction and stupidity."[112] Reminiscent of Kaplinski in his early twenties, the protagonist in *The Same River* is haunted and tormented by his hunger for sex.[113] Startled and exasperated "by the realization that there was something within him that was stronger than he was, something capable of suddenly taking the reins from him,"[114] he is left to wonder: "Why did his world have to be so erotic? Why did everything always have to remind him of sex, arouse him, take his peace of mind away?"[115] Is he also describing himself when he remarks in *Where the Night Came From* that sex is liable to change a "man's character beyond recognition?"[116] In his diary, he draws attention to the "forceful and uncaring" behaviour of men in intimate relations and to how it pains him.[117] This aspect of masculinity has "disgusted" him since childhood, he notes elsewhere.[118]

When he finds himself afflicted by his sexual desires, he easily feels that he too might be one of those men he abhors. His inner conflict deepens when he "loses self control" and, in his own words, is transformed into a "wild animal."[119] Love turns against itself and he becomes a "prisoner" of his emotions,[120] an "alcoholic" of sorts, chronically deprived of erotic love and at the same time ashamed of his sexual desires but unable to change.[121] Worse still, his "sexual hunger" not only "disgusts" him but makes initiating intimacy all but impossible.[122] He would betray his own account of love, the intimate and spontaneous mutual responsiveness between two people as he imagines it. What others might regard as an expression of assertiveness, he perceives as aggression. The collision between his sexuality and his larger vision of human fulfillment drives this already mostly concealed part of himself even further underground, adding to his despair.[123]

After some awkward and timid encounters as a teenager and the frustration of not finding a partner to satisfy his sexual needs – he was a university student when he experienced sex for the first time – Kaplinski tried to abstain in his twenties.[124] Torn, he imagined a world that does not know sex at all. Uncertain of himself, he asked: "Do I want sex or freedom from sex?"[125] In an article entitled "Avatusest ja armastusest" (Of Openness and Love), published in 1980, Kaplinski discusses his own "very personal and deep feelings of guilt and gratitude." He notes the destructive force inherent in love, as well as the reluctance to reveal one's weaknesses and desire for tenderness, but at the same time expresses hope that we might still mature sexually and arrive at a point where the border begins to vanish between "you and me, giving and taking."[126]

"ARTLESS" LOVE – INTIMACY AS UNFORCED FLOURISHING

Yet to be true to his own sense of loving also has meant sidestepping more commonly accepted behaviour and ways of thinking about intimate relationships. Elsewhere he refers to this vision as "artless" love: rather than finding mediated expression in "love signals" or "play," or drawing its inspiration from "passion," "intimacy," "commitment," or something else directing his behaviour and, as it were, taking the place of the love he envisions, Kaplinski desires a love that arises and unfolds "naturally," out of its own accord. In *The Same River,* he wrote of a force invisible and nameless, of love as unforced flourishing that "knows no boundaries, connects everything, makes everything one, man and woman, child and adult, brings everything into the light that has no boundaries or shadows."[127]

If we go back more than three decades to a diary entry from 5 November 1980, we find the author's notes on his frustrations about having had to be the one to initiate sex. He wanted this "fence" removed and more mutual attention paid to each other's bodies. He envisioned a relationship in which both partners are always ready to engage erotically. Directed against gender polarity and gender-based stereotypes where the male's love is active and the woman's receptive, Kaplinski's ideal of romantic love puts the woman into the leading role or altogether sidesteps the question of who initiates intimacy.[128] A heightened mutuality and spontaneity then simply merges into a togetherness unaware of itself. Although he did not call it unforced flourishing, Alan Watts, whose work Kaplinski read, expressed this sense of intimate fulfillment perhaps best when, in 1958, he wrote in his book *Nature, Man and Woman*: "The man does not lead and the woman does not follow; the man-and-woman-relationship acts of itself."[129]

Determined no longer to hide his innermost feelings, this vision of love, by Kaplinski's own account, became lived experience for him when he was sixty-seven years old.[130] For Kaplinski, the relationship with his new partner – a fellow Estonian – was one of "almost complete devotion." In a reversal of stereotypical male–female roles, he was the one who appeared openly vulnerable, exposed his sadness, revealed his pain, gave voice to his longing for intimacy, freely expressed what touched him most deeply. Even more importantly, as if embodying unforced flourishing, in this liaison much of what he desired happened without him having, or even knowing how, to ask.[131] Judging by his own account, probably for the first time in his life, he found himself sexually at peace.[132]

And yet, the bond did not last. The closeness, indeed his "absolute dependence on her," as Kaplinski put it, became not only uncomfortable for his lover but also turned into a burden for her, and even elicited a degree of anxiety and, finally, frustration.[133] In the end, she felt trapped and wanted out of the relationship, while he appeared unable to conceal his feelings for her, confessing time and again that he couldn't live without her. As if oblivious to the change in their affair, he was still surprised that his confession shocked her. Once he realized that she carried her love for him more lightly and harboured a more conventional understanding of the relationship between a man and a woman, despair soon followed.[134]

After about four years, Kaplinski reluctantly ended the love affair.[135] He was heartbroken, and, once more, issued barely veiled threats of suicide. But she simply did not share, or no longer had, the same strong feelings for him as he had for her.[136] She wanted more space between them and wished him to be a more independent partner rather than relying on her as much as he did.[137] Feeling diminished to a "beggar for love crumbs,"[138] he could not tolerate that there were so many things more important to her than being with him.[139] She was his life's focal point.[140] When she told him that she was unable to meet his expectations, he responded by saying that without her his life was meaningless. She still wanted to be with him but in a calmer, less dramatic way, committing to more distance and independence. Although he knew that he should not hold on to her with such intensity, he appeared unable to change. As soon as she devoted less time to him, he wrote to her about suicide, characterizing their relationship as a painful "seesaw between heaven and earth."[141]

He did not understand how she could love him but at the same time feel that there was too much love, that his love suffocated her. Describing their relationship in retrospect, Kaplinski recalls enjoying moments of "quite a balanced and creative togetherness"; they even collaborated on several book projects.[142] But eventually she outgrew his expressions of longing. We don't know how his "unsuccessful suicide attempt in December 2004" affected her[143] – he tried to end his life when she told him that she would not marry him.[144] Perhaps she not only experienced distress but also felt coerced, especially on those occasions when, in his despair, he told her that life without her would be a catastrophe.[145] We do, however, know that she resented being made responsible for his life and increasingly experienced the relationship as unduly limiting.[146] Although the letters are clearly subjective and expressive of concealed needs, momentary reactions, and past personal troubles, they nonetheless reveal that the rift between them deepened. What for Kaplinski was an honest acknowledgement of his sentiments, increasingly became over-identification in her eyes, indeed a burden.

Or was she perhaps merely reluctant to open up and let herself be carried away by her love for him? Looking back, this is what Kaplinski believes. "Thus, my passionate love was not always, up to the end of our relationship, just a burden for her, sometimes she was eager to answer to it with a lot of passion. My opinion is that perhaps she understood that her passion was becoming dangerous for her, and struggled with herself, sometimes suppressing it, sometimes letting go. She rarely spoke about our love story very openly."[147] This much we know from their correspondence: separateness was unbearable for him, but necessary for her.

No longer able to tolerate the "swaying from passionate love to anger and rejection," Kaplinski, heartbroken and at the brink of divorce, found himself drawn to his wife Tiia again as he was compelled to make a decision.[148] Once more, despite everything, she welcomed him back. This pattern of his unfaithfulness and her forgiveness had begun early in their marriage. In a private correspondence recalling their first and perhaps most devastating marriage crisis, in the mid-'70s, Tiia Toomet revealed how deeply she had felt betrayed by her husband's intimate relationship with another woman, a close friend of hers. His affair came as such a shock to her that she was ready to leave him:

> But at that time I had small children and had not yet finished my schooling. I didn't have a job, an income nor my own place. Perhaps I was looking for excuses to conceal my indecisiveness and shyness. Perhaps I still loved Jaan and, regardless of everything, wanted to stay with him. This is how I didn't leave him, nor did I make Jaan leave … and piece by piece tried to glue together what had broken … I knew that cracks would remain … I chose Jaan, this was my own free choice and perhaps not until this choice did I take on the responsibility for our future life together … Deeply convinced that this was also best for him, from then on I always wanted him to come back. And he always did, wounded, washed out, fragile.[149]

EROTIC RELIGION – CAN LOVE BE ITS OWN CURE?

Despite the turmoil and emotional pain that his mode of loving has caused, his account of love often takes on spiritual and religious contours.[150] The day before his 40th birthday he noted in his diary how he longed for "true" understanding and how this desire was connected to physical closeness.[151] Three years later he wrote of the vital role of love in his quest for a spiritual union and how he had never abandoned a belief in love as his "infinity."[152] Fed by the hope of finding "salvation," he maintains that "erotic love has had a ritualistic-religious significance" for him, and he loathes whatever threatens this "erotic religion."[153]

When he meets a woman to whom he is attracted, he hopes for a transformative "shamanic-mystical experience"[154] where the "border between religion, hope and love" vanishes.[155] This is how his understanding of love finds expression in his prose fiction: it is "like an encounter with God: complete surrender, fusion, becoming one total devotion, merging into one, becoming one."[156] "This was what he longed for," the protagonist in *The Same River* reveals, "even if this yearning was absurd, he could not live without it."[157]

But it would be a mistake to confuse his "erotic religion" with religiosity. On the contrary, Kaplinski asks, isn't "fervent devotion to some god a compensation for unhappy love?"[158] Raising the specter of religious fanaticism and personality cults, he cautions against substitutes for erotic love. Rather than turning it into an object, he believes, we should allow love to unfold and run its course.[159] "Much more dangerous" than love are replacements,[160] such as religiosity, that may lead to a destructive exploitation of our sexual energy.[161] Our "inability to find true love, not our alienation from religion" might be our real problem, Kaplinski concluded in a letter to Frank Tallis, the author of the book *Love Sick*.[162]

This distinction is important to remember or we will misunderstand Kaplinski: where others see "transitional objects" at work and value them as religiously charged or otherwise inspired subjective transformations, he, in contrast, sees frustrated human flourishing, inner conflict, and growing remoteness emerge, between him and the unmediated, spontaneous love he seeks.

For Rilke, love meant to welcome distance: "once the realization is accepted," Rilke wrote, "that even between the closest human beings infinite distances continue to exist, a wonderful living side by side can grow, if they succeed in loving the distance between them which makes it possible for each to see the other whole and against a wide sky!"[163] Rather than embracing distance, it bears repeating, Kaplinski, in contrast, yearns for a way of loving without "anything at all in between us," to borrow from his play *The Butterfly and the Mirror*.[164] Painfully aware of the propensity in his cultural environment to express love "through some objects, something third, external," one's creations, all he wants is the "minimum: bodies ... the coming together of two living substances ... like a baby in its mother's body."[165] Unsurprisingly, then, his quest for those elusive moments of "absolute unison" and "harmony" culminates in his seemingly simple advice:[166] to flourish, unforced, listen to your body![167] As troubling as its wordless message might be, ignoring it, he is convinced, is not only the greater risk but also constitutes a significant loss. In Kaplinski's words: to "escape from one's body ... means escaping from the most immediate and truest reality given to us."[168]

5

Desire for Dependence

Shunryu Suzuki
a little Japanese living
and teaching in California
couldn't be my teacher
one of my non-teachers
a little lit match from God's matchbox
sea wind soon blew out
somewhere between California and Estonia
somewhere between East and West
between somewhere and nowhere
nobody can find out what remained of him
after the wind has blown and the tide
come and gone – the white sand
as smooth as before – but his smile
from the back cover of *Zen Mind Beginner's Mind*
has silently infected book after book on my shelves
and perhaps shelves themselves and walls and wallpapers too[1]

Jaan Kaplinski

Amae is a dependency need which manifests itself in a longing to merge with others.[2]

Takeo Doi

In the summer of 1988 ... the crowd is in full throat protesting the Molotov-Ribbentrop Pact, whose secret protocol gave Estonia to the Soviets ... It seemed, finally, that independence was possible again.[3]

Priit Vesilind

Another seminal dimension of unforced flourishing, which is related to his way of loving described in the previous chapter, elucidates how profoundly Kaplinski's signature mental mode shaped his social self and emotional life. To gain access to it means reconsidering the prominence we tend to place in our thinking on the need to curb aggression by directing its energy towards behaviour considered socially useful or aesthetically pleasing, and in this way "set limits" to our "aggressive instincts."[4] Freud famously called this transformation of our "primary mutual hostility" *sublimation* and claimed that we owe our "civilized life" (in the German original Freud used the word "Kultur") in large measure to this transformation.[5] "The greatest impediment to civilization," in Freud's view, is our "instinct of destruction," which has in turn given such rise and standing to "Kultur" – our "higher psychical activities, scientific, artistic" and "ideological," as he notes in *Civilization and Its Discontents*.[6]

We can take the measure of Kaplinski's mentality and behaviour with greater precision if we invert this commonly held view and consider the possibility that we are not aggressive by nature, as we have been led to believe with Freud. What if we are in fact born altruists instead and not hostage to an inborn hostility?[7] Embracing such a view, our dependence on "civilized life," and the renunciation yoked to it, would diminish – and trust in our instincts and silent, non-verbal signals would grow correspondingly. Such is the shift in perspective derived from the proposition articulated by the Japanese psychologist Takeo Doi. He posits an "independent drive"[8] that is not only distinct from "the narcissistic sexual and aggressive instincts postulated by the individualistic psychology of Freud" but also more primary.[9] Doi calls it "*amae*," a Japanese word difficult to render into another language but which has generated interest beyond Japan. Doi defines it as a "craving for close contact" anchored in a dependency need that "takes the other person's love for granted."[10] "*Amae* is a good notion," Kaplinski comments in an e-mail.[11] "I recall some parallels from Chinese culture. Francis Hsu has written some articles where he stresses the importance of 'intimate' relations, first of all, family relations in China, saying that such intimacy is unknown in the West. Perhaps I have always sought something of that kind here, and learnt that probably one cannot find anything similar in Estonia. Thus, a good part of my personal history is a history of unrequited love."

Manifest in the "whole continuum of human life from infancy to adulthood" but in conflict with the individualistic psychology that predominates in the West, *amae* constitutes a primary need for loving care.[12] Unlike sublimation, *amae* is "constituted tacitly. It is telepathic, prelinguistic, and does not need the medium of language. It is communicated directly from heart to heart" and "totally hinges upon another person for its satisfaction."[13] In this unmediated sense, *amae* expresses the emotive dimension of unforced flourishing in human relationships, how the need for affection is met, invisibly, as one might say. Rather than approaching it as a condition that must be overcome and believing, as Freud did, that "men are not gentle creatures who want to be loved,"[14] Doi advocates that we trust this instinct, allow it to happen, and conceive of maturity in terms of our capacity to be receptive. Instead of encouraging independence and, as a consequence, forging a "morality of sublimation," the task, then, becomes to nurture our *amae* instinct to a greater extent, sanction it more broadly in a social context, and, in general, be more responsive to the desire to be taken care of.[15]

MEETING THE GURU – ELUSIVE ATTRACTION

It is Kaplinski's relationship with his most influential teacher, Uku Masing, that brings to light how dependence is woven into the fabric of unforced flourishing, how it guides Kaplinski's inner life and behaviour but, superficially at least, resonates with few in the culture into which he was born. When, in the late 1950s, Kaplinski was introduced to Masing, the encounter left the eighteen-year-old student awestruck. He was captivated by Masing's charisma, eloquence, extraordinary memory, and phenomenal capacity to absorb information. Enthralled with his astonishingly broad knowledge of foreign languages and remote cultures, he even found magic in Uku Masing's voice.[16] Always careful not to overstate the case and contribute to the mythologization of Masing, Kaplinski nevertheless unhesitatingly calls him a genius. The erudite intellectual influenced Kaplinski probably more than anyone else.[17] "I find it very difficult to imagine what would have become of me had I not met Uku Masing," Kaplinski wrote more than four decades after his first visit to Masing's home on Hurda Street in Tartu.[18]

Longing for his mother's love and mourning the lack of a father figure, in Uku Masing young Jaan Kaplinski also saw the other parent he never had. Feeling this "tremendous need for someone, for an elder man, whom to believe [and] trust," as he later revealed in an interview,[19] he confided in Uku Masing, even told him about his most private concerns and inner turmoils.[20] With him he could share the poems he had written as a teenager but that he had kept secret from most others. Although Uku Masing turned out to be a somewhat reluctant mentor, he did take interest in Kaplinski's work, encouraged him, read drafts of his poems, and even made suggestions for improvement. Although it was not Uku Masing who introduced Kaplinski to protestant theology, Uku Masing's strong sense for the spiritual dimension that one might say links poetry to religious experiences, on the one hand, and awareness of the paradoxical, on the other, resonated deeply with the young Jaan Kaplinski.[21]

For Kaplinski, Uku Masing provided an alternative to the impoverished and distorted intellectual atmosphere that marked the official face of totalitarian rule in Soviet Estonia. Public education, such as it was at the time, tended to be uninspired and uninspiring, and the obligatory lectures at the university on topics such as Marxist-Leninist doctrine and the history of the Communist Party were tedious at best. While Masing was a welcome breath of fresh air for many students, as an outspoken religious poet whose manuscripts had been smuggled into the West, who was unwilling to toe the party line, who had prominent contacts abroad, and who was known to inspire the young emerging generation of writers, theologians, and intellectuals, he was considered politically untrustworthy. In the eyes of the Soviet authorities, he remained *persona non grata* until his death. Largely as a result of this status as dissident-like outsider, his career as an academic and theologian was cut short. Hardly any of his many works were published and public acknowledgement of his achievements was virtually impossible. The strictly centralized and controlled media remained all but silent about him. The few times he was mentioned, as for example in honour of his 60th birthday, the coverage remained scant and the message mixed.[22]

As a consequence of a censorship machinery that only allowed publication of material deemed acceptable to the Communist Party, much of what Masing had written could only be circulated privately in manuscript form. Apart from the public lectures he was able to hold for a while at the Institute for Theology in Tallinn, the only other meaningful alternative for students, friends, and sympathizers to share in his knowledge was to go and visit him at home, his sphere of internal exile. Even this was not possible for everyone. Visitors from the West, who from time to time received permission to travel to Tartu, were typically kept from meeting with Masing.

It was not until Estonia regained independence in 1991 that his work began to appear in his native country. Since then, dozens of books by and about Uku Masing have been published. Even a three-part documentary about his life and impact on Estonia's cultural landscape was produced between 2000 and 2007 by Faama Film and Estinfilm. Although he is widely published and celebrated in Estonia today, his influence there was most keenly felt in the 1960s. It is this image of Masing as one of the major "unofficial trend-setters" of the literary scene in Estonia that has come down to us, showing him as a towering figure among like-minded contemporaries.[23] The fact that Uku Masing ranked among the most prominent "forbidden authors" was not without risk for those who associated with him,[24] and therein lay a certain seductive and liberating quality. This may have been what attracted Jaan Kaplinski to Uku Masing and compelled him to visit his teacher, with some interruptions here and there, about once a month for more than two decades of his life.

Here it is important to note, as this had a great influence on Kaplinski, that this "private tutor" was also critical of those who opposed Soviet rule and, in Masing's opinion, identified all too readily with the dominant culture of the European West, the other colonial force that had perhaps even more lastingly shaped Estonian history than the Soviet occupation. Advocating an unconventional and intellectually demanding third possibility – moving beyond the entrenched dichotomy that pitted Sovietness against Estonianness – Masing epitomized the pinnacle of Estonia's counter-cultural stance at the time. This, in any case, is how Kaplinski judged his teacher's importance in retrospect.[25]

But the essence of the attraction that created the unusually strong bond between Kaplinski and Masing has remained elusive. Even Kaplinski himself appears unable to say what really drew him to his teacher. We know that his attachment is intimately linked to Masing's "mystical philosophy."[26] In *The Same River,* Kaplinski very likely had one of his visits to Masing in mind when he wrote: "everything you've talked about today, it's been probably the most important and most interesting conversation I've had in my life … And now I'm here and listening to you, and it's an entirely different, vast, wonderful, colourful world. You've suddenly opened the door, and I've seen that world. And now I know I have to go there, I have to see it, touch it, experience it. I have no choice. Will you help me?"[27] If we are to believe Kaplinski's fictionalized account, this much is certain: from the moment he met Masing, he couldn't wait to see him again. "A couple of hours more, then he would go to the Teacher's ... What to do in the meantime?" we read in *The Same River*.[28]

SOUL MATES – ENTERING ANOTHER WORLD

The relationship with Masing developed into one of seemingly total dependence. Kaplinski once said in an interview that he felt as if "reduced to a mere speck of dust in the face of this genius."[29] Uku Masing wielded such "authority" over him that he even tried to practice what Masing preached.[30] Influenced by Masing's contemptuous views about women – he at times, perhaps provocatively, portrayed them as a threat to men – the young Jaan Kaplinski even tried to curb his sexual needs and, following in the footsteps of his teacher, for a while considered pursuing a career as a theologian.[31] Looking back, though, Kaplinski is left unsure whether he curbed his "sexual needs because of Masing's ideas or because [he] wished to be loyal to [his] girlfriend who was very afraid of sex."[32]

Masing, for his part, appears to have been of two minds about his disciple. When Kaplinski accidentally discovered that his idol had, in a letter, made some derogatory remarks about him, he was devastated.[33] We don't know the specific content of the injurious letter, but we do know that Kaplinski felt belittled and even shocked.[34] The thought of not being liked by Masing, of losing the one person whom he trusted and who seemed to understand him, was so traumatic that it pushed him to the brink of despair. Even long after Masing's death, he still struggled with this spellbinding and emotionally exhausting experience. In 1994, perhaps partly in an effort to come to terms with this transformative aspect of his past, he began to write a novel about his teacher. It would take him more than a decade to complete. Finally, in 2007, *The Same River* appeared in print.

The reasons for Masing's immense impact on Kaplinski may seem obvious: when they first met, sitting across from the eighteen-year-old Jaan Kaplinski was not only a man more than thirty years his senior but also a published author, accomplished poet, and academic who had studied abroad and developed into a man of exceptional learning. Hugo Albert Uku Masing, as he was known until 1937, had graduated from Tartu University in 1930 with an MA in Old Testament studies, and had even received a stipend to study abroad at the prestigious universities of Tübingen and Berlin (1931–33).

Upon his return to Estonia he was appointed lecturer in the Department of Theology at Tartu University, where from 1937 on he taught comparative theology and gave courses in Semitic languages and Oriental studies. His first collection of poems – *Promontories Into the Gulf of Rains* (*Neemed vihmade lahte*) was published in 1935, the year he completed his PhD thesis. In addition to his translation of the Bible, which appeared between 1938 and 1940, he also established himself as a prolific translator of European and Oriental literature. Masing translated from an astonishing array of languages, including Hebrew, Ethiopian, Syrian, Arabic, Coptic, Persian, Japanese, Hawaiian, Greek, Latin, Italian, Catalan, French, German, English, Yiddish, and Sanskrit.

When he first met his mentor, young Jaan Kaplinski had only recently finished high school. He listened in awe to a cultural icon and intellectual giant in the privacy of that idol's home. Masing was tutoring him in complex and at times esoteric topics. They engaged in discussions about the nature and limits of language. He introduced the young Kaplinski to myths of native American and Mayan culture. He explained the meaning of salvation and its relation to Buddhism, and elaborated on the incompatibility of Boreal with mainstream European culture, drawing his attention to resonances between Asian spiritual beliefs and currents of Estonian thought. Kaplinski may even have learned from him about the Mari – an ancient Finno-Ugric nation in the southern Ural region – and their reverence for the nonhuman world.[35] Uku Masing's deep connection to nature – he referred to plants as if they were his friends – probably left as much a mark on Kaplinski as did the conversations about philosophy, exotic cultures, shamanism, and how Lao-Tse, Buddha, and Jesus together might embody an ideal model of human fulfillment.[36] As Thomas Merton explained this sense of contentment, referring to the common ground concepts such as God, Krishna, Providence, and Tao share: "It is by remaining open to an infinite number of unexpected possibilities which transcend his own imagination and capacity to plan that man really fulfills his own need for freedom."[37]

Kaplinski's conversations with Masing may also have been influenced by one of the poems Masing had translated into Estonian, such as this famous Haiku written by Matsuo Bashō (1644–1694):

An old pond, ah!
A frog jumps in:
The water's sound![38]

Dwelling on possible meanings of the poem, Masing had written, "anything that disturbs quiet contemplation is as insignificant as the frog leaping," and whatever we might do, it is, in the end, equally unimportant.[39] The object of desire, then, is not intervention, assertive action, and clearly defined direction. What instead commands attention, Masing appears to suggest, is the undifferentiated, the diffuse, the plain. This perspective is not about definitions but instead focuses attention beyond the "communicative" and agenda-bound individual. And yet, according to Kaplinski it would be a mistake to see Masing as a "proponent of the Taoist 'natural' way of letting things develop by itself"; in Kaplinski's assessment, Masing was "first of all a Lutheran theologian."[40]

Kaplinski himself, on the other hand, "became immersed in the Chinese Buddhist-Taoist way of thinking."[41] What in this study is conceptualized as unforced flourishing would increasingly shape the habitus of Kaplinski as we know it, for example, from his philosophical magnum opus, entitled *Parallels and Parallelisms*. Several of his other publications support this claim. Perhaps most telling among them is his article "Filosoofia ja vaikus" (Philosophy and Silence). There he wrote that Estonians don't have a culture of "wordless communication," engagement without pre-established design, and that he has been able to share thoughts on this matter with only two people in Estonia.[42] Although "very much a man of words," like himself, one of them was Uku Masing.[43]

DESIRE FOR DEPENDENCE – JAAN KAPLINSKI'S UKU MASING

The way the relationship between Masing and Kaplinski has commonly been approached appears to sidestep what is most important to both. Informed opinion in Estonia prompts us to think about Kaplinski in terms of his "intellectual growth towards independence" and "independent thought,"[44] or of his finding an "individual creative style"[45] and coming into his own, as it were, by releasing himself from his teacher's hold over him. Others have concluded that "almost all of Jaan Kaplinski's intellectual activity was pre-structured by Uku Masing's intellect (like a formatted hard-disk),"[46] that he was a copy cat, a "miniature Uku Masing."[47] Already in 1968, Ivar Ivask described Kaplinski as being "one of Uku Masing's few true disciples," with obvious "ties" to his teacher.[48]

From a psychological point of view, pronouncements of this kind present a particular and widespread understanding of maturation in human development, namely as a process leading from absolute dependence towards increasing independence. Dependence, then, is cast as a condition to be overcome in favour of self-affirmation through disengagement. Its ideal is the "we-less I" (Elias). Public discourse about Kaplinski and Masing is largely shaped by this dichotomous perspective and the understanding of human advance associated with it. But it does not align with the view of the world they themselves shared and which bound them together.

At the same time, it must be acknowledged that the established public perception of Masing and Kaplinski chimes, in part, with Kaplinski's own anxieties about his relationship with Uku Masing and, as he sees it, the shadow his teacher cast over him, particularly in the early years of their acquaintance.[49] Ready to follow him blindly but unable to reconcile everything Masing held to be true with his own inclinations and circumstances often left Kaplinski "confused."[50] Eventually, the rift widened, yet in profound ways Kaplinski remained deeply attached.[51] He has referred to this predicament as a "double-bind" and in an unpublished e-mail writes of Uku Masing: "on the one hand [he] pulled me towards him, on the other he pushed me away and this created an unbearable psychological tension, almost a trauma, which was further deepened by personal difficulties. So that my relationship with Uku Masing would have almost come at the expense of my health if not my life."[52] Albeit slowly, he eventually appears to have recovered from the spell Masing cast: "I managed to free myself of the Uku Masing cult, began to see him as a human being with all his shortcomings and strengths and relate to him differently, no longer as to a guru."[53] It is true that Kaplinski gradually found his "own" path, as one might say. But equally true is that this path was shaped in no small measure by Masing. Importantly, however, neither Kaplinski nor Masing conceived of the world and themselves in categories that can be reduced to matters of influence or independence without missing the essence of their mutual point of view.

What, then, do they have in common? They share an inclination that pulls them away from a desire to stand out through their interventions and, instead, steers them in a less intrusive and agenda-free direction. Rather than seeking to establish individual qualities through confrontation and by illuminating their contours, they are guided by a different ideal: to borrow from François Jullien, they want "to slip into the world so discreetly that one no longer seems to make any intervention (nonaction) and to melt into its processivity in order to succeed."[54] To "be like a plant in the field," said Masing.[55] "It is but the unknown we have in common," wrote Kaplinski in his philosophical magnum opus.[56] He only forgot to say, as we now can begin to see, that it is a sense of unforced flourishing they shared, despite their differences. If this way of perceiving the world and understanding human fulfillment is what really concerned Masing and Kaplinski, and it seems to have been one of the most important sources of their inspiration, should it not therefore guide our approach when we ask, who is Jaan Kaplinski's Uku Masing?

This much is certain: to Kaplinski it seemed that Masing sensed and responded to his needs in a manner he had not experienced before. "For me," Kaplinski remembers, "Uku Masing was everything I had been consciously or subconsciously searching for in my hitherto brief life."[57] Masing indulged him, and Kaplinski didn't even have to ask. Much of what he had been longing for simply happened, as if naturally, silently and invisibly. Of course, he did receive loving attention at home, from his aunt in particular, and, in part, also from his mother and his grandparents. But their care, as well meant as it was, frustrated him. He felt it to be trivial and borne out of a sense of parental duty rather than deep inclination and unencumbered attachment to him and his need to talk freely about what was on his mind.[58] With Masing, the experience was profoundly different, not only intellectually but also emotionally: Kaplinski wanted to be with him and to be like him. In *The Same River*, Kaplinski writes about the desire "to be close to the Teacher, to be able to listen to him endlessly, work for him, be his secretary, servant, hired hand, anything so that he could be close to him. He yearned to see him, walk alongside him, hear a good word from the Teacher's mouth."[59] In this instance, Kaplinski's novel seems to have found direct inspiration from his relationship with Masing.

THE LOVE OF MY LIFE – FULFILLMENT AND FRUSTRATION

That Kaplinski finds it difficult to explain the essential nature of his attachment to Masing should come as no surprise.[60] There is no expression for it in Estonian, nor in many other languages. We have to turn to Japanese to find the word "amae" that takes us to the heart of Jaan Kaplinski's Uku Masing. The concept has gained international currency through the work of Takeo Doi, the Japanese psychologist for whom "amae" constitutes an "independent drive" that gives rise to an emotion we experience when we enjoy someone's generous affection, a pleasing attention that simply happens as part of an "implicit common expectation" to indulge each other.[61] "Amae," Doi claims, is not only distinct from "the narcissistic sexual and aggressive instincts postulated by the individualistic psychology of Freud"; it is also a more primary drive.[62] This means that "amae" is characterized by a "craving for close contact" anchored in a dependency need that "takes the other person's love for granted" and, unforced, simply occurs like wordless understanding between two people – if only we let it happen.[63]

As essential as this kind of mutual responsiveness without agenda was for Kaplinski, in his particular social, political, and cultural environment, revealing this "need-love" aroused feelings of shame in him: "for me, a northerner, it is embarrassing to write, even more so to say this," Kaplinski explained to Masing in the summer of 1979.[64] This is hardly surprising. Typically, "dependence" is not socially sanctioned and rarely used to describe a desirable condition. On the contrary, by and large, the word has overwhelmingly negative connotations: these range from helplessness and vulnerability to addiction and neurosis. The litany of pejorative associations includes immaturity, being spoiled, weak, sentimental, entrapped, poor, exploited, and selfish.[65] Treated as a sign of regression unbecoming of a healthy adult, dependence is often seen as pitiful maladaptation, stifled creativity, and even illness.

There is, in short, a critical, primarily dismissive, if not "condemning," attitude towards dependency, particularly in the West.[66] While it is a fact of life for infants, escaping from a state of dependence is the apparently obvious goal in the journey towards adulthood. The mature and healthy adult is self-reliant. Dependence, by contrast, thwarts growth. This is the general bias in which the lack of social sanction for expressions of dependence is rooted.

This stance can also be expanded to include a national-political dimension. In the specific case of Estonia, particularly during Communist colonial times, the local population probably drove such sentiments expressing dependency even further underground. Overt manifestations of *amae* easily would have provoked resistance and been regarded as a sign of passive victimhood, if not complicity. They would have given rise to anxieties linked to the struggle for political and cultural survival of a people under threat. Driven by a collective ideal marked by a particularly strong desire for independence, "dependence" could not easily be regarded as meaning "amae," or "passive love," or "cherishment." Indeed, if anything, it meant lack: lack of love, lack of freedom, lack of fulfillment. "How long will we be able to sacrifice ourselves," asked then President of Estonia, Lennart Meri, in a 1994 speech given on the occasion of Estonia's 76th Independence Day celebrations in Tallinn, "to feed ourselves on this immense longing for independence, which we accumulated in our hearts during the long night that was the fifty years of Soviet occupation?"[67] In fact, for most who lived under communism, dependence meant being kept, against their will, in "permanent fear" and "much like children."[68]

In the absence of cultural and social support for dependence as an expression of unforced flourishing, Kaplinski was more likely to find himself marginalized and his desires frustrated or repressed because his need to lean on others appeared not only age-inappropriate, but also misguided, undesirable, and "potentially humiliating"[69] – even during the post-Soviet era. Kaplinski's relationship with Masing was probably also fraught with the kind of anxieties and suspicion to which strong emotional bonds between men used to give rise. Although himself a heterosexual, his attachment to Masing was initially so strong, he wrote in an e-mail in 2005, that he even would have agreed to a homosexual relationship had his teacher asked.[70] Masing apparently never did. In *The Same River*, Kaplinski wrote: "Or was his attachment to the Teacher homosexuality? No, perhaps the homo part was right but not the sexuality bit ... Love, yes, but not sexual love."[71] As much as Masing himself may have been longing for more emotional or even sexual intimacy – he was in many ways a very lonely man – he instead pushed Kaplinski away. In part, this is how Kaplinski appears to have experienced the relationship with his teacher.[72]

In more closely examining Masing's character, one might consider this: he tended to be blunt and could treat others in a harsh and even hurtful manner.[73] He "could be very tolerant," the contemporary Estonian writer Viivi Luik said in an interview, "but also very angry" and "arrogant."[74] Those who knew Masing do not see his ambiguous and sometimes hurtful behaviour towards Kaplinski as being unusual. It was in keeping with his character and predicament.

To some extent, his behaviour was probably borne out of a life marred by illness – he suffered from tuberculosis – and exacerbated by the politically, socially, and intellectually oppressive and often absurd conditions prevalent during most of his life, a life that saw a career cut short and largely reduced to an inner exile of sorts. Perhaps also fuelled by self-doubts that apparently plagued him, all this was likely to breed sarcasm and arouse bitter feelings. Prone to extremes, intellectually and emotionally, he was known for his misogyny and the startlingly antagonistic pronouncements that sharply contradicted his own ideals. He, for example, had an exaggerated and stubbornly unsympathetic view of what he referred to as "Indogerman" culture and mentality, as Kaplinski remembers.[75] A collective mindset that favours conquest and control and believes that human flourishing is above all a matter of human intervention is what he saw at work in powerful nations in general, but mostly in the Germany he experienced first-hand during his student years in the 1930s, and later during Communist rule in Estonia.

Masing's at times sweeping judgments, together with his reluctance to assume the explicit role of teacher and caregiver of sorts, the often uneven quality of his work,[76] and Kaplinski's heightened sensitivity for "need-love," all contributed to the distance that eventually developed between them.[77] But this, we can conclude with some certainty, is not only the self-assessment and retrospective rationalization of an individual who had outgrown his most influential teacher. Rather, it is also a manifestation of disguised "amae," an expression of the unfulfilled need of an adult for wordless affection, for being nurtured and cherished without having to ask, for receiving love without seeking it.

This interpretation sheds a rather different light on Kaplinski's controversial article about Uku Masing, entitled "Haige Geenius," which in English means sick genius. In it he claims that Masing's "work remains incomplete, fragmentary and unfinished."[78] But, considering what has emerged about the relationship between the two men, as well as their specific characteristics, could one not assume that Uku Masing's "love," in Takeo Doi's sense, "remains incomplete, fragmentary and unfinished?" In other words, "amae" – fulfilled and frustrated indulgent dependence – lies at the heart of Jaan Kaplinski's Uku Masing.

On 1 May 1985, the day after Masing's funeral, Kaplinski noted in his diary: "Yesterday then Uku's funeral and wake. Since mother's death I haven't been so emotionally exhausted from anything ... At church it was hard to pull myself together and keep from weeping … in the evening I thought that I really did love Uku very much and would have liked nothing more than being near him, yet I did not have the courage. I was afraid to bother him and thought he didn't think much of me. He was the love of my life."[79] "Yes, it was a love story," Kaplinski confirmed almost twenty-five years later, when, in 2009, Estonians celebrated the 100th birthday of Uku Masing. "But not a happy one."[80]

As we will see in the next chapter, Kaplinski's struggle to extend unforced flourishing from the private world of *amae* to his public life under totalitarian rule leads to another fateful encounter, a confrontation with dissent.

6

Beyond Dissidence

I opened the Russian-Chinese dictionary:
there between two pages was a tiny insect.
It spread its wings and flew away.
I lost sight of it, maybe
it's still struggling on the window pane
or has died there like so many insects or succeeded
in getting out into the open. Like some of us.
For a while I wondered if it couldn't have been
a word, a sign from the dictionary
which had had enough and wanted to become
something else, something more than a sign,
a hieroglyph under the cold glass covers
of this world, of this life.[1]

Jaan Kaplinski

I used to dream I was in Berlin or Paris, then wake up and be so disappointed: "I'm still here. I can't get out of the USSR."[2]

Jaan Kaplinski

The better we understand what elsewhere has been called a "character without character," the more we will uncover the identity-shaping underpinnings of unforced flourishing and the perception of self to which Kaplinski was drawn throughout much of his life: in spite of his eminence, he remained partial to a sense of personality that overturns everything that might be "perceived by others as striking or remarkable."[3] Ironically, it is this fundamentally Buddhist sensibility that made him stand out – at times in dramatic, if not traumatic, ways. Judging by his own assessment, already as a child he found it difficult to think of himself in unambiguous and more common terms. Since then a personal puzzle has occupied him and animated his quest for a more real and deeper self: how is it possible, he has kept asking himself, that he is both "a man without qualities" (Musil) and the distinct individual known as "Jaan Kaplinski"?[4]

In an unpublished letter from 5 July 1980, Kaplinski offers comments that resonate with his experience of Communist rule but are not limited to it: "I once read a 'Manual of [an] Inquisitor' and the most horrible thing I found there was not the tortures but the basic idea of the whole thing: that man must conform to a definition, man must define himself with the aid of various symbols and credos. The inquisitor had to be vigilant and take notice of the slightest deformation of the sacred formulas by potential heretics."[5] Decades later, Kaplinski would still see himself as being "different from any meaning, from any word, any idea," as he told French filmmaker Raphaël Gianelli-Meriano in 2009.[6] This kind of self-awareness that resists definition also finds expression in Kaplinski's collection of poems and texts entitled *Evening Brings Everything Back*. There he evokes the image of a man who grows smaller until he is so indistinct and diffuse that he is "nearly nothing."[7]

To deepen the exploration of this alternative path to "character," it is also instructive to look at Kaplinski's essay "The Mystical Non-Action." First published in 1993 and written "partly under the influence" of Finnish philosopher Georg Henrik von Wright, "a friend and student of Wittgenstein," it draws attention to an essential aspect of Western culture, namely the importance assigned to action and to how closely linked it is to our sense of self.[8] To imagine action means to imagine a "doing" subject. All this changes fundamentally, Kaplinski argued in his essay, when we think of a human being as "a psycho-physiological complex without a center, or an 'ego' that coordinates its activities," and assume that everything "in our body and mind happens spontaneously, by itself."[9] What we do, then, "cannot be analyzed as intentional action with its motives, goals and means."[10] Instead, it becomes "mystical non-action," activity without an agenda, cleansed of the confines and pressures yoked to pursuing a path narrowed to a specific image of one's self.

Kaplinski's "mystical non-action" aligns with a key concept of Daoism, which he knew well, namely "wu-wei."[11] Although it implies a spontaneous engagement unencumbered by the calculative aspect normally associated with activity, it does not lack efficacy. It is merely conceived differently. Rather than collapsing into irrational behaviour or indicating passivity or even unquestioned acceptance, *wu-wei* conveys the capacity to "allow effects to come about," or to "implicate an effect" and "engage the present in non-instrumental ways."[12] The efficacy of an action, then, is not one "measured by calculating future gains against present costs, but one that takes into account how far the acting individual is in fact in tune with the rhythm of his or her environment."[13]

This expression of unforced flourishing contrasts sharply with the pursuits of the "men of action" prominent in Western literature, and the conflict and confrontation that lies at the heart of their quests to reach a goal, often at great cost, to themselves and others. In contrast to the heroic or tragic mode in which such narratives are typically cast, unforced flourishing replaces daring and intrusive action with non-calculating, spontaneous, and relational behaviour. Such a "natural" flow involves harmony with the propensity of a situation.[14] Neither necessarily a form of "quietism" nor a retreat into "primitive naturalism," the critical capacity of this approach lies in its potential to provide what one might call a virtually "continuous calibration" – a highly attentive, context-sensitive focus on the present and means to adjust and readjust the response to a challenge from moment to moment, guided by the circumstances on hand.[15] While Kaplinski struggled with issues of such fundamental concern and magnitude, he emerged convinced that we should not conceive of individuals and their actions in terms of what makes them stand out. Rather, for him, the key to individual growth, indeed human advance and fulfillment, lies in the capacity to blend in.

The consequences of this understanding of character and efficacy are immense. For Kaplinski, they grew dramatically clear under totalitarian rule when he questioned the value of dissent as a response to the oppressive Communist regime. Kaplinski arrived at a startling and for many unsettling conclusion: not only did dissent fail effectively to address the conditions that brought it about, in important ways, Kaplinski believed, this form of protest was potentially complicit in the "slow suicide" of his native country.

RUSSIFICATION – A "SLOW SUICIDE"

Looking back later in time at his life in the Soviet Union, he finds that it was not a "horror story."[16] But when asked about his attitude towards Russian-Soviet rule, Kaplinski's disapproval is unequivocal. It "exposed itself right away through absolute physical and mental violence," he says. "It was prepared to kill, rape, burn books and suffocate every free thought."[17] Even after Stalin's death and Khrushchev's so-called "Thaw," in his eyes the Communist regime remained "most malicious against individuals with an honest and unconventional mentality."[18] Relentlessly demanding unconditional conformity, casting everyone into a mould, indeed attempting to "create a new people,"[19] the Kremlin behaved like "terrorists," raising the specter of turning its own citizens into complicit "prisoners" of a dysfunctional system.[20]

Judging by his diary entries of the 1980s, Kaplinski saw Soviet Estonia as a place under siege,[21] illegally occupied by a secretive, powerful, and at times particularly devastatingly destructive regime, not unlike the worst radioactive fallout in human history, the meltdown of the Chernobyl nuclear plant.[22] Kaplinski was not only furious about the rampant political propaganda and a broken bureaucracy, but also deeply concerned about rising alcoholism, the abuse of conscripts serving time in the Red Army, deteriorating ethnic relations, and rapidly increasing environmental degradation. In his view, Moscow's autocratic leaders "lied to themselves, their people and the entire world."[23] Totalitarian rule amounted to nothing but a "slow suicide," the poet in him said.[24]

In 1980 and the following years, Kaplinski experienced the events that unfolded in the Estonian SSR as particularly troubling. During this time he had grown increasingly worried about the escalating "hatred and violence" that had poisoned the general social and ethnic climate in Estonia.[25] Fuelling the discord was a widespread and deepening sense that Russification had reached a new height, if not a tipping point.[26] The Radio Free Europe "background report" of 17 December 1984 noted: "The single most pressing concern to Estonians has been and continues to be Russification, the Bête noire of Estonian culture since Czar Alexander III decreed Russian the only language to be taught in Estonian schools. Some 100 years later the issue remains the most volatile of any facing the republic."[27]

In a telling departure from past practice, the Russification of Estonia was now increasingly enforced using Russian rather than Estonian as a medium of communication. The impact was unmistakable: the percentage of non-Estonian immigrants rose; Russian became more widespread at public events; politicians with little knowledge of Estonian and appreciation for its culture were appointed to high-ranking positions; Estonian authors writing in Russian received preferential treatment; Russian was introduced in public schools already at the kindergarten level and given decidedly more prominence in Estonian theaters and universities.[28] These centrally orchestrated initiatives threatened to diminish the existence of a viable and influential Estonian-educated segment of the population. The potential brain drain benefiting other Soviet republics, and the Russification of the educational as well as public landscape in general, was likely to increase the already high number of immigrants sent to Estonia even further.[29] All this left Estonian culture in peril to an extent not seen before in the Soviet era.

Trapped in the closed system of a one-party dictatorship with a union-wide power monopoly and an ill-functioning bureaucracy, the absurdity of the entire political system stirred Kaplinski and many of his peers to ask: What, if anything, could they do? "We see how the work ought to be done, and we see that the system makes it impossible," he wrote at the time.[30] Convinced, as he was, that it was "useless to fight the regime" and that a meaningful response required more than settling in the certainties of opposition, one thing grew particularly clear in his mind: the need to dispense with dissent.[31]

THE LETTER OF 40 – THE CZAR'S MADMEN

Especially after demonstrations of mostly Estonian high school students in Tallinn in the fall of 1980, Kaplinski feared that tensions in Estonia might escalate. Overzealous police already had resorted to beatings and arrests of a number of protesters. Compelled to make the authorities aware of the link he perceived between the rising social unrest and the unprecedented acceleration of Russification of Estonia, he drafted an open letter.[32] To garner support, he introduced friends in Tallinn to the text. It would form the basis of what later became known as "The Letter of 40." Following discussions and revisions in October of 1980, a final version was produced. After signatures had been solicited, the text was sent, on 4 November 1980, to two Estonian dailies and to the leading Russian-language newspaper, *Pravda*. Strictly controlled by the Communist authorities, none of the papers published the letter.

It has been called "one of the most remarkable documents of the Soviet era in Estonia."[33] Never before had a group of Estonian intellectuals come together in this way and endorsed an open letter directed at the Communist authorities. Also unprecedented was its popularity among the population at large. Borrowing from the title of Jaan Kross's 1978 historical novel, the signatories soon became known as the "40 Czar's Madmen." But they were very much unlike Timotheus von Bock, the protagonist of Kross's novel. The "mad dissident," as he has been called, promises to always tell the Czar the truth.[34] An audacious man of honour and unyielding principles, he keeps his word and openly speaks his mind in front of Alexander I. His frank and bold criticism earns Timotheus von Bock nine years in prison. With the same, "somewhat merciless, consistency" and relentlessness[35] the Baltic German nobleman pursues the "grand plan he had drawn up for his life" and marries an Estonian peasant.[36] Regardless of the cost, to him and others, to the very end he remains defiant and true to convictions rooted in "categorical imperatives and abstract principles and ideas."[37] Unsurprisingly, Timotheus von Bock feels that he must be "like an iron nail in the body of the empire" and not flee his "battle ... against the Czar."[38] In contrast, "The 40 Czar's Madmen" did not pursue Timo's path of "suicidal public resistance."[39] In part, perhaps, this is why the largely modestly phrased letter not only struck a chord with many, but to everyone's surprise also united the Estonian population across the main ideological divide: among the supporters and signatories were both members of the Communist Party and non-Communists.[40]

The immediate point of departure of the letter was the youth unrest in Estonia's capital. "The violence associated with the events in Tallinn is cause for concern," the letter stated.[41] "There have been subsequent calls for more of the same. The use of force is an indication that perilous splits have formed in our society, splits indicative of antagonism between the teachers and those they teach, of conflict between the leaders and the led." Important though such concerns were, the letter focused on another troublesome worry: the deeply rooted and very sensitive native language issue. As the letter makes clear, already the German and later the Czarist government had "attempted to convince the Estonians of the impotence, uselessness, and even the detrimental nature of a culture relying on the Estonian language as a keystone." And yet, against all odds, Estonian continued to flourish and remained at the heart of the Estonians' sense of self. As the authors of the letter noted, the "[a]ttitude towards the Estonian language is a key question in the development of relations between Estonians and other nationality groups in Estonia." Calling for an honest and thorough discussion of this issue "at all levels" and a "guarantee that the native inhabitants of Estonia will always have the final word on the destiny of their land and people," the letter concludes with a conciliatory vision of a culturally tolerant and thriving Estonia, "where understanding prevails in the absence of hate among nationality groups, where cultural unity reigns amidst diversity, and where no one feels any injury to his national pride or endangerment to his national culture."[42]

TO SIGN OR NOT TO SIGN? – SOUL SEARCHING

Although Soviet law did not distinguish between dissidents and criminals, and the authorities continued to deal with regime critics in an intimidating and at times violent way, Kaplinski did not openly fear that he might be prosecuted and sent to prison, or worse, that his life might be in danger. By any measure, the Soviet Union of 1980 was still distressingly oppressive, but it was also no longer a place of Stalinist purges and deportations. Still, the participants, including Kaplinski, worried that the authorities might once again react in a hostile manner and misconstrue the letter as an expression of dissent, although its stated intention was to engage in conversation and open discussion. Mostly, however, Kaplinski was wary of possible aggravations, such as so-called prophylactic measures and other forms of harassment. Meant to intimidate, these were routinely employed by the authorities. Mindful of the often unpredictable behaviour of the KGB, his first reaction was to continue writing the letter, but to err on the side of caution and not sign it.[43]

Indeed, not everyone who had the opportunity did sign, including some prominent and influential figures, such as the writer Jaan Kross or the composer Veljo Tormis. Their reasons varied: for some, the letter provided legitimacy to a political system they despised. Others felt that it invited further repressions, and, in the end, would do more harm than good. Some of those who had in the past suffered at the hands of the Soviet regime applauded the courage of the signatories and supported the initiative, but fear of renewed harassment and even punishment kept them from further involvement. A number of Communists distanced themselves from the letter because it amounted to an admission of failure, and of having supported an ideology that had emerged as deeply wanting. Still others thought the letter a trap set by the KGB, or, for political reasons, did not want to be associated with some of the signatories. There were also some who had simply lost all hope that change was still possible at all. For them, the Soviet Union was unreformable, and signing, therefore, seemed futile.[44]

After a period of soul searching and embarrassment at harbouring doubts and letting others carry the brunt of responsibility, Kaplinski did indeed sign the letter. Little did he know then that he would soon be singled out by the authorities as the primary instigator, labeled a dissident both in the West and the East, and, in his eyes, diminished to a pawn in the Cold War. To shed the unwanted role, stay true to his convictions, and satisfy some of his and his family's practical needs, he would end up doing the unthinkable – recant. Worse still, to the satisfaction of the regime, their "Intellectual Enemy Number 1," Jaan Kaplinski, would become an outcast among many, perhaps even most, who had previously held him in high esteem. It all began with the search of his home.

THE SEARCH – 42 PAGES BETWEEN RED COVERS

Late in the afternoon on 6 November 1980, four KGB agents arrived at 20 Arukűla Street in Tartu, then the home of the Kaplinski family. The agent in charge informed Kaplinski that a criminal investigation against him had been launched. Allegedly, he had been involved in the youth unrest in Tallinn, which had taken place about a month earlier. Armed with a warrant, issued on the basis of this charge, groundless though it was, the KGB conducted a search of the apartment. The agents were to look for so called "anti-Soviet and nationalist materials."[45]

Except for the occasional "slightly cynical remark," as Kaplinski noted in his diary two days after the search, apparently the conduct of the KGB was reasonably civilized.[46] We may take him at his word that they had behaved "properly,"[47] displaying none of the "sadism and brutish self-confidence" for which they were known.[48] The agents appeared to treat the entire matter as a mere formality and even seemed somewhat embarrassed.[49] True, they certainly could have conducted a more thorough search and, for example, also inspected Kaplinski's work space in the basement. But they chose not to. In all, they spent more than three hours with the Kaplinskis, checking their books and documents in the living room, "rummaging" through both the master and the boys' bedrooms, and confiscating several items.[50] According to the official report of the KGB, among the seized documents were: (1) a list of 37 names, most likely including people Kaplinski himself had approached for signature of the Letter of 40; (2) a letter written by his mentor and friend Ain Kaalep, in which he explained his reasons for not signing the letter and even advised the group to abort their initiative – he believed it would lead to further repressions and, in this sense, do more harm than good; (3) 1 page of copy paper used to copy the letter or a version of it; (4) 42 pages between red covers, *i.e.*, Kaplinski's diary; (5) an 8-page manuscript, probably of an essay; (6) another manuscript of 12 pages, likely his essay "Kust tuli öö" or a version of it; (7) an additional 5 pages of the letter. In the course of the search they also questioned Kaplinski. Who had written the letter, they asked? From whom had he received it? To whom had he given it, and who had composed the original text?

All of this and most of the other evidence the KGB seized, Kaplinski considered relatively harmless. But both he and his wife were clearly concerned about the double-sided "42 pages between red covers" taken from his diary. Now in the possession of the KGB, would the information contained in the diary be used by the authorities against him and against others whom he had mentioned and possibly, though unintentionally, implicated in some way?[51] "Conceivably, it ranks among the most candid any Estonian writer has ever written," he recorded in his diary shortly after the search.[52] As he would soon learn, high-ranking officials in the Estonian Socialist Soviet Republic, including the Estonian Communist Party chief, Karl Vaino, probably took note of the diary.[53] Since it was returned to Kaplinski, we know what the diary revealed about him.

THE DIARY – DISSENT CONSOLES; IT DOES NOT LIBERATE

The entries, dated from 5 September 1980 to 5 November 1980, contain comments about the Letter of 40 and its context, a fairly detailed account of marital issues, including rather intimate matters and indiscretions, and other, more mundane domestic concerns, as well as remarks about his contacts in the West. That he listened to the BBC and, occasionally, the Voice of America, forbidden at the time, can also be gleaned from the diary. He mentions books received from friends abroad. Other entries reveal his rather frank criticism of fellow Estonian writers who, presumably, were too caught up in the "dark" side of Soviet life.[54] Most importantly, though, shining through the diary is his account of what might constitute a more meaningful response to the irremediable hypocrisy and inhumanity of the neo-Stalinist regime.

From Kaplinski and his diary we learn that there was only one viable alternative for the Estonians: to have any hope of making a difference, they had to turn inward and change their behaviour and thought patterns. Rather than cultivating conflict, their predicament demanded humanizing but dispassionate engagement – non-confrontational, honest, and transparent. In his own words, "not wanting to belong to any 'anti-world,'"[55] he believed that everyone, even the KGB, should be told the "truth, neutrally, being neither abjectly submissive nor rebellious."[56] As he would say much later in his autobiographical novel *Seesama jõgi* (*The Same River*): "He had to write down everything as it was, without embarrassment, without embellishment, because there can be beauty only in truth, not in falsehood."[57]

Here Kaplinski's account recalls Havel's signature essay of 1978, "The Power of the Powerless." This deserves comment. Havel draws attention to the complicity of individuals, partially unaware, in sustaining a repressive regime. His path out of this conundrum is based on moral integrity and a sense of individual responsibility unconcerned with the power politics of "denying or rejecting anything."[58] In Havel's celebrated words, it means to "live within the truth,"[59] a mode of being that "cannot be coerced" – and, if Havel is right, must grow from inner values and relationships "built on tolerance and acceptance of everyone, *especially* the other."[60] But Havel also understood that the roots of living in the truth have to reach even deeper to bring about a truly transformative change and dislodge ingrained habits of thought and behaviour, not only behind the Iron Curtain but in Western civilization at large. If Havel was right, corrosively at work was a "rationalist spirit" founded on an impoverished sense of humanity and the "presumption of impersonal objectivity."[61] To drive this spirit "out of our own souls," he famously wrote, and to "banish it from contemporary humankind" would be the "best defence against totalitarianism."[62]

Both the philosophical and the spiritual dimensions of Havel's "existential attitude" emerge with particular clarity from his "Anti-Political Politics," a speech he had prepared for an event held in 1984 at the University of Toulouse, where he was to receive an honorary doctorate.[63] In his address he asserts that we "must draw our standards from our natural world," and "honour with the humility of the wise the bounds of that natural world and the mystery which lies beyond them, admitting that there is something in the order of Being which evidently exceeds all our competence."[64] Similarly, Havel noted in "The Power of the Powerless" that "life, in its essence, moves towards plurality, diversity, independent self-constitution and self-organization."[65]

This "deep," one might indeed say "organicist," identification with the human and nonhuman world, non-political and in its intention unburdened of preconceived designs, unites Kaplinski with Havel. Put differently, both struggle in their own ways to reach beyond a world dominated by antagonism. "If someone thinks of us as their enemy and also behaves towards us in this way," Kaplinski wrote in his diary, "then let us not look at him as our enemy!"[66]

As we can begin to see, living in the truth, at its core converges with unforced flourishing. But unforced flourishing and dissidence have between them a profound gap. For Kaplinski, dissidence evokes what its etymology suggests: being apart (Lat. *dis-sedere*) rather than growing together. Ironically, though, adhering to his signature mental mode would steer Kaplinski onto a collision course even with those closest to him rather than permit positive or transformative change. Also critical of the term "dissident," Havel called it "truly a cruel paradox that the more some citizens stand up in defence of other citizens, the more they are labelled with a word that in effect separates them from those 'other citizens.'"[67]

Of course, both Havel and Kaplinski lived in already deeply divided worlds, largely inhospitable, if not inimical, to their non-intrumental responsiveness and sense of human fulfillment rooted in the spontaneous and intuitive. The contrast of this vision to Kaplinski's life under Communist rule was made particularly clear, for instance, by the fact that school-aged Estonians were taught that "there [was] a fierce battle going on, the battle for existence between the Socialist and Capitalist countries, and there [was] no third way. We [had to choose] between Socialism and Capitalism."[68] During the Brezhnev–Reagan era, the rift separating the East from the West grew ever wider. It was the peak of the "Second" Cold War (1979–85). Kaplinski understood that the dissidents "were seditious according to the prevailing norms of the party-state."[69] And, if we are to believe the Russian philosopher Alexander Piatigorsky, many dissidents themselves "were just as likely as conformist apparatchiks to be stuck in outmoded ideological frameworks."[70] Moreover, the diary also reveals Kaplinski's belief that, in hidden ways and unintentionally, the Estonians, too, were complicit in their own malaise. This gave the already-controversial notion of reform from within an even sharper edge.

But embarking on his "third way" was fraught with additional pitfalls. For one, it easily obscured the courage and sacrifice of the political activists who pursued a more openly defiant approach. Considering confrontation a wanting response to the absolute rule of the Communist authorities, Kaplinski was at risk of surrendering his influence as a writer to the whim of the regime. Equally important, and raising even broader concerns, Kaplinski presupposed the reformability of a system most critics of the Soviet Union believed to be inherently unreformable.[71] In other words, he had to contend with the fact that the Cold War operated in a world of rigid boundaries drawn by firmly entrenched ideologies. Unyieldingly pitting "good" against "evil," such certitudes could not easily, if at all, accommodate dialogue in a meaningful, self-organizing rather than self-asserting way. Kaplinski's intention to engage in conversation with the Communist regime was thus liable to be misunderstood. As a consequence, even those who knew him well were at times left unsure of his intentions. Had he succumbed to conformism and become a pawn of the regime? Remaining vulnerable to such doubts and possibilities that would almost certainly impact on his ability to secure a living under already difficult circumstances was the price he had to pay for trying to stay true to his convictions.

The diary also reveals that Kaplinski detected two diverging but, in his opinion, fundamentally wanting reactions among Estonians to their predicament. By his account, they unwittingly deepened their complicity. One large group of Estonians pinned its hopes on the "West, God, or luck."[72] Those who did not believe that they would be rescued, Kaplinski went on to argue, or were too traumatized by the past and perhaps even consumed by a sense of abandonment and helplessness, reacted in a surprising way.[73] Rather than becoming more hostile, they, paradoxically, developed an emotional bond with their captors – not unlike the "Stockholm syndrome," although Kaplinski did not use this term.

Ultimately, the most important claim Kaplinski made in his diary was this: dissent consoles, it does not liberate. Although neither resistance nor empathy with the "terrorists," as Kaplinski put it, provided more than temporary relief, many Estonians confused seeking solace with a resolution of their woes. Judging by his diary, Kaplinski appeared convinced that this was not merely a mistake but a root cause of their tragedy.[74] In addition to suffering the immediate consequences of totalitarianism and, in some cases, even being manipulated into welcoming their subjugation, Estonians demonstrated a need for consolation that, Kaplinski felt, was the real obstacle to be overcome. It remained insurmountable for as long as they confused it with a way out of totalitarian rule. Or, as political prisoner and critic of the Soviet regime Vladimir Bukovsky observed, dissenters were not necessarily "expecting any victory" but "wanted to have the right to say ... 'I did all I could.'"[75]

Their existence as a people besieged and the threat overwhelming, what else could the imperiled Estonians have done? Certain that radical political change was unlikely, that direct intervention was no option, that passive resistance was ineffective, and that Estonian independence was perhaps ultimately unsustainable, all this led Kaplinski at the time to conclude that an entirely different approach to human flourishing under the constraints of Soviet rule was needed – and indeed possible. Dissent, he felt, was merely an escape into solace that flattened social complexities and narrowed them to a rigid dualism. It was coercive to such an extent, he argued, that it ultimately eroded any sense of well-being and left but "severed links" behind. In the end, it diminished human relations to two deeply sedimented and mutually exclusive extremes: allies and – pitted against them – enemies.[76]

Kaplinski's sense of the social and political world told him that the Estonians had to unburden themselves of this way of thinking. But he knew that ushering in a transformative change would require more than openness and transparency. It would mean "sharing everything with everyone," from treasured and even intimate feelings to hidden dimensions of their collective histories.[77] Dovetailing with his understanding of "living in the truth," and equally important for Kaplinski, this approach also meant refraining from enmity directed at those hostile towards them. Instead, the Estonians had to not only speak their minds but also identify with their enemies on a human level and do what for many amounted to a counterintuitive proposition: trust them.[78] Although public life in the Soviet Union favoured and indeed rewarded those who did not say what they really thought,[79] it was essential, Kaplinski argued, to resist adopting that role.[80]

This unburdening from identity formed the basis of his hope for a "third way," a transformative, non-intrusive engagement from within.[81] He was convinced that embarking on this path would not only help a traumatized people reclaim lost vitality. Causing the target of aggression to vanish, as it were, would also dissolve the *raison d'être* for rule by force. In his own words: moving forward in this "third way" would provide access to "power … no terrorist can match."[82] This was the hope that marked the trajectory of his thought, idealist though it may seem.

At the time immersed in books by authors such as Japanese Buddhist Shunryu Suzuki, Kaplinski was also concerned with wider processes of questioning that resonated with Eastern modes of perception. In this he seemed to draw inspiration from Daoism. Not a "philosophy of power," it is the "wisdom of renouncing the game, of contenting oneself with being only an insignificant particle of indifferent nature," as the Polish journalist Ryszard Kapuścinśki wrote about Chinese thought in his *Travels with Herodotus*.[83]

Did the Daodejing and a way of life aligned with its basic tenets perhaps yield, in Kaplinski's imagination, a meaningful survival strategy for a small nation, such as Estonia, especially during the decades of Soviet occupation? The following advice, based on Kapuścinśki's reading of the Daoist text, invites such a parallel: "So do not become attached to anything. All that exists will perish; therefore rise above it, maintain your distance, do not try to become somebody, do not try to pursue or possess something. Act through inaction: your strength is weakness and helplessness your wisdom."[84] This we can state with some certainty: to relieve one's self from any identification, to resist any role, lies at the heart of Kaplinski's vision of liberation from within. To simplify a complex matter, one might say that this process begins with an examination of one's own sense of self and leads from concentration and domination to a diffusion of dualist thought. As he has repeatedly stated, his sense of self is informed by "non-existent borders" such as the lines we like to draw between summer and fall, night and day, old and young, warm and cold. We create them, Kaplinski believes, but beyond language they don't exist.[85] Or, as the semiotician Kalevi Kull summed up this aspect of Kaplinski's thinking in his afterword to one of Kaplinski's books, although "in life we are one," language separates.[86] Elsewhere Kaplinski has noted: "I am what the Chinese call 'yun-shui' (Japanese unsui) – cloud and water."[87] Elaborating on this metaphor in an article about definitions and identity published in *The Guardian*, Kaplinski explains: "My homeland is here, in Estonia, but my spiritual homeland is the nebulous border region between literature and science, poetry and prose, fiction and non-fiction. I share this borderland with some Chinese literati of the past. I think these people, too, had an aversion to definitions and characterizations, ... stressing their affinity with things that have no clear-cut borderlines, no well-defined form. I like the ancient fuzzy logic of these Daoists, and feel at home in their company."[88]

It would be a mistake, however, to conclude from this statement that, for Kaplinski, the importance of the individual is diminished. Rather, from his perspective, it amounts to a "decrease in egocentricity," as Arne Naess formulated it, and an increase in mutual identification extending as far as possible, even to the nonhuman world:[89] "The self to be realized is not the ego, but the larger Self created when we identify with all living creatures and ultimately with the whole universe."[90] This affirms the individual, indeed allows her to grow, as Naess has argued, but calls for a different path towards self-realization, one functionally dependent on the flourishing of everything and everyone else. François Jullien has noted that this point of view "alone allows an individual to possess all aptitudes equally and to bring the appropriate faculty into play when needed" without giving preference to "any single trait ... to the detriment of another."[91]

For Kaplinski, turning this dimension of unforced flourishing into lived experience also meant disentangling himself from the dichotomies that shaped Brezhnev's neo-Stalinist world and those trapped in it. Deeply fragmented, the social order divided Russians from Estonians, the Left from the Right, Communist Party members from non-members, authorities from citizens, secret service agents from the public, and regime critics from its advocates, to name but a few of the divisions particular to this time and place.

In broad strokes, this constitutes the account of himself Kaplinski adopted and presented in his diary. Although dissidence "is not an ideologically unified phenomenon,"[92] at times it made for very clear distinctions, "the way they are in fairy tales: evil was evil and good was good," to borrow from Czech sociologist Jiřina Šiklová.[93] "We are always, / in a way, wandering knights; we are always looking /

for what to fight for and against, whom / to hate with a just hatred," Kaplinski, calling this an "unlived life," wrote in a poem published in 1985.[94] In Kaplinski's view, it bears repeating, dissidence, understood in this limiting, indeed divisive, sense, did not constitute a meaningful response to totalitarian rule. "I am not suited to be a dissident," he wrote two days after the search of his home, as if to confirm what the KGB now knew to be true about him. The dissidents' "hostility towards the KGB" made "any kind of humane relationship" with them "altogether impossible," he added.[95] Regardless of how one might describe dissent, he wanted to see this animosity dissolved. Such a transformation demands much, Kaplinski knew: above all, distance from a sense of fulfillment bound to a reified understanding of self, both collective and individual.

Rather than defining positions, which then easily gives rise to conflict, Kaplinski advocated careful and open attending to the other. In his imagination, replacing confrontation with conversation was also the main intention of the Letter of 40.[96] But, as if in a blind spot, this dimension of his approach was destined to remain invisible to most. Intuitively drawn towards a view of the world imbued with more permeable boundaries, Kaplinski's convictions seemed politically naive to most, if not foreign or ideologically inadmissible, both inside Estonia and outside. Worse still, as the events unfolded from the fall of 1980 to the summer of the following year, the ideal articulated in the letter did not repair any rifts and, in the end, did not create new common ground. Instead, the gap widened and Kaplinski saw himself marginalized to an extent he had never before experienced. How could it have been otherwise? One might say, in the midst of the Cold War and a perception largely "framed through [its] bipolar lens," his approach, conceptualized in this book as unforced flourishing, had to remain anathema to most, East and West.[97]

A PAWN IN THE SECOND COLD WAR – MISSION IMPOSSIBLE

To this day, it is unclear who leaked the Letter of 40 to the West.[98] But there appears to be general agreement among the signatories that it was neither meant to be published abroad nor intended to advocate dissent. And for a time it seems as if this was generally understood. Indeed, for many, the attraction of the letter lay precisely in the absence of anything inflammatory or confrontational. Kaplinski described its tenor as ethnographic-sociological and distanced rather than ethno-politically engaged.[99]

According to his own account, internationally renowned conductor Tõnu Kaljuste, one of the 40 who signed the letter, immediately felt drawn to a spirit of sincere concern he detected in its text and a genuine interest in tackling problems together with the Communist authorities rather than confronting them by, for example, dwelling on demands for independence, legitimate though they were.[100] It was faith in the possibility of at least a modicum of cooperation and good will from the authorities that many of the signatories shared. Although Kaplinski harboured doubts about the final outcome of their initiative, he did not at all dismiss the possibility that the letter just might persuade the officials of the Communist Party to listen to their concerns. If nothing more, it would at least facilitate the appointment of "more sensible leaders."[101] Others also seemed optimistic. "We indeed expected dialogue," wrote journalism scholar Marju Lauristin.[102]

Naive as their hopes may seem in retrospect, they knew the letter could become a successful vehicle of change only if it remained a domestic matter, avoided any inflammatory rhetoric, and conveyed a spirit of mutual respect. In other words, the political objective of the letter had to be, and was, a transformation, but one that took place from the inside. On 21 June 1981, Kaplinski noted in his diary: "Even though we travel in turbulent seas on a dilapidated and dingy raft, it still is not right to knock it over or demolish it – then we drown. Persistently, one has to try to fix and modify the platform ... there is no other way."[103] To some extent, history would prove him right. A transformation from within was possible, but not until years later when the regime was about to collapse and the Soviet empire finally ceased to exist.

There was indeed nothing explicitly radical in the letter – certainly not compared to appeals penned by dissidents. It did not contain a plea for help from the West. Nor did it address the then particularly prominent issue of human rights violations, or align itself with organizations such as Amnesty International. None of the international accords about fundamental freedoms, that had previously circulated as *samizdat* publications, or other dissident activities were mentioned. The letter was also silent about the illegality of Estonia's incorporation into the Soviet Union and, yoked to it, the infamous Molotov-Ribbentrop Pact and the stubborn denial of its existence by the Soviet regime.

In short, it was not a letter of dissent. None of the 40 who signed it were dissidents, least of all Kaplinski. Wary of the potentially corrosive effects of confrontational thinking and behaviour, Kaplinski did not seek contacts with dissidents, neither in Estonia nor elsewhere in the former Soviet Union. Of course, he did follow events related to the dissident movement, such as the tragic story of Jüri Kukk (1940–1981), as did many in Estonia at the time.[104] Kukk, a chemistry professor at the University of Tartu, had resigned from the Communist Party of the Soviet Union. Quitting "the organization did not trigger automatic execution," wrote Rein Taagepera in his book about Kukk, "but it started a long chain of events which ended with death under questionable circumstances."[105] Kaplinski kept a newspaper clipping of the obituary for his diary and noted that Voice of America had reported Kukk's passing, which confirmed what he had heard earlier in the day on Swiss radio.[106]

As much as Kukk's death touched him, Kaplinski did not identify with the dissident movement. It is therefore all the more surprising that he was singled out by the authorities and, even more astonishing still, that he was cast in the role of dissident. Did he, then, belong to those individuals Václav Havel described in "The Power of the Powerless" who have not "consciously decided to be professional malcontents" but "are merely doing what they feel they must and, consequently … find themselves in open conflict with the regime?"[107] This we know: when the entire text of the letter was first published in the West, its intended purpose – to engage in dialogue, maintain a conciliatory tone, and treat the concerns raised in it as an internal matter – was quickly lost. The *Estniska Dagbladet*, an Estonian émigré newspaper published in Stockholm, framed the letter as a dissident appeal: "Obviously" also aimed at readers "all over the world," one commentator noted, the open letter was a "courageous protest and at the same time a desperate cry for help against the rapists of Estonian language and culture."[108] Calling it an "open letter with 40 signatures," the *Frankfurter Allgemeine Zeitung*, a respected German daily, was considerably less confrontational but still referred to the letter as an "open counter-reaction."[109] *The London Times* aligned it more directly with dissent when the widely read daily noted that the "signatories … are not known to have been associated with the dissident movement before," implying that they now were.[110] Under the headline "KGB campaign against dissidents in Estonia," *The Times of India* also depicted the 40 Estonian intellectuals as resistance fighters "expected to be subject to arrests and house searches."[111]

Soon this tendency to align the letter with the dissident movement, both implicitly and at times explicitly, became common practice also in scholarly discourse. In 1981, for example, an article appeared in the *Journal of Baltic Studies* that associated the letter with Soviet "counterculture," "Baltic human rights activism," and "national sovereignty."[112] An influential scholarly account of Latvian, Lithuanian, and Estonian history, published in 1983, interpreted the letter as the beginning of a "new major phase in Baltic dissent."[113] In the following year, Radio Free Europe's "background report" on Estonia also drew attention to the Letter of 40 in conjunction with the dissident movement.[114] Not until after the collapse of the Soviet Union was it more fully acknowledged that the letter had "called for debate" and had been penned "in contrast to the uncompromisingly independence-oriented demands of the radical freedom workers."[115]

In the absence of more nuanced and balanced assessments of the letter, a frustrated Kaplinski saw its intended purpose of contesting totalitarian rule in a non-confrontational manner slip away as it was increasingly transformed into a seditious act of dissent. Left with the impression that foreign media outlets largely missed or ignored the "diplomatic" intent of the letter, Kaplinski felt pushed into a role he could not accept.[116] He feared that the Estonian people might become victims "in the stupid game of the Cold War," and he was at risk of being reduced to "a pawn in a propaganda conflict."[117]

IMPOSED SILENCE – "THE PARTY AND THE PEOPLE ARE ONE"

In Moscow's eyes, the mere fact that the letter had become public in the West constituted an act of dissent. The letter was declared secret and its publication actively suppressed. Its signatories were censored and subjected to pressure tactics by the authorities[118] that left them with little or no access at all to print and any other media.[119] Though the Letter of 40 remained in circulation abroad, it was not published in the Estonian SSR until 1988 when, finally, it appeared in the Estonian periodical *Vikerkaar*. For eight years, it was as if the letter did not exist, although it was common knowledge, certainly in Estonia but to some extent also abroad.[120]

As self-defeating as this kind of censorship often turned out to be, before Gorbachev ushered in *glasnost* and *perestroika*, it was general practice in the Soviet Union to silence any expression of public opposition. The roots of this censorship originated in the Soviet constitution. Soviet law regarded the Communist Party and the citizens of the Soviet Union as one. "All power in the USSR belongs to the people," stated Article 2 of the Constitution. Article 6 made explicit that the "leading and guiding force of the Soviet society and the nucleus of its political system, of all state … and public organisations, is the Communist Party of the Soviet Union."[121] To maintain the illusion that the will of the Communist Party indeed coincided with the will of the people – "The People and the Party are One," was among the most widely used slogans – dissent could not exist. Public opposition was unconstitutional and therefore subject to prosecution.

Since dissent constituted a criminal act, for "almost five decades the existence of political opposition was entirely denied by Soviet Estonia. While the press, television, and radio presented pictures of a happy and prospering Soviet republic that was content with the leadership of the CPSU, the USSR State Security Committee (KGB) was putting dissidents behind bolt and bar."[122] As a consequence, expressions of independent thought and individual initiative were driven underground. This was also the fate of the Letter of 40.

THE MAKING OF A DISSIDENT – KGB AT WORK

Nevertheless, it spread like wildfire.[123] Copied by machine and by hand, read aloud to others, and broadcast by forbidden radio stations from the West – Voice of America in Washington and Radio Liberty in Munich – the Letter of 40 increasingly took on the appearance of *samizdat* and even carried the potential of leading to a "mass rebellion."[124] Rumours that some of the signatories had been fired, searches conducted, and some distributors of the letter punished by the authorities buttressed the dissident aura and further diminished its original intent.

Seen as the main author of the letter, also among his fellow Estonians at home, Kaplinski soon had garnered the "reputation of a resistance fighter and national hero," as he put it.[125] Unwittingly – but, as we shall see, not accidentally – he had become a symbol of standing up against a repressive regime. Concerned about their well-being, perhaps even about their future, and to show their appreciation for his courage and the risk he had taken on their behalf, people visited the Kaplinskis bearing gifts, offering to collect money or send clothes.[126]

Although he himself wanted to avoid "blind nationalism" and at the same time maintain a "critical, but not inimical" relationship with the Soviet authorities, the regime adopted a rhetoric implicating Kaplinski in dissent.[127] At a gathering of the Estonian Writers' Union, a high-ranking official singled out Kaplinski as the main author and driving force behind the Letter of 40 and alleged that he maintained subversive connections with the West. In Kaplinski's view, they essentially had declared him a heretic, an intellectual dissident.[128] Indeed, all but in name, soon the entire Group of 40 was treated as if they were dissidents.

In January of 1981, another leading official of the Estonian Communist Party had branded the content of the letter "hostile."[129] As if a resistance fighter, a member of the Group of 40 was told that he would suffer the same fate as Jüri Kukk, the dissident whose life tragically and under suspicious circumstances ended in a Soviet psychiatric asylum where he had been placed by the Communist authorities.[130] Although the authors of the letter "were not dissidents," as Rein Taagepera explicitly noted in 1983,[131] the line that separated them "from the fate of the so-called dissidents was paper thin"; they were "almost-dissidents," wrote former members of the Group of 40 in their monograph about the history of the letter.[132]

It may seem curious that the "imposed dissident role" had been magnified in Kaplinski's case.[133] Already the search of his home suggested a possible "witch hunt" against him, as one member of the Group of 40 remarked.[134] Kaplinski himself became increasingly convinced that the leaders of the Estonian Communist Party considered him their worst enemy among all the Estonian intellectuals.[135] He was worried that a public campaign would be waged against him to punish, and perhaps even silence, the "dissident Kaplinski."[136]

On the whole, his fears were warranted. A controversial member of the Estonian Academy of Science, Gustav Naan, known at the time for his Stalinist tendencies, wrote a letter addressed to the Central Committee of the Estonian Communist Party. Bearing witness and contributing to the branding of Kaplinski as anti-Soviet, it contained a vitriolic characterization of Kaplinski and a recommendation to step up the campaign against the "gang of 40" and "crush" them, including, in particular, their "leader" Kaplinski.[137] Naan had previously published an article aiming to discredit Kaplinski and undermine the trust placed in him by his peers and the Estonian public at large.[138] Reviewing two articles Kaplinski had published in 1980, Naan spoke of an "ahistorical" approach, a "pseudoscientific" introduction, an account of society that amounts to a "caricature" replete with "factual errors," mistakes in logic, and a "scandalously confused" level of knowledge. Naan also situated Kaplinski in opposition to assumptions fundamental to Marx and Engels, an attempt to render Kaplinski's work not only intellectually but also ideologically suspect and thus unworthy of publication.[139] Hardly surprising, Kaplinski was not given an opportunity to publish a reply to this crudely biased and politically motivated critique.

Instead, in the 1980s, the KGB "incrementally intensified" its interest in Kaplinski.[140] In addition, the authorities assigned a senior member of the prosecutor's office to lead the investigation against him. He was, of all things, a "well-known specialist in dissident matters," with experience in cases against such prominent dissidents as Jüri Kukk and Mart Niklus.[141] As was common practice in the case of dissidents, the authorities had all of Kaplinski's correspondence scrutinized, not only mail from abroad. He was also shadowed by secret agents. Even at his country retreat, a neighbour was charged with the task of reporting on him to the KGB. Kaplinski was summoned to the prosecutor's office in Tartu and, for years, was called upon to meet with the KGB on a regular basis.

The class of files opened by the KGB regarding Kaplinski, three categories altogether, underscores the fact that scrutiny of him had increased. As we can begin to see from this, he was not only suspected of "anti-Soviet" behaviour (*Delo operativnoj proverki*), but was also believed to be engaged in "criminal" activities that called for special measures to "anticipate and prevent the spread of hostile conduct" (*Delo operativnoj razrabotki*). Finally, Kaplinski had been assigned a criminal record for "particularly dangerous illegal acts" (*Delo operativnogo nabludenija*), probably on account of his involvement in the Letter of 40.[142] Not only was he a marked man, but in the eyes of the KGB and particularly the top-ranking Communist officials, he now also firmly belonged to the core of Estonian dissidents – a fact confirmed by the former KGB chief in Tartu.[143]

CRACKDOWN – END OF DISSENT

To make matters worse for Kaplinski, the late 1970s and early 1980s also led to a general crackdown on dissent in the Soviet Union. Looming large in the broader international background were the "Charter 77" in Czechoslovakia, Poland's massive labour protest movement (*Solidarność*), the invasion of Afghanistan, an accelerated arms race pitting the "Capitalists" against the "Communists," as well as increased international attention to security and human rights issues in Europe.

As *The New York Times* of 10 January 1981 reported, the Kremlin responded with more arrests of dissidents in the Baltic States: "Two Estonians have been sentenced to labour camps on charges of anti-Soviet agitation." The front page of *The Washington Post* carried the headline "Kremlin Breaks Dissident Movement."[144] *The Christian Science Monitor* reported that Moscow had stepped up its "4-year assault on Baltic dissidents."[145] In a headline, *The Washington Post* referred to a "Crack Down on Dissidents in Estonia,"[146] where a wave of dissident activity had led to searches, confiscation of *samizdat* materials, arrests, interrogations, imprisonments, and other forms of repression.[147] The large-scale intervention by the authorities meant that by 1983 almost all overt opposition, including protest letters, had ceased to exist in Estonia and the Soviet Union as a whole.[148]

THE INFAMOUS ARTICLE – CREATING CONFUSION

Kaplinski himself considered it "accidental" that the authorities associated him with dissidence, a view he expressed in later years.[149] But he was convinced that the KGB was behind the rise of dissidence. By "intervening in everything that brings people together," they fragmented society, drove people underground, and helped create hostile splinter groups, including dissidents.[150] It is also conceivable that the KGB knowingly created dissidents. Certainly, in Kaplinski's case, the fact that he was cast in this role against his own will and inclination provided the KGB with a unique opportunity to take advantage of him.[151]

What grew clear from the KGB's efforts was the importance of the confiscated diary in achieving their main objective: unable to turn

Kaplinski into an informant, the KGB shifted their strategy towards "isolating"[152] and using him to create "confusion" among his peers and the émigré community in the West.[153] Turning the letter into an act of dissidence and him, as its main author, into a dissident provided the perfect opportunity. But would he renounce his role and recant, as they hoped and as his diary suggested?

This much we know with certainty: although at the time he referred to it as a "compromise article," finding it "difficult" and even "drudgery" to write what the KGB "expected" of him, as he put it in his diary at the beginning of July 1981, he nevertheless delivered his text to authorities in Tartu.[154] The KGB chief was "satisfied," Kaplinski laconically noted in his diary.[155]

He had indeed recanted – and had done so of his own accord, one might say. On 19 August 1981, the text appeared in *Kodumaa* (Homeland), a weekly published under the auspices of the KGB. As a propaganda tool, it was sent to the émigré communities abroad. But in spite of its dubious status, it was also widely read in Estonia, especially by the intellectuals. They scanned it for any information not available elsewhere in the local media which the authorities were known to include in an effort to raise the profile of the publication and ensure a degree of influence and interest among the public at large.

In his article, Kaplinski aligned the West, mostly the US, with a "reactionary worldview" characterized above all by a rigid "dualism" and what he called "right-wing propaganda."[156] Not wishing for Estonia "to be cannon fodder ... in the Cold War,"[157] he spoke out against the "primitive black-and-white myths" that, according to him, prevailed in the West and were at the heart of Estonia's predicament. Although he continued to advocate against a confrontational approach and stressed the need for better mutual understanding between East and West, this time he remained silent about such matters as the Russification of Estonia.[158] More importantly, he slipped into a one-sided depiction of the West, and, albeit without telling any untruths, painted an overly benign picture of Soviet censorship and cultural intolerance.[159]

BREACH OF TRUST – OR ZEN KOAN

Unsurprisingly, Kaplinski's friends and allies were disappointed. The poet, philosopher, and humanist they once knew had turned hostage to politics, they thought.[160] The broader public's reaction to Kaplinski's recantation was swift and equally devastating. "It is becoming increasingly clear that my article ... has saddened and annoyed many," an initially somewhat surprised Kaplinski noted.[161] Although he was accused of "intellectual surrender" and even betrayal,[162] he also felt a sense of relief, initially: "At least I am no longer in opposition to the authorities as I have been, *nolens volens*, for twenty years and more. Resistance is painful and tiresome."[163] But the feeling that a tremendous weight had been lifted off his shoulders would not last long. With each passing day, the realization grew of how broad and deep was the wave of condemnation that his article had triggered. The hostile reaction soon rendered him desolate. He had nightmares, felt "rotten," even suicidal.[164] Accused of complicity and breach of trust, he had become an outcast. To add insult to injury, the Communist authorities praised him for his "manly" deed, an embarrassed and distraught Kaplinski noted in his diary.[165]

It is not an exaggeration to say that his reputation never really fully recovered from his decision to write the article and comply with the request presented to him by the KGB. The "social isolation and contempt" that followed in the wake of the article[166] was "very painful" for Kaplinski; and the "pain has lasted to this day," he wrote in his diary five years after the publication of his infamous article in August of 1981.[167] In the memory of many Estonians, perhaps even most, he had defected and become one of "them."

In retrospect, Kaplinski admits that in his frustration he had "foolishly" cast the article in a language that was too close to the rhetoric and interests of the authorities.[168] Having in this way "played Soviet citizen" obscured his struggle to shed the role of dissident, into which he had been cast, and return to the path that had inspired him to write the Letter of 40 in the first place.[169] Refusing to be a symbol of resistance and be dragged into a dualist mode of thought and behaviour, he would come to call his recantation a "koan," the famous riddle invoked in Far Eastern cultures.[170] It is designed to expand our awareness beyond logic and the boundaries of the definable whenever a seemingly insurmountable mental impasse is reached. In other words, Kaplinski asked his fellow Estonians to see what must have seemed impossible at first: "To demand of a person (including oneself) to define himself, to say who he is, what he believes, what his worldview is," Kaplinski wrote in his diary, is "tyrannical and wrong."[171] If we are to thrive, we need to think of ourselves in other, less coercive and confrontational ways. In his view, to dissolve the divisions, lines of separation that also form the core of totalitarian rule, we need to resist conceiving of individuals and their actions in terms of what makes them stand out. The key to human advance lies in the capacity to blend in.

Perhaps it now becomes easier to understand that Kaplinski had not renounced the spirit of the Letter of 40, what Havel had called "living within the truth." Rather, he had renounced dissent – and the reified mode of thinking about identity, efficacy, and fulfillment aligned with it. To those unable to make this distinction or see merit in it, it appeared as if he had betrayed their trust.

SOFT COLLABORATION – THE GREY ZONE

The disparity between his intention and public perception may also help explain why, to this day, some believe that the KGB coerced Kaplinski into retracting the letter.[172] If we are to believe his own words and the memory of the former chief of the KGB in Tartu, this is not what happened. As a matter of fact, Kaplinski has stated repeatedly that he was indeed the sole author of the infamous article and wrote the recantation without being forced.[173] But it is equally clear that in addition to Kaplinski's desire to live in the light of his convictions, "some kind of pressure" did exist, as he noted in retrospect.[174]

His formulation and stated ideal of non-confrontational, open, and honest engagement mask his vulnerability at the time and the extent and effect of the oppressive measures exercised by the authorities. Although much of it was not readily visible and Kaplinski would probably disagree, he was under considerable duress. After all, on 12 March 1981, the KGB chief in Tartu informed Kaplinski that he could be charged with libel against the state.[175] According to his account of the meeting, Kaplinski had erred not in what he had done when he wrote the Letter of 40. Rather, his mistake was that he had not anticipated what others would do with the text, namely publish it abroad and use it against the Soviet Union.[176] Kaplinski "promised to counter the hostile propaganda."[177] Two months later, on May 18, he was again scheduled to appear in the KGB office in Tartu. The officials asked Kaplinski whether he had given the matter further thought and let him know that, mostly, they would like him to speak out against the "claim" that the Estonians were being Russified. Kaplinski agreed "in principle."[178]

Unsurprisingly, this would not remain the KGB's last such request. A few years later, in 1985 they asked Kaplinski whether he would be prepared to write a "sequel" to the article in which he had recanted.[179] Kaplinski initially declined, but the KGB persisted. The result was that he eventually consented to an interview meant to counter Western "propaganda."[180] Like his recantation, it was published in *Kodumaa* (Homeland), the Communist Party newspaper distributed to the émigré community.[181] The article painted a factually accurate but idyllic picture of his life and work in Soviet Estonia. The West, on the other hand, was portrayed as intentionally spreading false information about him.

To be fair, what appeared in the *New York Times* and elsewhere about Kaplinski was indeed not always accurate. Perhaps overstating the case but nevertheless with some justification, Kaplinski in his diary called the information published abroad about him, in part, "utter nonsense."[182] He referred to broadcasts of Radio Free Europe and articles such as "Oppression Hasn't Stilled Estonian Literature" in which Kaplinski had been falsely reported as having been dismissed from a teaching position at Tartu University.[183]

It is true that in 1980–81 Kaplinski's financial troubles had worsened considerably. On 27 November 1980, he noted in his diary that he "hardly [had] any warm socks" and his winter boots were falling apart. At about the same time he learned that his wife was pregnant. They already had four children to look after, Maarja (born 1964), Ott Siim (born 1970), Lauris (born 1971) and Lemmit (born 1980). Serious marital difficulties exacerbated the couple's already precarious private and material circumstances. The relationship deteriorated even further on account of Kaplinski's bouts of depression, their poor living conditions, and the sanctions issued against him by the authorities.

On 16 December 1980, he was to travel to Lithuania to participate in a workshop with other writers and theater professionals. On the day of his departure, he was informed that the meeting had been postponed.[184] A few days later, he learned that the decision to award him an annual literary prize had been rescinded. A song with lyrics written by Kaplinski had been removed from the record[185] and his contributions to a theater magazine would most likely not be published, he noted in his diary in January of 1981.[186] He began to suspect that he wouldn't see any of his work in print any time soon, except perhaps some translations.[187] Money owed to him for publications was not forthcoming, and manuscripts of her own work that his wife had submitted remained unacknowledged. He was even cut out of a film that had been produced about his hometown.[188]

The Kaplinskis' apartment in Tartu, where they had been living since their return from Tallinn in 1980, was so small that every night they had to move their living room table so that they could use their pull-out couch as a bed. For the purpose of a study space, Kaplinski had to make do with a corner he had cleared for himself in the cellar where the coal was kept to heat the apartment building. No help was forthcoming from the authorities. As it turned out, even though his material circumstances remained difficult for several years, his work was again published and payment resumed as a result of his recantation. However, not until 1985 would he be able to express with some confidence that the worst for him and his family appeared to be over, at least financially.[189]

Meanwhile, another worry arose and loomed larger with each passing year. As his sons grew, Kaplinski's fears began to mount about the war in Afghanistan and the possibility that his boys might suffer the fate of other conscripts who had been brutalized by fellow soldiers or killed in combat. "Afghanistan's meat grinder" haunted him to such an extent that he approached the KGB for support.[190] In January of 1985, he noted in his diary that the Tartu KGB chief had "promised to assist him in the matter of the boys' military [service], when the time came."[191] To his great relief, the Soviet Union signed a peace treaty with Afghanistan in 1988, the very year his eldest son turned 18 and could have been conscripted.

Another source of frustration, and at times even despair, were the travel restrictions the authorities imposed on individuals in the Soviet Union. Kaplinski could not accept that he was being kept against his will and, as he noted in his diary, confined like a prisoner.[192] After yet another negative reply from the authorities, he even contemplated entering into a hunger strike or emigrating, as the world-renowned composer Arvo Pärt and famed conductor Neeme Järvi found themselves compelled to do.[193] Finally, in 1986, when travel restrictions were about to be lifted Union-wide, he received permission to travel abroad, for the first time in his life. He was forfty-five years old. But there was a price to pay for this "favour." A KGB document reveals what the Communist authorities asked in return. They wanted to use Kaplinski as a "counter-propaganda" tool aimed against "reactionary" elements in the Estonian émigré community, and "once and for all tear Kaplinski away" from his peers.[194]

After his first trips abroad – to Finland, in 1986, and to Sweden, in 1987 – he did what most, perhaps even all, who received exit visas were required to do: he provided the KGB with information about some of the people he had met abroad. Innocent as much if not all of the information he provided might have been[195] – mostly descriptive character sketches and a short account of the political-ideological leanings of his main contacts in Finland, Norway, Sweden, and the US – the exchange troubled Kaplinski: "Have mercy on this sinner," is the last entry in the diary that contains his account of this trip.[196] He had done "what a free citizen of a free country would not do," as he put it on 3 March 1984, when he had named for the KGB "most of his Swedish acquaintances and exiled Estonians and said more or less who they might be politically."[197]

It is easy to see why he had grown weary of being black-listed by the authorities. He had been under surveillance since the late 1950s and from the mid-1960s on was known to the KGB as an author opposed to Party principles and Socialist Realism, who had contacts in the West, who listened to foreign radio broadcasts, and whose works had been published abroad without permission from the Communist authorities.[198] After years of regular meetings with the KGB, on 9 April 1987, he noted in his diary: "I have learned a thing or two from these conversations but also suffered a lot. In any case, it would be easier, if they came to an end."[199]

But had he categorically declined any involvement with the KGB, the former chief of the KGB in Tartu confirmed, life for the Kaplinskis would have been even more difficult.[200] In addition to material restrictions, such a refusal also would have amounted to a betrayal of what Kaplinski knew to be a meaningful response to totalitarian rule and human advance in general – his sense of unforced flourishing. In this vexed way, then, external, self-imposed, and internalized pressures converged, making him both unable and unwilling to draw a line between himself and "them." Instead, he pursued a path to identity not in league with independence and difference, and to a behaviour unburdened, as much as possible, by the calculating and heroic – at times tragic – dimensions that could and often did define dissent.

AHEAD OF HIS TIME – CONVERSATION NOT CONFRONTATION

Inside Estonia, many found fault with Kaplinski for his recantation, but few ultimately blamed him for his "soft" collaboration with the KGB. This should not come as a surprise. As citizens under a totalitarian regime, in one way or another, everyone inescapably inhabited this "grey zone." Although it was fraught with moral and ethical challenges and undoubtedly a source of much anguish, "soft" collaboration was no sin. If anything, it was expressive of the absurdity of the entire political system. Rather, when he recanted, Kaplinski was above all criticized for having betrayed the spirit of the Letter of 40 and the trust that people had placed in him. True, in renouncing the letter, he had denied it as an expression of dissent, but not as a critique of what, in his view, ultimately lay at the heart of their predicament: the dominant presumption of antagonism. Seemingly inescapable, this logic and belief in intrinsic superiority and human design as key to fulfillment had captivated the imagination on both sides of the Iron Curtain. His contrasting perspective – rooted in a non-hierarchical and organicist impulse – left Kaplinski feeling abandoned by both the West and the East.

One of his peers, the writer Viivi Luik, was perhaps right when she said that Kaplinski may have been politically naïve and probably should never have become involved with the letter.[201] This much we now know: the certitudes of the Cold War era cast a long shadow over many, including Kaplinski and his struggle to move beyond dissent. Not until Gorbachev would a partial transformation of totalitarianism from within succeed and, though far from Kaplinski's ideal of unforced flourishing, concentrate attention on conversation rather than confrontation.

7

Self-colonization

The washing never gets done.
The furnace never gets heated.
Books never get read.
Life is never completed.
Life is like a ball which one must continually
catch and hit so it won't fall.
When the fence is repaired at one end,
it collapses on the other. The roof leaks,
the kitchen door won't close, there are cracks in the foundation,
the torn knees of children's pants …
One can't keep everything in mind. The wonder is
that beside all this one can notice
the spring which is so full of everything
continuing in all directions – into the evening clouds,
into the redwing's song and into every
drop of dew on every blade of grass in the meadow,
as far as the eye can see, into the dusk.[1]

Jaan Kaplinski

Evil can abate only when we give up dualism.[2]

Jaan Kaplinski

To this day, Kaplinski's views about dissent remain little understood. But it is his critique of culture that truly runs like a fault line between him and most of his fellow Estonians. For them, culture paved the path to freedom – for him, by contrast, culture easily put it at risk. Guided by the philosophical dimensions of his thought, he understood that unforced flourishing raises a question of broader concern to the survival of small nations such as his native Estonia: is there a "wisdom of the weak," or perhaps a shared inescapable need that makes it less meaningful than his fellow Estonians commonly thought to strive for independence and cultural achievement – all in the hope of making freedom unassailable and leaving aggression behind? Or is it impossible, as history has taught us, to escape domination by the more powerful only, perhaps even worse, to be remade in the image of outsiders destined to colonize ourselves?

Although it struck a largely unacknowledged chord with many, if not most Estonians, reimagining human advance and fulfillment as unforced flourishing, to Kaplinski's mind, pointed the way out of this conundrum. But gaining access to this path, Kaplinski knew, would mean revisiting and reimagining the Estonians' response not only to totalitarian rule, but also to their more distant colonial past.

HARDWIRED FOR PEACE – CIVILIZED FOR COERCION

During the Soviet occupation many Estonians withdrew into their own culture, hoping to find shelter in it from the turmoils of Communist power and, in a manner reminiscent of the young Kaplinski's discovery of poetry, retain a sense of cohesion, thus securing their survival as a people. But at the same time, this retreat into their native language and customs fuelled the antagonism between Russians and Estonians. The stronger their sense of self grew, the wider became the gulf between the occupied and the occupiers. In a kind of double-bind, the Estonians' survival was yoked to the very thinking that had put their collective future at risk throughout much of their history, namely the presumption of human fulfillment rooted in difference – a path demanding division, disruption, and coercion.

"But another direction is also possible," Kaplinski would write much later – one requiring a "huge effort and practice," and involving a radical shift in perspective.[3] Such a shift would unsettle the understanding that we are hardwired for confrontation and that the monopolization of the means of violence – a function of nation building and growing self-discipline – has made life more peaceful.[4] At its most fundamental, for Kaplinski the inverse has appeared to be true. Reaching beyond strong voices of the past, such as Freud's and Elias's, he began to understand that violence is "not primordial" and, moreover, that "civilization does not tame it."[5] When he has tried to explain his personal view of what it means to be mature as an individual and as a society, he has often returned to the image of the child in us as an ideal to uphold. In other words – and in marked contrast to widely held opinion – violence, for him, is not in our nature. We can trust our instincts. Although scarcely any "cultural discourse admits this," it is as if violence stems more from our social-situational and civilizational rather than neurological organization.[6] If normally they are seen as pacifying powers, then nations, for Kaplinski, are better understood as "coercion-wielding," and their license to civilize as rooted in a misunderstanding of our psychological, perhaps even neurobiological, make-up.[7]

The other important assertion that informs Kaplinski's competing mode of perception concerns culture. As Freud famously argued, the relationship between civilization ("Kultur") and violence rests on the belief that we are hardwired for violence. We are "not gentle creatures who want to be loved," he claimed in *Civilization and Its Discontents.* We are, "on the contrary, creatures among whose instinctual endowments is to be reckoned a powerful share of aggressiveness"; "[h]omo homini lupus" – man is a wolf to his fellow man.[8] The need to control our violent nature thus gives rise to demands for discipline and a view of art in which even acts of violence are said to merge with pleasure when they are depicted through the mediated lens of the creative artist. The entire "order of culture," this transformation of violence into the sublime, in turn sustains the belief that we are innately aggressive. In other words, culture constitutes not only an act of symbolic taming but forms a symbiotic relationship with violence.

The trajectory of Kaplinski's thinking is even more complex. It culminates in his critique of "westernization." Inevitably, he remained caught up in the discursive maintenance of boundaries. But rather than being anxious about specific manifestations of difference – such as ethnicity, nation, or Eastern versus Western patterns of thought – he was primarily worried about falling into a self-defeating over-dependence on "shadows of reality," the world of symbols, representation, language, culture.

For Kaplinski, then, retreating into the realm of culture constituted only seemingly a nonviolent response to totalitarian rule – not merely because symbols are in league with violence. The trouble with culture ran even deeper for him: it implicated the Estonians in self-colonization – the psychologically double-edged process of making one's own what is owed to colonizers, for many contemporary

Estonian intellectuals a contentious proposition.[9] As essential as self-colonization may have been for Estonia's independence and its social, cultural, and political history, as well as its process of identity formation in general, Kaplinski has argued that it constitutes a fundamentally flawed response to colonial power. Not only did the Estonians increasingly identify with European culture, but, more importantly for him, in this process they became too dependent on the symbolic order, on "communicative culture."[10] This "addiction" to taming through culture, as one might say, feeds into colonialism, sustains it, and values what lies at its heart: namely, the assumption that we are hardwired for violence, that we need to be civilized, and therefore must submit to the "rule" of culture. Convinced that our ills are rooted in culture, not primarily in the individual, for Kaplinski, in contrast to Freud, the task then became to diminish the influence of culture and weaken the belief in the "transformation of the raw energy of the instincts into products of utility and beauty."[11] Woven into the fabric of Kaplinski's personality and experience, this critique of culture also put him on a collision course with many of his fellow Estonians, especially those "who assert that they have belonged to the West for 700 years already and thank … the Baltic Germans for their westernization."[12] For Kaplinski, however, this history is one that, above all, aligns with the waging of war.[13] About his hometown he wrote in *The Guardian*: "Once I tried to find out how many times and by whom … Tartu, has been invaded. I counted 15. First by the Teutonic knights during their crusades against the Estonian heathen in 1223, then by Russians, Poles, Swedes, Russians, Estonians, Soviets, Germans."[14]

Indeed, Kaplinski's account of Tartu mirrors the history of Estonia at large: from the day the first colonizers arrived on Estonian territory in the thirteenth century to the close of the twentieth when the last left, a complex and violent legacy followed in their wake. It includes the double colonization by Czarist Russians and Baltic Germans, who competed for and exercised control over Estonia in the nineteenth century, and the occupation of Estonia by the Soviet Union in the twentieth century (1940–41 and 1944–91). All this was further complicated by militant Baltic German state-building aspirations in neighbouring Latvia as well as Estonia (1919), other past colonist interventions and reverberations of Estonian's War of Independence (1918–20), and, finally, secured statehood (1918–39). Whether they were reduced to servitude by a religious order of crusading knights, or fell to the rule of other alien forces, this, in broad strokes, is the history of Estonia: while variously influenced by commercial, religious, cultural, territorial, and political motives, it is a seemingly endless sequence of multiple, and at times simultaneously occurring, colonisations or occupations and violent confrontations. The past is nothing but a "big and merciless battle," a character in Kaplinski's play *The Day of the Four Kings* notes matter of factly, "where the stronger conquers the weaker in order to stay strong, and become even stronger."[15]

Kaplinski knows that, in the history of Europe, there is nothing exceptional about Estonia's bellicose past. Indeed, it has been claimed that "war has remained the defining activity of national states" over the past centuries.[16] Of course, being on the "wrong" side of this history of coercion and war has for the Estonians meant that, ever since the first invasion in medieval times, any ensuing battle on their territory was almost always already lost before it could even begin. It has also meant that being colonized has provided the main thread that Estonians weave into the fabric of their national narratives. Subjugation became their history and is overwhelmingly part of their collective sense of self.

Although he distanced himself from a perspective focused on nation making, ethnicity, victims, and perpetrators, it bears repeating that Kaplinski's reflections grew from a different, even more profound concern: the aim of his thinking about the colonized was to find out what lay at the root of their vulnerability and how one might sidestep a seemingly endless and inevitable cycle of violence, flourishing unforced instead. Isn't this an ideal shared by us all? he asked in a text accompanying a graphic of the Estonian artist Kaljo Põllu entitled "Nurmekund" (1979): "How many have a dream about a sheltered haven, a place where you can be quite on your own, secure, at home and alone? ... A place where, coming from a long trip, you would find peace and quiet, where the rustling of the forest would soothe you ... A naive, outdated dream, promptly rejected by our reason in the daytime, yet invading our mind at night and accompanying us even in our waking hours, in the form of a strange longing. Who dares affirm he has never dreamed of anything like it?"[17]

The germ of this dream to live in peace and quiet can also be found in his conviction that the political, economic, social, and cultural subjugation of his native country need not be regarded as inevitable. While this hope constitutes "one of the fundamental axes" in his work, it is also crucial to recognize that his perspective presents a consciousness and sensibility anchored in a distinctly "different understanding of life, of values and of the world."[18] Ironically, this led to a rift between him and the majority of his fellow Estonians. All too simply put: to flourish, they turned to culture – he, by contrast, turned away from it.

CULTURAL RESISTANCE – THE LOCATION OF NATION

But what else could the Estonians have done? With the Soviet occupation Estonia's cultural fabric underwent radical change.[19] No "invading culture except the Soviet Union has ever insisted on a complete agenda of cultural genocide, that included the suppression of local customs, education, religion, and, most important, language," Karl Jirgens wrote; a grand-scale process of "renaming" was implemented with the aim of creating a new subject: *homo sovieticus.*[20]

While some might argue that the distance between culture and colony is so vast that a focus on the relationship between symbols and aggression easily leads to distorting extremes, Kaplinski believed that their common existential underpinnings must neither be confused with physical violence nor go unnoticed. Symbolic violence exposes a face of culture that Kaplinski associated with the "masculine," the desire to "rule, define and determine," and, at its most extreme, "destroy" what appears alien to it.[21]

We know how, in Kaplinski's eyes, most Estonians dealt with the disorienting experience of occupation. They "did not accept the imposed Soviet identity, and, encouraged by [the] proximity to Finland, clung instead to a real or imaginary western one."[22] Members of the war generation, who, unlike Kaplinski, had grown up in prewar Estonia, especially turned to their memories of symbols, rites of passage, customs and traditions associated with independent Estonia of 1918–39. For them, culture was a *condicio sine qua non.* Indeed, culture was the nation: to borrow from Franco-Czech novelist Milan Kundera – another writer born into a small "kidnapped" nation – being inescapably caught on the "wrong side" of history drove the Estonians ever deeper into the past cultural realm until culture itself became "the living value around which all people rally."[23]

This is not surprising, especially since atrocities are not easily forgotten, and Estonians suffered immensely during World War II and the terror regime of Stalin that followed. Fuelled by linguistic differences between Estonian and Russian as well as dividing lines between Russian Orthodox and Lutheran Protestant religious practices, the Estonians found themselves locked into a downward spiral of "existential insecurity."[24] This led to distrust of others and a dichotomized self-perception, rigidly pitting Europeanization against Russification, West against East, collective national memory against imposed foreign ideology, home against exile.[25] As a consequence, the "Russian-speaking post-World War II ... immigrants were until very recently considered illegitimate and thus functioned as the internal negative Others against whom Estonians asserted their nationness."[26] While this return to the past was meant to serve as a collective refuge of sorts from the trauma of imposed and disorienting alien cultural practices, it also constituted an act of resistance. Ranging from unprecedented mass participation in their song festivals to the immense popularity of all the arts among Estonians during Soviet times, cultural resistance gained an extraordinary status.[27] One might say, it rose to become their "one hope."[28]

Perhaps this thinking even underlies today's widely accepted notion that culture not only "saved" the Estonian nation but also won the battle against the occupiers, as *National Geographic* photographer Priit Vesilind famously wrote in his book about Estonia's *Singing Revolution:* "It was as early as the late 1860s that Jakob Hurt suggested that if Estonia contributed anything to the world it would have to be in the cultural rather than any political or military field. A small, defenseless, sparsely populated nation, eternally vulnerable on the edge of the European plain, living for 700 years between imperial powers, has only psychological weapons. That contribution is now understood: It is the Singing Revolution. Estonia's break from the prison of the Soviet empire was unique – a primer in intellectual and spiritual strength."[29] Similar to other nations that suffered under totalitarian rule, it is, as Marek Tamm rightfully noted, above all the belief in cultural power that animated the Estonians when they turned to their language, music, and historical and literary narratives to remember who they were; they resisted totalitarian intrusion through words and song.[30] The former President of Estonia, Lennart Meri, echoed this sentiment when he noted in a speech delivered at the University of Helsinki in 1999 that the Estonians "cannot really conceive of [their] independence otherwise than as a cultural, and not only political, notion."[31]

Even after the collapse of the Soviet Union, this particular belief in cultural capital characterized the political struggles of Estonia and other Central European countries. They re-emerged on the international scene with a new breed of top civil servants, "cultural politicians" – writers, historians, former professors, and other intellectuals rich in cultural knowledge and distinguished credentials in the arts and humanities.[32] Among them was Jaan Kaplinski, who served as Member of the Estonian Parliament in the early 1990s. Indeed, "[n]owhere else in modern times has there developed such a deep belief in the well-nigh magical power of the word and of cultural symbols in general," another observer wrote about the extraordinary role of culture in the early years of post-Communist Central Europe.[33] Expressing hope for a future of "sincere cultural openness," poet and academic Jüri Talvet in his book of 2005 envisioned a "cultural symbiosis" grounded in a "permanent dialogue" between the centres and the peripheries of power.[34]

That culture constitutes a formidable force, perceived or real, Kaplinski discovered, holds especially true when social imbalances are at an extreme, as they tend to be under totalitarian rule. For most of his life he was subjected to such conditions. They magnified this potential of culture to a point where it became considerably more than a means of social organization and physical survival. It transformed Estonia into "a country where poetry and poets were feared, admired, persecuted, oppressed and exalted," as Kaplinski wrote in *The Same River*.[35] Poets mattered. In that semi-autobiographical novel, set in Nikita Khrushchev's Soviet Estonia of the 1960s, a student-poet who closely mirrors Kaplinski himself attracts the attention of the KGB for no other reason than possessing a few poems that had been "classified as anti-Soviet."[36] Until Stalin's death, texts even remotely critical of the occupying powers were carefully monitored, translated, and filed by the KGB as evidence constituting "literary resistance," which was punishable by years, if not decades, of hard labour.[37]

Perhaps it is an exaggeration to regard it as the "greatest enemy of any totalitarian super power," but to young Kaplinski, and most Estonians at the time, their culture appeared endowed with such extraordinary force.[38] While the Communist authorities saw their own form of culture as a means to legitimize their power, for the Estonians it served as an encoded, secret system of symbols. This substitute for public discourse became their weapon against the occupying regime.[39] Its arsenal included Kaplinski's earlier poetry, and one poem in particular.

"VERCINGETORIX SAID" – MISREADING A CELEBRATED POEM

In his highly regarded collection *Tolmust ja värvidest* (Of Dust and Colors) – published in 1967 – Kaplinski wrote in overt opposition to a world characterized by conquest, control, confinement, reification, violence, and destruction. In contrast to such a world, he imagined a kind of "paradise" where

> no one anywhere needs your history, your ends and / beginnings. / Peace. Simple peace to the jellyfish, and to grouse eggs; peace, / to the ant's rushing pathways; peace, to birds of paradise / and the ginko / peace, to the sky; peace, to you snipe's flight / peace, to apples, pears, plums, apricots, oranges, / wild roses growing on the railroad guardshack: / Requiem, Requiem aeternum.[40]

This eternal peace can be imagined, as many of the poems in *Tolmust ja värvidest* suggest – and perhaps even briefly experienced in a shamanistic-like trance, mystically invoked by the power of words – but, in the final analysis, it remains out of reach. Consequently, the collection ends in the resignation of someone who has lost hope that it is in his power to effect change: "there is no solace," he laments in the concluding poem of this collection.[41] Instead of this imagined paradise, we remain trapped, as the poem "Tüütus tüütus" (Bother bother) suggests, in a rigid, lifeless world.[42]

As some have argued, at its most fundamental we owe this fate to an egocentric mentality. But, in Kaplinski's eyes, this sense of self is rooted in a misunderstanding: that human beings are divided "within themselves, between themselves, and from the natural world."[43] As this internalized pattern of thought has come to be associated with the European West, several poems in *Tolmust ja värvidest* are, explicitly or implicitly, directed against mainstream European culture that draws upon dualist means of orientation and modes of seeing as its all-absorbing guide. Kaplinski "fights against an expansionist Faustian mentality," some of his friends and fellow poets noted in 1968, evoking Goethe's masterpiece and its much admired but in in fact ruthlessly goal-oriented and blindly self-serving protagonist.[44] In a 1983 lecture, Kaplinski remarked that when he wrote the poems of this collection in his early twenties, he felt that "this world had to disappear, this world and also this culture ... it had to be replaced by something else."[45]

But these early poems were often read with a national sentiment: as a protest against the long-ago invasion of the Teutonic Knights or the subjugation of the Celts by the Romans, as a sign of collapsing colonialism and Eurocentrism,[46] and, above all, as allegories of the Soviet occupation of Estonia.[47] For the world-renowned Estonian composer Veljo Tormis, who set Kaplinski's "Ballad of Mary's Own Land" to music in 1969, Mary's Land, as the German missionaries used to refer to Estonia, is a synonym for a colonized country and the poem as a whole is an allegory that captures the anti-Soviet feelings of Estonians in the '60s and the fear of seeing their culture vanish:[48] "No strength any more ... One random shriek of an eagle, the flight of the one-day moth – / if you lose your songs and your language, it is total loss."[49] Responses to the internationally widely read poem about Vercingetorix, the Gallic tribe leader of the Arverni who rebelled against Caesar, often exemplified the typical tendency at the time to regard Kaplinski's early work as a protest against colonial, and specifically Soviet, intrusion into his native land and the threat of loosing one's identity and own language. "Vercingetorix Said" includes the following lines that easily chime with this view:

> Caesar, you can take / the land where we live away from us, / but you cannot take the land from us where we have died: / I've thrown down my sword at your feet. / That is how we are, my people and I; / I know what is coming. / All those who deserved to live / in the Arvernian land are dead, / and I do not want to live / with those who are left / ... So be it, Imperator. Let there be one language / in your republic, one faith and one people, ... It is my hand and the hand of my people / that will bring you down, / my hand wielding the sword of the Vandals.[50]

Introduced as "A Poem from Estonia," "Vercingetorix Said" was reviewed in 1984 in the *New York Times*. The reviewer wrote: "Mr. Kaplinski has never explained his allegorical poem, but readers have had little trouble understanding that it was directed at the Russians."[51] In distinction to Kaplinski's own view of the poem, already "at the time of publication, his verses were seen as an allegory of the relationship of peaceful, rural Estonia – represented by Gaul – with the imperialistic new Rome, that is, the U.S.S.R."[52] Indeed, it is a poem evoking several "allegorical parallels between the Celts under Roman domination and the Estonians under Soviet Russian domination," including the threats of assimilation and loss of cultural identity.[53] As much as the allegorical dimension appears to be "immediately intelligible,"[54] the poem is also expressive of Kaplinski's broader "concern for all endangered groups."[55] Although Kaplinski is partial to the latter reading, he himself has called the poem "audacious" (hulljulge), which possibly supports prevailing allegorical interpretations.[56]

The problem, then, is this: whether directed against a dominant European culture and its pervasive conception of a split between self and other, or, more specifically, against the Soviet occupation of Estonia, the critique of colonialism characteristic of Kaplinski's collection finds expression within an antithetical frame of reference. In other words, it mirrors the roots of a rationality that so often has dragged Estonia down. Acknowledged by Kaplinski, the dualistic perspective is informed by the desire to replace one homogenizing view of the world with another, rather than letting things arise of their own accord.[57] As such, this volume of poems also turns against its own anti-colonial stance and unintentionally perpetuates what it seeks to eradicate. In this sense, it constitutes an act of "self-colonization," a term used elsewhere to describe a process of "voluntarily absorb[ing] the basic values and categories of colonial Europe," of acknowledging Europe as "master signifier" and "civilizational superego."[58] To step away from the logic that governs this process of self-colonization lies at the heart of the mature Kaplinski's work and constitutes a core aspect of what we here have called unforced flourishing.

Shortly before his first collection of poems in English translation appeared in 1985, he told his co-translator and North American editor, Sam Hamill: "I do not consider it right to be called primarily the poet of the oppressed Est[onian] people. I think my background is larger. If I write about Estonians, I mean Estonians, but if I write about Indians, I mean Indians."[59] Similarly, to Ilse Lehiste he wrote already in 1969 that for him native "Indians don't mean Estonians," but added that it would be even more truthful to say that we are "dealing with one and the same, regardless where it happens."[60]

More than three decades after the first publication of *Tolmust ja värvidest,* in the 1990s, Kaplinski's position had evolved further. About his Vercingetorix poem he said that it constituted a protest aimed against those "who accept as their own the culture and values of the colonizers."[61] In other words, it was also intended to be critical of self-colonization, of wanting, not merely being coerced into certitudes. Self-colonization thus erodes Kaplinski's all-absorbing quest: a sense of human flourishing anchored in the unforced – the spontaneous, undifferentiated, non-calculative, and naturally unfolding.

ALLERGIC TO CULTURE – RESISTING DEEP SELF-COLONIZATION

For Kaplinski, this fundamental attribute of the occupation – the complicity of its victims – reached even deeper. Looking beyond the Russification of Estonia and "a system that remained totalitarian while pretending to be something else entirely," one concern in particular stood out for him:[62] while "Estonianness" was meant to be a refuge from the traumatic experience of Russification, from the 1960s on Kaplinski became increasingly anxious about it – and not only because it expressed and cultivated a limiting mentality, most visibly in dualist patterns. Estonianness, he discovered, also carried a double imprint. Barely noticeable but firmly lodged in the indigenous population were two distinct patterns of orientation and modes of perception: one rooted in a non-Western, "Finno-Ugric" imagination; and the other in a "Western European" one. This realization took Kaplinski further into Estonia's colonial past.

Although the members of the ruling Baltic German upper class of merchants and nobility were "deeply resented by the Estonian population until the middle of the twentieth century,"[63] in their culture-making process the Estonians internalized the "Germanic notion of what culture must be"; they "acquired the German cultural model and structure, and began to shape their own culture according to this model."[64] The impact of Baltic German colonial culture was long-lasting, complex, and "deep," as Jaan Undusk has noted.[65] Felt well into the first decades of the twentieth century,[66] it can be regarded as pivotal to the "dominant rhetoric of Estonian culture," which, according to Estonian writer Jaak Rähesoo, "has always been that of catching up with more developed nations."[67] Not only did the Estonians identify with the mentality and way of life of the

Baltic Germans, but, more importantly, they also increasingly looked at the world and themselves through the prism of "Kultur" as such. The Germans had long since internalized this perspective.[68] Far into the nineteenth century, they had referred to the conquered Estonian territory as "Kulturboden," and presented themselves as agents of culture, "Kulturträger" (literally "carriers of culture") charged with a mission of "Kulturarbeit" ("cultural work"), or even "Kulturkampf," the battle to cultivate those who, like the Estonians, were deemed cultureless, an inferior people equipped only with "Unkultur."[69] "Kultur," for them, stood above all for "human products," such as "works of art, books, religious or philosophical systems, in which the individuality of a people expresses itself." The concept, as Elias notes, "delimits" and "places special stress on national differences and the particular identity of groups."[70] The Estonians had grown accustomed to this quality inherent in culture, and with their own agenda in mind would soon begin to exploit, and in doing so at the same time sustain, the cardinal lesson they had learned from their subjugators: Kaplinski would come to call it "communicative culture."[71] In the case of the Estonians, this meant concentrating the collective attention not only on "large dichotomies" generally – such as "self" and "other"[72] – but also on aligning national identity with cultural achievement.[73]

In response, some Estonians, such as the prominent folklorist Oskar Loorits, urged a return to their Finno-Ugric heritage, to escape the influence of their Indo-European colonizers and take pride in their own cultural achievements.[74] Not unlike the Estonian Juhan Luiga before him, Loorits aimed to expose as groundless the charge often levelled by the colonizers that the Estonians lacked cultural capital of their own. On the contrary: they too were champions of culture, the mind and spirit, ready and eager to give expression to their individuality as a people.

Particularly with respect to their Finno-Ugric, indeed Eastern rather than European orientation, Kaplinski aligned himself with Luiga's and Loorits's views. But the primary importance the latter two attributed to culture elicited a decisively different response from him.[75] Put provocatively, Kaplinski did not come to think of "Unkultur" as a condition to overcome. Unlike Luiga and Loorits, who believed that culture sets us free, Kaplinski saw in the "demarcation" and "differences between groups," that culture addressed and expressed a limiting rather than liberating force.[76] Worse, whether "we want it or not," Kaplinski noted in an article first published in 1989, "culture means violence directed at oneself and other living beings, pains and strain that ... take us further away from life."[77] For this reason, Kaplinski advocated a diminished dependence on what is commonly understood by culture. "What is culture anyways?" he asked:

> [We] consider the products we create too important ...
> We think the city-building Aztecs a highly cultured people,
> a people who punished their children by hanging them by
> the feet above a smoking fire of smoldering peppers and
> don't consider the Papago's culture as highly advanced, a
> people who were able to raise their children entirely without
> punishment, but whose handiwork didn't extend much beyond
> simple baskets and ceramics.[78]

Later, when he used the term "culture," Kaplinski thought above all of dominant European culture, a culture that tends to marginalize the "undifferentiated" as a core value, relegate it to the mystical and spiritual domain. In his own words, it is "not oriented towards the beginning, birth and becoming but towards the end, death and completion."[79]

From a historical perspective, rather than seeing the Estonians' reliance on culture decrease, Kaplinski perceived an overdependence on it. Already beginning with the so-called National Awakening in the second half of the nineteenth century, the Estonians used mass cultural events to develop a collective sense of self as a cultured people and fast-tracked a process of "assimilation of the best of European culture." All this was rooted in the belief that they had to "create a modern culture of their own."[80] While Kaplinski remained convinced that one couldn't create a people, and that one had to instead nurture and protect it,[81] it is this period in particular that is generally identified as "the actual birth of the Estonian nation and culture."[82] As Hennoste explained,[83] adopting European cultural models of the time – the decades around the turn of the century – coincided with the struggle for independence; but it also meant falling into a discourse that defined itself in sharp contrast to the so-called "uncivilized" world and, importantly, adopting "the central idea and ideal of the colonizers," namely to civilize.[84]

Drawing attention to the link between culture and war making, Kaplinski invoked Estonia's heroic tale *Kalevipoeg* (Son of Kalev). Written in the tradition of the quintessential medieval Germanic epic, the *Nibelungenlied,* but created only in the nineteenth century,

> Kalevipoeg, along with the creation of Estonian choral groups, brass ensembles and theater companies, were our period of National Awakening's biggest achievements. In some aspects, the period of Awakening was directed acculturation, during the course of which gaps were filled and Estonians were shown to have all the characteristics that distinguish a so-called civilized people [*kultuurrahvas*]. It is interesting that one of those characteristics of the nineteenth century happened to be something typical of the war-prone barbarians, who a few millennia earlier created political and cultural structures and ideologies, which became a model for all civilized nations [*kultuurrahvastele*].[85]

While Estonian "intellectuals remained powerfully under German cultural influence, including the use of German as a means of communication among themselves," they increasingly sought to widen their exposure to other European cultures, most notably French and English and to some extent Scandinavian.[86] And indeed, during the first decades of the twentieth century, "to be in the closest contact with the deepest and clearest springs of Europe" – its cultural capitals – became the stated aim of the then leading intellectuals, like the prominent Estonian cultural critic Ants Oras in the 1930s.[87] Unsurprisingly, then, the guiding slogan of the Young Estonians reflects this goal: "More culture! Let there be more European culture! Let us be Estonians, but let us also become Europeans!" Oras would go on to add that the achievements of the Estonians should "surpass those of the nations with long cultural traditions ... The smaller a national unit is, the more vigorous its mental life has to be."[88]

Kaplinski remained critical of this influential early twentieth-century Estonian cultural and intellectual movement. Their Eurocentric legacy and effort to expand Estonia's cultural self-definition beyond Russia and Germany in no small measure had co-determined Estonia's cultural history and identity throughout much of the twentieth century. In 2005, Kaplinski wrote of Young Estonia that, since the time of this movement, Estonian literature has shared the same path with much of European literature, but added that "sooner or later people here will understand that Europe is no manor house, where one has to sit and walk as if one had swallowed a steelyard."[89] Yet Estonia's identification with Europe continued to gather strength until Western culture and "national survival" had merged in the collective imagination of the Estonian people. It forms the visible core of their self-image to this day.[90]

TERRA MARIANA – FROM THE TEUTONIC ORDER TO THE EURO ORDER

Generally celebrated as a return to the European West, the collapse of the Soviet Union made it again possible to more fully reconnect with the cultural, social, and political space of Europe from which Estonians had been separated during the Soviet occupation. Indeed, it has been argued that their "wish to be accepted again by the West and to be recognized as an integral part of the Western cultural realm is a more substantial driving force in their development than mere economic or political motivation could ever be."[91] In an effort to secure EU membership, Estonia appeared particularly keen to present itself in the international arena as belonging to Western Europe. So much so that, in 1995, the then Estonian president, Lennart Meri, introduced an order of merit named the "Cross of Terra Mariana" – to be awarded to foreigners in recognition of their services to Estonia.

Kaplinski did not approve of the name chosen for the order of merit, which, in his view, amounted to an expression of gratitude for centuries of subjugation. The explanation for Kaplinski's criticism is simple: Mary's Land – in reference to the Virgin Mary of Christian mythology – is a longstanding synonym for Estonia. It was introduced and used by the Christian conquerors and missionaries who invaded Estonia. Then known as Livonia, the Catholic Church had dedicated this territory to the Virgin Mary. For Kaplinski, in this sense, the order is not an Estonian order. Instead, it is a Euro-order,[92] a symbol of a kind of "masochistic" desire to belong to a Europe that honours self-colonization.[93] Are the Estonians the "only people in the world who mark their subjugation with an order?" Kaplinski wondered in the pages of a major Estonian newspaper.[94]

As this example illustrates, even in the 1990s, Estonia's Baltic German colonial past had not receded into distant memory but remained a current and sensitive point of reference in public discourse, at least for Kaplinski. For most Estonians today, "Terra Mariana," including the medieval core of Tallinn built primarily by Estonian workers but for German merchants using German architectural designs, constitutes Estonian and not alien history. Indeed, for many Estonians "Maarjamaa" also resonates with patriotic sentiments. The emotional connection and sense of national identity the word "Maarjamaa" tends to evoke was particularly strong during Soviet times. But the seeds had already been sown almost a century earlier with its perhaps most prominent poetic evocation and idealization by the best-known writer of Estonia's period of National Awakening, Lydia Koidula (1843–1886). Her anthology of verse, published in 1866 and entitled *Emajõe ööbik* (The nightingale of the Emajõgi), includes the poem "Sind surmani" (You until death) in which "homeland" and "Maarjamaa" are synonymous. In distinction, still others, among them composer Veljo Tormis, have been decidedly critical in their assessment. They largely align with Kaplinski's position, and view "Maarjamaa" primarily as a symbolic representation of Estonia's colonial past. For them, "Maarjamaa" is a name given to their homeland by those who invaded and conquered it.[95]

In Kaplinski's view, this identification with colonialism constitutes more than simply an expression of self-colonization. It also casts a different light on both the "heroic" advances in the late nineteenth and early twentieth century towards nationhood, and then the retreat of the Estonians during the Soviet occupation into the "territory of the mind and the spirit."[96] Meant to be a place safe from the foreign intruders, it turned out to be the belly of the beast. One might say that, for Kaplinski, this overdependence on European culture amounts to a license to civilize: throughout their history the Estonians were "civilized" by invading forces. By adopting "culture" as their "weapon" of choice, they unwittingly lent legitimacy to the cultural power of their subjugators and became vulnerable to culture wars, wars they were unlikely to win. In this fundamental sense, colonization deepened into self-colonization – and unforced flourishing, the alternative to the "incessant and doomed alignment/competition with the colonial center" Kaplinski imagined, was destined to remain at the margins of the collective mind.[97]

During the Soviet occupation, in his drama *Day of the Four Kings*, Kaplinski evoked the Estonians' complicity in this unintended consequence of their quest for more culture and self-determination. First performed on 26 February 1977, but probably written in 1972, it is a play within a play set in contemporary Estonia. At its core lies the staging of a commemorative performance about four Estonian Kings who meet with a representative of the Teutonic Order in 1343, the year of the St. George's Night rebellion. Some call it an uprising, others a fight for freedom of Estonian peasants against their colonizers. The Estonian kings insist that it is wrong to occupy their land and force them to adopt the values, beliefs, and customs of Western civilization and serve their foreign rulers. The Master of the Order tries to convince the four kings that their ambition is naïve and has no hope of succeeding, and so he scolds them: "For one hundred years, the Order and the Church have gone through the trouble of spreading enlightenment in Mary's Land. But still the Estonians have remained foolish pagans, dogs who bite their master's hand."[98] The participants in the play are then given a choice: take on the role of the ancient Estonians or act as men of the Order. Opting for the latter, in the end, the four kings are killed, not by the Master of the Order but by members of the audience, Estonians who had agreed to participate in the play. It is as if, for Kaplinski, culture, colonization, and self-colonization have merged.

This raises a more general question about Kaplinski himself. How are we to reconcile his long and prolific career as a writer and his status as an Estonian cultural icon with his conviction that culture easily diminishes rather than enriches life and that the greatest risk to human fulfillment results from human beings themselves? Kaplinski's diaries show that this conundrum affected him. Indeed, it may have "paralyzed" his "literary activity" – but only "for a while," as he noted in a letter written towards the end of 1980.[99]

Although he understood how culture tracks a decline, and ever more firmly believed that "reality is more amazing" and "life considerably richer" than anything we are able to imagine, it would be a mistake to conclude that he had lost all confidence in our creative impulse.[100] But if we believe Kaplinski, how, then, was it possible for him to envision human culture and creativity so that he, as a writer, could "be free with it," remain discreet, and, in Gary Snyder's words, find it a "vehicle of self-transcending insight?"[101] Kaplinski discovered his answer in an ancient tradition at a time when it had receded so far into memory that it was all but forgotten by many, and perhaps even most. In his heritage he had detected a way for culture to converge with unforced flourishing.

8

The Art of Unforced Flourishing

What, after all, can I write?
About what was – memories.
About what could come to be – dreams.

I do not want either.
I want to write
above all about what is.

About the present. But the present is
the meeting of two walls – the very same
memories and dreams. And between them
is only a corner, too tight
to write in it, *it is*.

Now I understand:
I stand once more in the corner
as once in University Street
and want to believe that from there
from that elusive hue
a door opens to somewhere else
Somewhere far away.[1]

Jaan Kaplinski

Our songs are tendrils of a primeval forest which refuse to be transformed into artful gardens of modern culture.[2]

Jakob Hurt

The deeper resources of Kaplinski's habits of thought lead to an uncommon but conceivably timely notion of creativity: from the underlying motives of his life and work issues the intriguing and seemingly impossible challenge to be creative but, at the same time, resist creating more. Compelled to undo creativity in this fashion, or, more precisely, seek creative advance in a decidedly different manner, for Kaplinski means to channel his creative impulses into a way of living, as a man and a writer, that is predominantly receptive. According to this approach to creativity, "one constantly cuts back on one's involvement and reduces one's activity."[3] Does this, then, put him on a path to a "world of meaningless plenty," impoverish him as a creative human being, and cast doubt over his eminence as a poet?[4] This much is certain: captivated by a mainly meditative rather than communicative mode, Kaplinski finds himself at odds with those who believe that giving vitality to our lives means being "the interpreters … of our experience"[5] so that we can claim our "right to separate existence and individual identity."[6] Otherwise, as much of common wisdom has it, we run the risk of being "simply reflexively reactive to … stimuli that do not represent anything, but simply are."[7]

To summarize a complex matter, one might say that, for Kaplinski, creative advance means to illuminate rather than transform what exists. This path, in his view, does not spell the eclipse of the creative element in personality. Rather than being impoverishing, such a path promises fuller access to life's abundance. Importantly for Kaplinski, it gives rise to the hope that he does fit into this world and is, after all, not destined to remain in conflict with himself and his environment.

A good example illustrating this contrasting approach to creativity and fulfillment can be found in Chinese and Japanese art where "using a bare minimum of form," as Thomas Merton explained, is meant to "awaken us to the formless."[8] In other words, in order to counter the tendency based on the conviction that "everything has to mysteriously signify something else," we need to de-symbolize, turn sublimation on its head,[9] place our trust in a "process of discovery without intentional design."[10]

Coinciding with this approach and sentiment, Kaplinski's poems frequently evoke an "almost wordless / wordmanship,"[11] as if to make clear: "what / remains unspoken is always the most important" – and bound to elude language.[12] But he is not merely holding "language at bay."[13] He knows that it is our shared human-made culture which makes communal life possible. He also knows that we are part of a larger world, a world more important than all of us. As Gary Snyder wrote in "The Practice of the Wild" about self-organizing systems – which include the human and the nonhuman, culture and nature – this calls for a "civilization that can live fully and creatively together with wildness,"[14] a view that chimes with Kaplinski's sense of the art of unforced flourishing. Rather than retreat into a self-imposed inner exile, the traditional response of the sage and hermit, essentially saying that we are ill-suited for this earth, as a writer he moves towards "equalizing poetic activity with any process ... occurring in the living world."[15] Kaplinski understands that the more art aligns with everything and everyone, the more it approaches the artless. In this sense much of his poetry steps away from subjective transformations, harnesses a residual aesthetics, and thus engages, rather than resists, a world unfolding on its own.

With the help of two strong voices of the past one might say that Kaplinski overruns the framework created by Freud's notion of sublimation and reaches beyond Winnicott's "transitional space" to another location of cultural experience and creative expression. Kaplinski's understanding of creative expression reveals a sense of fullness and strength rooted in the seemingly unremarkable, "sooner reached by way of reduction than by growing complexity," purposeful silence and frugal simplicity rather than self-indulgent abundance of artistic modalities. This is how Kaplinski's contemporary and in some ways equally unconventional fellow Estonian, Arvo Pärt, described significant aspects of his thought, minimalist music, and deep spirituality.[16] To borrow from François Jullien, it could be said that Kaplinski's understanding of art also "brings us to experience a world beyond," but it does not "open onto another, metaphysical world, cut off from the senses"; rhetorically unrefined and largely unconcerned with the ego of the creative mind, it "simply unfurls and expands this world."[17] Kaplinski's most memorable poems, then, do not settle into representations, but, as much as possible, let the symbolic fade away, almost disappear together with all the things we employ to evoke another reality;[18] in short, his intention as a writer, to use Gerhard Richter's credo, is to "invent nothing," nearly nothing, and in this way claim a place for the arts in nature.[19]

TARTU 1961 – ENCOUNTER WITH ANOTHER WORLD

Kaplinski caught a glimpse of the art of unforced flourishing, perhaps for the first time, on 28 November 1961, when he attended a most unusual musical performance in Tartu. The event took place in the auditorium of the university, across the street from his childhood home. The venerable venue, adorned with neo-classical designs and located in the heart of the city, was familiar to him also from previous concerts to which his mother had taken him when he was still a teenager. At that time, the concert culture in Tartu was defined by classical European music, occasionally even including guest performances of virtuosos such as the then prominent Estonian opera singer Georg Ots and Russian cellist Mstislav Rostropovich.

Kaplinski's early exposure to "high" culture reflects an affinity for the arts and music that runs through his family, at least in part. Kaplinski's father, Jerzy, played the piano; his Polish grandmother was a professional singer; his mother, Nora, studied modern dance in Germany and France; and one of his sons, Märt-Matis Lill, is a composer and instructor of music theory. Although he did not inherit a similar talent (he has trouble carrying a tune and has not learned to sing or to play an instrument himself), over the years, perhaps beginning with his childhood, Kaplinski acquired a quiet passion for music – Mozart and Beethoven above all. Ever since a friend introduced him to the music of John Coltrane, he has also been fond of jazz. This is unsurprising, especially in view of the improvisational dimension of jazz, its particular convergence of virtuosity with intuition.[20] Indeed, for a musician like John Coltrane, whose name is synonymous with free jazz, a performance only comes "alive again" at the point when it is at its most "spontaneous."[21] This sentiment aligns Coltrane with Kaplinski's signature mental mode. Not unlike improvisation in jazz, unforced flourishing, too, places the highest value on what arises of its own accord. It embraces the unpredictable, is fluid and evolving, and, in this way, resists being subject to coordination and a predetermined outcome. But unlike improvisation in jazz, which rests on "a lifetime of preparation and knowledge" of conventions and models, the art of unforced flourishing uproots cultural mastery and lets artistic expression grow even more deeply from the unrehearsed.[22]

But the most important clue to understanding the larger role of music in Kaplinski's life is contained elsewhere, namely in the concert of 1961. It took him into altogether unfamiliar territory, musically and philosophically. He saw at work a cultural mode that derived its power from the "inartistic," from pointing away from itself as art. We can't be certain how he felt, but if we are to believe his recollection, the event left him stunned. Although such judgements are too easy to make and may seem exaggerated, there are indications from Kaplinski later in life suggesting that this performance even stirred something in him that changed how he saw what surrounded him and how he imagined himself. One might say, it opened a new chapter in his thinking about the nature and capacity of art.

This we know directly from Kaplinski: appearing insipid at first, the music mesmerized him, and this despite the fact that the songs were anything but spectacular, dramatic, or artful – at least not to someone used to classical music or the popular tunes played on radio during the 1950s and '60s in Soviet Estonia. Remarkably, for Kaplinski, the magic of the music lay precisely in its monotony; and the strong appeal of the lyrics was found not in their rhethorical sophistication and polish but in their stunning simplicity and unembellished directness. He had stumbled upon something remarkable when he realized: there is no need for great art to be extraordinary. Recalling the memorable event less than a decade after the performance, he wrote:

> But then three ... women came ... They weren't wearing folk costumes and they didn't stand out in their appearance; they were like old village women are; they sat down in chairs, put their hands in their laps and began to sing. And this was already something strange. The words of the song were so clearly audible. The women's voices were old, they cracked now and then, perhaps from excitement, maybe from tiredness, but this did not interfere with listening to them. At first there was something odd in the singing; it was so dispassionate, and, as it felt then, formalistic; all the attention was on scansion. No expressiveness at all, no emotion.[23]

The absence of artsy sophistication intrigued him. The simplicity of the music evoked an altogether different time and place. Removed from familiar aesthetics, melodic structures, lyrics, patterns, and poetics, the music delved into Estonia's pre-colonial pagan past. In the years that followed, Kaplinski began to understand and value this kind of art, and to "grow ever more close to folk poetry" and folklore.[24]

THE REGI SONG – LOST TOUCHSTONE OF ESTONIAN CULTURE

Convinced he had discovered "the core of Estonianness, the soul of the people," what the twenty-year-old Kaplinski had witnessed was a performance of indigenous Estonian folk songs, music which predates the Christianization and colonization of Estonians in the Middle Ages.[25] Estonians call it *regilaul*, the regi song. Its origin probably reaching back more than two millennia and traditionally performed only by women, the regi song lies at the heart of Estonia's ancient singing tradition. They were the only songs that Kaplinski, not being musical himself, would sing to his children and occasionally even perform in public.

In his introduction to Veljo Tormis's millennium cantata *Birth Spells*, Kaplinski quoted an Estonian regi song entitled "At Mother's Grave."[26] Widely known in Estonia, this moving song exists in a great variety of written versions. The first one was most likely recorded in 1871, but the song itself may date as far back as the Middle Ages, or perhaps even further. Although it was not part of the repertoire performed by the three women in Tartu when Kaplinski heard the regi song for the first time, the passages he selected for commentary in *Birth Spells* may serve here as an example of this archaic oral tradition that captivated his imagination. The song tells the story of an orphan who goes to her mother's grave and calls her. Unable to help her daughter, it is left to nature to console and care for the orphan:

Tõuse hauast, emmekene,
tõuse mu pääd sugema,
Veimevakka valmistama.
…
Ei saa tõusta, tütar noori,
mul on liiva laugudella,
sinililled silmadella.
Jalakas on jalge päälla,
pärnapuud on pää päälla.
…
Tuleb tuuli, soeb tukka,
paistab päeva, pääd silitab.

Rise from the grave dearest mother,
rise to comb my hair,
to prepare the dowry chest,
…
I cannot rise, my young daughter,
I have sand on my eyelids,
violets in my eyes,
an elm on my feet
a linden tree on my head.
…
The wind comes, combs your hair,
the sun shines, strokes your head.

Of course, the archetypical regi song is not formless: it has a nonstanzaic structure[27] and distinct tonal, metric, and rhythmic characteristics, including a verse line of eight syllables grouped into four pairs with each disyllabic verse foot consisting of alternating stressed (long) and unstressed (short) syllables.[28] One might add that in the case of "Mother's Grave," alliteration and assonance of words in a line also stand out. But the real source of Kaplinski's fascination with the old songs lay elsewhere.[29] We find it in his deeper, existential and philosophical affinities. His commentary accompanying the millennium cantata he co-authored with Veljo Tormis, and which is composed in the tradition of the regi song, provides a sense of his true interest. As if pouring out of him with angry, righteous passion, he wrote:

> [A]dvertisers and prophets want us to believe in their messages, to buy their products, their creeds, their ideologies. What is the price? Do they want us to pay them with our soul, to exchange our soul for something interesting, sweet, colourful, for things, a way of life, a religion? Is the coming new millennium itself such a preacher who wants us to rush into its embrace, to believe in it, to trust it, forgetting everything else – our past, our ancestors, our songs and our souls? Surrounded by all the nice things, phrases, pictures and promises we suddenly feel lonely, lonely as a bee who has lost its way to the beehive ... Isn't it the old archaic song that can tell us something about our soul?[30]

It was all the more astonishing for Kaplinski to see "how thoroughly Estonians [had] been able to forget their old folk songs," as he wrote in an article entitled "Heritage and Heirs," published in 1969, the year that also marked the 100th anniversary of the Estonian Song Festival.[31] True, the regi songs had been written down in the nineteenth century, the melodies transcribed later on, and many of the songs recorded in the 1930s.[32] However, important as this was, Kaplinski argued, for the majority of Estonians, the songs represented "dead culture."[33] "I am quite certain," he wrote about the collective Estonian cultural memory in the 1960s, "that ninety per cent or possibly more of our even modestly serious music fans do not have the slightest idea how *regilaulud* [regi songs] sounded."[34] "We all know, that the regi songs are not in fashion," he noted a year later, in 1970.[35]

And yet, for Kaplinski himself, clearly the opposite appeared to be true: throughout his adult life, ever since 1961, he would return to the regi song, time and time again.[36] There are even indications that no other form of Finno-Ugric cultural expression influenced him more than the old Estonian songs. Why, then, he asked, had this touchstone underlying Estonian culture and thought, as he saw it, all but vanished from general public consciousness? Intrigued by this question, in the late 1960s and early 1970s he immersed himself in the regi song and began to explore its history and inner architecture.

DECLINE OF THE REGI SONG – THE RISE OF THE SONG FESTIVAL

As noted in one of his early essays about the regi song, Kaplinski had discovered that from the nineteenth century on, Estonians increasingly looked down on their pagan Finno-Ugric heritage, and even came to regard it as "their dark past."[37] "We know that feeling ashamed of our elders' black coats and even our language was widespread among urbanized Estonians," Kaplinski wrote about nineteenth-century Estonia.[38] "My grandmother recalled that in her youth, when some old women began to sing a [regi song], younger ladies interrupted them saying that these songs were ugly."[39] Is this attitude the main reason why the regi songs all but vanished?

Although there were exceptions, and ethnographic interest in them flourished already in the nineteenth century, in the more distant past the regi songs were regarded by the colonizers with suspicion, if not outright disdain. Some of the lyrics contained demonizing portrayals of the Baltic German lords; other songs betrayed a deep-seated devotion to pagan beliefs. In the eyes of the colonizers, both constituted heresy and perhaps even grounds for prosecution. In fact, the ancient Estonian songs were at times used as incriminating legal testimony in witch trials.[40]

On a less intrusive level, this prejudice and the power imbalance that pitted the local Estonian peasants against their foreign masters was reflected in the eighteenth century in the work of a German writer who referred to the ancient oral tradition as "wüstes Gesänge," a "terribly chaotic singsong."[41] Although some German intellectuals developed an interest in Estonian folklore, and in small measure the local cultural heritage may even have influenced them, most Baltic German poets ignored the regi songs. Preferring established German models, the regi songs "probably seemed to be too primitive to be used as a poetic means of expression."[42] Echoing the same sentiment, soon, even leading Estonian cultural figures themselves would make disparaging remarks about the regi song. Most prominent among them was the nineteenth-century journalist Johann Voldemar Jannsen. In an article published in his influential newspaper, *Postimees*, Jannsen criticized the regi song for not having a "real melody" and lyrics. In his opinion, the songs were confusing, repetitive, and even mindless. They were best suited as drinking songs, he continued, but certainly not worthy of being performed in public or part of the cultural capital of a people with "higher" aspirations.[43] Even proponents and avid collectors of regi songs at times perpetuated the common primitivist stereotype, albeit unintentionally. For example, in 1902, the Estonian folklorist Jakob Hurt referred to the songs as "tendrils of a primeval forest [Schlinggewächse eines Urwaldes] which refuse to be transformed into artful gardens [künstlerische Gartenbeete] of modern culture."[44] The undomesticated as a value disappeared from view.

Having become more a source of shame than of pride, by the end of the nineteenth century the regi songs were performed less and less often. As a living part of Estonian culture, soon they had all but ceased to exist and, in the minds of many, were at best destined for the archives as a folkloristic curiosity of Estonia's so-called primitive pagan past. With the decline came the endangerment of what, for Kaplinski, lay at the heart of the regi song, namely its unique "cosmology"[45] – a deep sense of unforced flourishing, a way of expressing that the human and nonhuman are woven together into a "civilization that wildness can endure."[46]

Filling the gap left by the vanishing regi song, the tradition of the Estonian Song Festival was born. Influenced by congregational singing, music lessons at school taught mostly by German Lutheran clergy and Baltic German song events arranged by the Baltic Germans paved the way to the first Estonian Song Festival in 1869. Although it was also meant to commemorate the abolition of serfdom in Estonia fifty years earlier and serve national aspirations, its origins were clearly not indigenous. Restricted to male choirs, the Song Festival did not – and could not – include a single regi song.

Even though the regi song has remained in the shadow of the Song Festival ever since, it is nonetheless widely regarded today. Indeed, it has become iconic of Estonia's indigenous cultural heritage to the extent that "[s]ome observers might [even] contend that the regi song is the only genuinely original aspect of Estonian culture."[47] According to the musicologist Mimi Daitz, the melodic/rhythmic source of the regi song is "unlike others to which we are accustomed."[48] Veljo Tormis, one of Estonia's internationally best-known composers, master of the regi song, and, together with Kaplinski, a driving force behind its revival in Estonia, wrote already in 1972 that one of the regi song's "greatest values is its artistic originality."[49] To capture the essence of its unique appeal for Kaplinski, however, means to recognize and welcome the regi song's astonishing inartistic modality, a remarkable "blandness," as we shall see. But this seemingly paradoxical consideration has done little to further appreciation of the regi song. In Estonia's contemporary cultural landscape, it is the Song Festival, the massive open-air choral concert with its European "harmonic music" and not the regi song that Estonians are said to regard as their "*primum mobile*," the primary foundation and driving force of their culture.[50] "It is safe to say," wrote the historian Toivo Raun in his widely read monograph on Estonian history, "that no other Estonian cultural tradition of the past century and a quarter has proved as powerful or as durable."[51] Moreover, this UNESCO-designated heritage event has come to symbolize the end of the Soviet Empire and the peaceful beginning of Estonia's regained independence. It was a nonviolent fight for freedom, ushered in by the "Singing Revolution," with the Song Festival as its signature event.

But for Kaplinski the Song Festival does not represent the unforced flourishing of a people. As popular as it is, and as much as it may constitute a ritual of restraint, the Song Festival also masks a history of violent intervention, a profound disruption of spontaneous indigenous cultural expression, and, finally, acceptance of a "culture by design," as one might say. In this complex sense, then, the regi songs and the Song Festival point to fundamentally different paths, rather than merely "differing layers" of cultural heritage.[52]

The shift in favour of the Song Festival coincides with two diverse yet closely related processes reaching back into Estonia's nineteenth-century past: emergent nationhood and self-colonization.[53] Intertwined, they gave rise to a deeply unsettling and fragile collective consciousness. Independence as a people – informed by European modes of seeing – promoted a sense of equality and worthiness amongst other nations. In the second half of the nineteenth century, this Europeanization provided the foundation for Estonia's nation-building and paved the path to Estonia's birth as an independent nation in 1918. While at the same time distancing themselves from the ruling Baltic German minority and dismantling their power structures, Estonians imported alien values and patterns that were eventually assimilated, thus forging a firm association with Western European civilization. A new Estonian identity as a European nation-state was the result. It has come to dominate Estonia's self-image to this day.[54]

In Kaplinski's view, however, the denial of a Finno-Ugric peasant past perceived as inferior, and the mimicry of a mostly Baltic German culture misunderstood as inherently superior, fostered feelings of intense insecurity and low self esteem. Instead of affirming their own native traditions during the National Awakening in the 1860s and 1870s, the Estonians increasingly saw themselves through the eyes of the dominant perspective of the colonizers, and imagined gaps in their own history and culture where there had been none before. European colonization created holes and Europeanization was meant to fill them. "As is known," Kaplinksi wrote in 1970, "the model for our poetry during the period of National Awakening was German Romantic poetry, which in its turn has been greatly influenced by German folk songs."[55]

According to Kaplinski, the models borrowed from established German traditions – such as the four-line *Volkslied* with its characteristic end-rhyme, strophic text structure, and Western melodic harmonies – were entirely unlike the regi songs. "The old *regilaul* [regi song] differs so greatly from the music we are accustomed to," Kaplinski noted in 1969, "that by accommodating its melody to European harmony, by performing it in the style of the European school of voice production, nothing remains of it."[56] In particular, the end-rhymes do not suit the Estonian language. Its extensive case system, which utilizes a fixed set of endings to indicate the function of nouns in a sentence, generates far fewer options for end-rhymes. Poetry of inferior quality was the potential result of this mismatch. Including its non-harmonically oriented nature and quantitatively based rhythm – a function of the duration and not only the stress of a syllable – the structural principles and prosody of the regi song were also ill-suited to the models borrowed from the Germans or other Europeans. "Just as the European tradition of reciting fixed texts is in obvious opposition to the structure and artistic details of [the regi song], likewise the rules of classical music are incompatible with the melody and structure of [regi song] tunes," wrote Veljo Tormis in 1972.[57] Yet, as Kaplinski expressed it, the new models

Estonians desired in the hope that they would put them on a more equal footing with their colonizers "definitely had to be such that the Germans would also consider them to be culture."[58] The pressure exerted by the colonizers together with the self-imposed "other"-orientation of the Estonians and their conflicted collective sense of self resulted in "psychological chaos," Kaplinski argued. One might say, they themselves intervened in their collective ability to flourish naturally. They felt compelled to abolish anything that was "significantly different from the Germans," as if their own way of living and perceiving the world "amounted to 'unculture,' a lack of culture."[59]

This put the regi song in peril, which, in Kaplinski's eyes, was doubly misfortunate for Estonians: its loss marked a deep alienation from their own culture and the obstruction of a path away from a seemingly endless history of subjugation. At its core essentially untranslatable and representing a profoundly different mode of perceiving the world, the regi song, Kaplinski understood, was not adaptable to the dominant Western culture. First imposed and then serving as the model for creating a unique sense of self as a people, the "invented," or one might say "translated," Estonian culture was meant to do the impossible: be both their own and at the same time fit into the adopted alien model introduced by the colonizers.[60] In the end, regarded as exotic or pushed aside, the regi song seemed out of place in the very culture to which it belonged. Kaplinski argued that the Estonians had internalized the values of the colonizers until, finally, most Estonians had removed themselves so far from their heritage that they didn't have "the slightest idea how *regilaulud* sounded."[61] As if in a hurry to catch up and overshooting the target in their rush, the Estonians wanted to prove their cultural competence and capacity for self-creation, but, instead, Kaplinski maintained, they often merely became more proficient "in copying classical ballet, classical music, modern poetry or Parisian fashion."[62]

Even more troubling for him was another consequence he noticed in the regi song's demise: not only had the Estonians sacrificed an important part of what is commonly regarded as their indigenous culture, they now also lacked easy access to a significant alternate mode of perceiving the world and expressing themselves. It now lay hidden at the heart of the ancient songs: a sense of human fulfillment that thrives on the ordinary and embraces the unrehearsed and spontaneously unfolding.

THE HEART OF THE REGI SONG – "IN PRAISE OF BLANDNESS"

Although Kaplinski was influential in the revival of the regi song, the growing interest in Finno-Ugric heritage was also part of a broader, often politically and ideologically charged, revitalization and instrumentalization of national cultures in the Soviet Union. It gathered momentum during the "Thaw," the period of relative liberalization under Khrushchev. For the local Estonian population, particularly in the latter part of the 1960s, the turn towards Estonia's indigenous past also constituted an act of symbolic resistance aimed at the cultural curtailment and general repression characteristic of Brezhnev's regime (1964–82).

In Estonia, among the most prominent voices shaping the renaissance of Finno-Ugric culture were Lennart Meri, producer of ethnographic documentaries such as *The Waterfowl People* (1969–70) and *Winds of the Milky Way* (1967–77); the composer Veljo Tormis, widely known for his choir music rooted deeply in ancient Estonian song; and the graphic artist Kaljo Põllu, who led expeditions to other Finno-Ugrian peoples and in the early 1970s radically changed his own artistic style to artwork focused on Finno-Ugric traditions reaching back to ancient cave drawings.

Kaplinski collaborated on several projects with Tormis and Põllu. Internationally perhaps best known among them are Kaplinski's texts for Tormis's choir piece *Curse Upon Iron* (1972) and, more recently, the commissioned millennium cantata *Birth Spells* (1999), as well as Põllu's two series of graphics, "Kodalased" ("Ancient Dwellers," 1973–75) and "Kalivägi" ("Power of the Kalevs," 1978–84). The latter were inspired by fieldwork among the Finno-Ugric peoples, and probably also influenced by the well-known Finno-Ugric specialist Paul Ariste who taught at Tartu University. Evoking the past life of Finno-Ugric and Samoyed tribes, as it once may have been, "Kalivägi" is said to be a "pictorial epic," but, importantly, "one without a central hero and glorious warriors."[63]

Although ethnic and national considerations furnished Kaplinski with a powerful sense of motivation, still missing in this revival, he argued in an essay published in 1972, was the "real bridge" that would connect old to new cultural forms and breathe life into Estonia's forgotten folkloric past.[64] Convinced that concealed in the regi songs lay a unique world view obscured only by a lack of deeper understanding of their structure, music, and language, Kaplinski set out to explore the regi songs in more detail and reintroduce the Estonian public to their own (but by then largely invisible) culture.[65]

This turned out to be a difficult, if not impossible, task: difficult, because it meant reacquainting Estonians with a seemingly outdated style of music; impossible, because it also required a seemingly insurmountable shift in thinking.[66] As curious as it may seem, early on he sensed in this music a connection with cultures apparently far removed from the shores of the Baltic Sea: "This was an encounter with a tradition whose roots reach somewhere into ancient Siberia, China and even all the way to the American Indians," he noted in 1970–72.[67] He must have thought about it a lot: ever more clearly he would see parallels, especially to ways of perceiving represented by "radical critics of culture" as distant in time and space as Lao-Tse, the author of the Daodejing.[68] He soon found that at work was an uncommon ideal the regi song shares with Chinese culture: at the root of the regi song's aesthetics, musicality, and currents of thought lies what one might call a propensity for simplicity that extends into the "unremarkable." In Kaplinski's assessment, this does not constitute a condition to be overcome. On the contrary, for him the unremarkable constitutes a valuable opportunity, not only to be cherished but to be cultivated and even given priority over its counterpart, the "remarkable" products of "progress" and "high culture." How are we to understand this undoubtedly crucial but seemingly strange turn in his thinking?

To begin with, rather than making political or narrow ethnic concerns his primary target – which in his mind would have flattened and reduced the currents of thought operating within the regi song – he focussed on the "oriental mood" of the ancient tradition.[69] Paradoxically, then, it was the Far East that led him, the "cosmopolitan," not only back into his native culture but to the "core of Estonianness."[70] Barely visible behind Estonia's deeply layered colonial past, Eastern modes of perception provided access to a largely forgotten dimension of the "soul" of Estonian culture as Kaplinski began to understand it. More importantly, apart from his experience of nature, the East would reveal the signature of his own mentality and work as a writer – his sense of unforced flourishing – perhaps more clearly than anything else in his life.

Instead of carrying a European imprint and underscoring Estonia's connection to the West, this meeting of the Finno-Ugric with the

Oriental world also coincided with Kaplinski's general interest in Eastern cultures and their revival in Estonia at the time. Already in the mid-'60s, towards the end of his student years at Tartu University, Kaplinski began to learn Chinese. Earlier, probably influenced by Uku Masing, he became a devotee of Mahajana Buddhism. In 1960–61 he read Lao-Tse in Finnish translation and, years later, even published his own Estonian rendering of the Daodejing. It appeared in 2001. In Chinese and Finno-Ugric cultures, he argued, it is easier to refer to "fuzzy, indistinct things" and to speak of "Truth" as something that extends beyond the limits of language.[71] In other words, increasingly Kaplinski found himself drawn towards a "conception of the universe where it is not a text, cannot be described by any text."[72]

Much of his knowledge about Eastern spiritual thought came from publications widely read in the 1960s and '70s, such as Alan Watts's introduction to Zen, and the books of one of the most prominent mediators of Eastern culture in the West, Daisetz Teitaro Suzuki, author of *The Essence of Buddhism*, among others. By the late 1960s, Kaplinski was also familiar with a sizable body of classical Chinese and Japanese poetry. Throughout the '70s he would continue his exploration of Oriental thought and culture, immersing himself in such books as H.V. Guenther's *Tibetan Buddhism in Western Perspective* and his *The Tantric View of Life*. Not only did Kaplinski draw inspiration from Asian culture, but by the end of the 1970s he had, in his own words, moved "ever closer to the Far East" as a writer;[73] and he was not "just reading" about it in such books as Shunryu Suzuki's popular *Zen Mind, Beginner's Mind* of 1970, "but living through it."[74] The concluding lines of a poem published in *The Wandering Border* make clear that Suzuki and his smile had "silently infected book after book on my shelves / and perhaps shelves themselves and walls and wallpapers too."[75] In this book Shunryu Suzuki associates Zen with the richness of the ordinary and unrehearsed that eludes language and a way of living governed by foresight. Buddhism for him means: to "exist right here, right now," "as if drinking water when you are thirsty," and not let "self-centred thoughts" or the desire to "attain something special" limit the "many possibilities" open to the beginner's mind;[76] to "forget all gaining ideas" or "fancy ornaments" and, instead, support an "ordinary practice" unburdened of "philosophical understanding" and adorned accounts.[77] "When we hear the sound of the pine trees on a windy day," Suzuki writes, "perhaps the wind is just blowing, and the pine tree is just standing in the wind" – nothing more, nothing less.[78]

Ten years after his encounter with Suzuki's book, in March of 1989, a journey to China deepened Kaplinski's affinity for Asian cultures. To use his own words, where others were drawn towards "Kant, Goethe or Heidegger," he preferred "Zhuangzi, Li Bo as well as Lin ji."[79] Several of his essays, many of them published in the 1990s, also bear witness to his propensity for salient aspects of Oriental thought. More importantly, what drew Kaplinski to the Far East elucidates and merges with his sense of unforced flourishing, above all the primary value he attributes to the undifferentiated. This link becomes particularly visible when we consider the meaning accorded to "blandness" in Chinese culture. There, in contrast to predominant Western modes of thought, it is not aligned with lack but, instead, constitutes a desirable quality.

In the view of the philosopher and sinologist François Jullien, blandness is characterized by an "uncluttered sparseness"; it presents "nothing that might be perceived by others as remarkable" as it charts a course toward "plainness," toward the "formless and the "toneless," the "discreet and unobtrusive."[80] With "the natural" as its basis, the bland "does not open up onto another, metaphysical world, cut off from the senses."[81] It does not "fulfill the sign's 'natural' role of representing"; as it "de-represents" instead, it does not "demand that we look for another meaning."[82] "[D]eepening toward the simple, the natural, the essential," it "provides access to the undifferentiated foundation of all things."[83] Taken together, these are also core qualities characteristic of unforced flourishing. They blend into a pattern of thought and behaviour not based on a preconceived, dominant design but one that emerges spontaneously.

Unforced flourishing also coincides with much in Kaplinski's understanding of Chinese poetry, as it, for example, becomes apparent in his introduction to a selection of poems by Li Bo and Du Fu. Rather than turning towards the symbolic and abstract or expressing an idea, the poems convey a series of loosely connected and very concrete images. They, according to Kaplinski, invite the reader's meditative-contemplative attention to arise from and remain anchored in the specific and tangible.[84] As if following in Li Bo and Du Fu's footsteps and on a trajectory that leads from poetry to prose and finally speech, he writes in a poem about the forest near his country retreat: "I duck beneath a fallen birch tree. The leaves are still green, but / much of the bark is loose: it has fallen between two nearby alders."[85] Similarly, in the regi song, the "images evoked are always concrete, never abstract. It is never just *eerie*, but: 'The night is long and dark, / The sky wide, the earth barren.' A girl does not just *not love* somebody, but: 'Her body did not desire him, / Her heart did not fancy him.'"[86]

About his collection of poems entitled *Valge Joon Võrumaa Kohale*, published in 1972, Kaplinski once said in a public lecture that it constituted a step towards the Far East. In his words, it was the search for "the sacred," that "other reality," that led him to rather than away from the seemingly insignificant, everyday moments and aspects of ordinary life.[87] This shift in his thinking, expressed in his turn towards the regi song, gave rise to poems that focus on the unremarkable as an ideal:

Under blue stars
the old sauna slowly cooling
it is Saturday night
the moon illuminates the icy
broom in front of the stairs[88]

Largely unburdened of anything "artful," Kaplinski's verse evokes a sparse solitude, still, unobtrusive, and plain, yet direct and sharply focussed on the ordinary – not unlike ancient Chinese landscapes painted in praise of the bland where the aim is to blend in rather than stand out, to present rather than represent, aligning with Kaplinski's ideal of the character without character and logic without hinge, both key to his sense of unforced flourishing.[89] Calling to mind the seemingly simplistic and "bland," his collection *Ôhtu toob tagasi kõik* (*Evening Brings Everything Back*), which was published in 1985, contains a number of runo song texts, several translations of poems (Li Bo, Petronius, Sappho, Harry Martinson, Bo Carpelan), and more than a hundred original poems by Kaplinski. Regarding it as part of a "natural" development in his thinking, they perhaps best exemplify his turn "towards the concrete, the simple," and his striving as a poet in general.[90] As Hasso Krull fittingly remarked in reference to another, later collection of poems: "Kaplinski wishes to avoid all manner of word fetishism."[91]

This articulation of the "bland" in his poetry also converges with the autobiographical. Where the regi songs provide a window into the life of the peasants – with songs ranging from weddings and harvesting, to milking, forests, animals, and husbands – Kaplinski's poems provide access to minutiae of his own life.[92] About *Evening Brings Everything Back* he wrote, it "is a kind of lyrical diary of 1983, which begins in March and ends in November and tells the story of everything, doing laundry, cooking cereal, going for walks with the children, skiing, writing, news on the radio. The raw material of this book is my life."[93] This chronicle-like tendency in his poetry is perhaps best exemplified by lines such as "The morning began with sunshine – we brought the rugs out / to be aired, sent the children to the sand pit / and ourselves went to the garden where / the dandelions and couch grass were already rampant, the strawberry bed / full of flowering corn mint buzzing with bumblebees."[94]

Also mirrored in his poems is the "dispassionate" quality of runo singing, "displaying none of the variations of expression common to art music," even when the text evokes dramatic tensions. As Kaplinski has noted: "By allowing the content to speak for itself, our ancestors sang with equal lack of emotion about trying out a swing, serfdom, or wife slaying."[95] A reviewer of a concert directed by Veljo Tormis in Soviet Estonia in 1977 aptly characterized this pivotal equalizing feature of the regi song, its absence of expressiveness, as an "intensive monotony" rooted not in tediousness and limitation but a concentration of inner strength instead.[96] Emphasizing their ritualistic and incantational function, Tormis detected in the monotony of the regi song its primary merit and spellbinding effect.[97]

The plain and unremarkable quality on which the regi song thrives in large part issues from its melodic characteristics: closer to Gregorian chants or classical Indian music (Ragas) than traditional European folk songs, the melodic structure of the regi song is monophonic and not dictated by pre-existing harmonic patterns. This means it is not set in a particular fixed key – instead, it is modal – and not restricted to the two typically Western "flavours," minor or major. Nor is it "controlled by harmonic direction." Rather, its "tonality is determined by the initial and final tones as well as the tone with maximum duration."[98] Usually unaccompanied, the tune of a classical regi song is cast in a simple syllabic setting, composed of one note per syllable. Except for "varying the first note of the melody," the same melody line is, as a rule, repeated throughout the song.[99] All notes are similar in length (isochronal) and relatively narrow in range and pitch, which means that the expressive qualities and potential for individual articulation of a performer's own technique and interpretation are kept to a minimum. Blandness and blending in, rather than standing out, distinguish the regi song.

But if the regi song's ideal is in this sense more Oriental than Occidental, one might ask why Chinese music has remained "very foreign" to Kaplinski, as he noted in a television feature.[100] Despite the shared desire for openness, blandness for him would not be entirely identical with the unforced flourishing in the regi song. If to "refrain from even beginning to play" lies at the heart of Chinese music, the regi song points in another direction: it does not know silence, one might say.[101] Rather, it keeps going without pause. As a *perpetuum carmen*, the seam- and endless song, in a "call and response" pattern, one singer sings one line, the next singer or chorus joins in before the first line ends and continues with the second line while the first singer takes a breath before again joining in shortly before the second line ends.[102] There is also no division into strophes.[103] Coinciding with this non-stanzaic verse form, the singing continues uninterrupted, even without the pauses for breathing customary in Western music. The effect of this "grammatical phrasing" is "a seemingly endless chain of song,"[104] evoking "an endless and beginningless microcosm," Kaplinski wrote in 1999.[105] In this sense, then, the regi song not only aligns with the undifferentiated but also presents a ceaseless responsiveness.

Here, too, an autobiographical connection suggests itself: as if transforming it into a *perpetuum scriptum*, a never-ending text, Estonia's *perpetuum carmen* coincides with Kaplinski's seemingly boundless need to express and, perhaps, explain himself as a writer. Rather than refraining from giving voice to his thoughts and moving toward silence, Kaplinski has continued writing for over half a century, and has penned hundreds of poems, volumes of essays, short stories, autobiographical accounts, children's books, website pages, and blogs – addressing topics ranging from war and politics to obesity and Christmas kitsch – and a seemingly unending cascade of newspaper articles that bear witness to his "verbose love of silence."[106] "Could you stop writing [altogether]?" the filmmaker Raphaël Gianelli-Meriano asked Kaplinski. "Probably not... not now," he replied.[107]

Indeed, Kaplinski conceived of the *perpetuum carmen* as an elaboration on a way of thinking that is neither Indo-European nor entirely Finno-Ugric but particular to him.[108] Borrowing from Swedish poet Gunnar Ekelöf, he linked this ideal of the ceaseless in the regi song to his "something-else" philosophy,[109] a reference to Ekelöf's poem "The Gymnosophist": "What I mean / What I want / is something else / always something else / … And still the greatest secret is / kept somewhere else / always elsewhere."[110] Mindful of the limiting nature of language, he does not "settle down in words and concepts."[111] To "be free" with them, he nurtures a "non-attached" view of words,[112] acknowledging that everything always also means "something other than what we say, think, know."[113]

PARALLELISM – FROM HIERARCHICAL TO "COMPOUND THINKING"

Probably most expressive of his "something-else" philosophy and unforced flourishing is another striking, yet simple, feature of the regi song that Kaplinski finds especially compelling. It is called "parallelism." Commonly regarded as a constitutive element of the regi song, for him it is one of its linguistically and conceptually most significant and revealing characteristics.[114] Take the regi song "Mother's Grave":

> Ei saa tõusta, tütar noori,
> mul on liiva laugudella,
> sinililled silmadella.
> Jalakas on jalge päälla,
> pärnapuud on pää päälla.

> I cannot rise, my young daughter,
> I have sand on my eyelids,
> violets in my eyes,
> an elm on my feet
> a linden tree on my head.

At its most fundamental level, parallelism constitutes a rhyme scheme, but it is one based on shared thoughts, not shared sounds.[115] Comprised of the associated words "eyelids," "eyes," "feet," and "head"; and "sand," "violets," "elm," and "linden," the parallelism in "Mother's Grave" alludes to the interdependence of the human and nonhuman world but without deepening into the symbolic and rhethorically refined. What we witness here, then, is an unusual "inner" symmetry aptly referred to as "thought rhyme." In this way – through a semantic parallel construction, rather than formal poetic devices such as end-rhymes – individual verses are bound together in the regi song to evoke a special sense of coherence that remains anchored in the concrete.

As Kaplinski has pointed out elsewhere, at work in the ancient songs is an element rooted in the Finno-Ugric languages.[116] Although as a means of generating a generalization it has become archaic, traces of this concrete-abstract mode can still be found in Estonian language today. Later in life, and with reference to Nobel laureate and in many ways like-minded poet Tomas Tranströmer, Kaplinski would call it "'semantic' music."[117] Formed without a conjunction, the word pair "kopsud-maksad" (lungs-livers), for example, denotes organs, or "õed-vennad" (sisters-brothers) means siblings, and "sood-rabad" (marshes-bogs) signifies wetlands. The latter example also illustrates the liminal quality of the word pairs. As Kaplinski explains, although marshes are distinguished from bogs, being bound together in this "parallel" way could also be an indication that there was no need or desire to separate one from the other. Instead, it was meant to emphasize the absence of a clear-cut boundary between bogs and marshes, which only exists in language but not in nature, or else it was meant to draw attention to what bogs and marshes share – both are wetlands. "Being precise, clear demarcation is not always and necessarily a virtue," Kaplinski noted.[118]

In addition to such archaic linguistic elements, Kaplinski detected further dimensions in the regi song. They, too, are intimately connected to his self-image and way of perceiving: "As a child of war I am unable to appreciate heroes," Kaplinski wrote in his published correspondence with Swedish-Finnish writer Johannes Salminen.[119] Kaplinski's statement dovetails well with his attraction to the regi song. Epic elements, especially heroic narratives, are virtually unknown to it. The heroic sentiment that characterizes the grand ancient narratives of Western culture – from the *Iliad* to the *Nibelungenlied* – "became the civilized people's *condicio sine qua non* and many nations created their own epic," Kaplinski noted in 1978; but in Estonia this genre did not have a "folkloric foundation," and therefore heroism also remained foreign to the regi songs.[120] The ideal regi song does not link efficacy with audacity and hope with great deeds, as does the epic, including Estonia's own national epic, *Kalevipoeg*, a nineteenth-century creation. The *Kalevipoeg*'s prominence and popularity came, in part, at the expense of the regi song and the fundamentally different, unobtrusive, unheroic mentality it represents.[121] Pagan and pre-Christian in origin, the regi songs resist and even sidestep in important ways any expression of dualist and hierarchical thinking. Rarely, if at all, do they feature themes fundamental to a Christian worldview, including the notion of an otherworldly paradise. Characteristically, the paradise evoked by the regi song resides in this world, not in a metaphysical one. Mirroring this notion, Kaplinski wrote: "For the awakened chopping wood is a mystical activity and the view from the door of one's home towards the forest as miraculous as the view into paradise. He who arrived from the ordinary to the extraordinary, finally understands that the extraordinary is even in the ordinary. And returns to the ordinary."[122]

Addressing broader contemporary concerns of ecological degradation and social and inner alienation, the former editor of *World Literature Today*, Ivar Ivask, an Estonian himself, put it bluntly if somewhat vaguely when, in 1968, he argued that Estonians had to "find a way out of the more than two thousand year old tradition of the Western world which since the Greeks and Jews has been deeply dualistic."[123] According to Kaplinski, however, the Estonians had already discovered a different path. Convinced that "evil can abate only when we give up dualism," he found this existential ideal expressed in the ancient Estonian tradition of song.[124] As Kaplinski remarked in his philosophical *magnum opus*, not only are heroes and heroic action largely absent from the lyrics of the regi songs, but their entire structure tends to be non-hierarchical and, instead, leads toward a largely lost way of seeing and speaking about the world.[125] Thus, in the regi song, things are placed side by side without a connecting word defining their mutual relationship.[126] This open and "equalizing" style is a characteristic tendency of Kaplinski's verse,[127] and traces of it can be found in his more recent prose work, where his texts are often presented in numbered, mostly short individual paragraphs.[128]

At times, Kaplinski has observed, the parallelisms of the regi song defy logic, and mutually exclusive elements are brought together.[129] Moreover, as if expressing a "spontaneous coexistence of things," any shared meaning to which the parallelism gives rise, shifts as the inventory of compound components changes.[130] Articulated differently, any generalization is at all times evolving or, in Kaplinski's words, is potentially "always something else," not unlike the melody and the text of a regi song. Over time, even from one performance to the next, the melody would be modified and the lyrics altered. In other words, the presentation of a regi song is "essentially improvisational," or more precisely, it remains open to variation, free of immediate concern for authorship, artistic fidelity, authenticity, and mastery of formal modalities.[131]

Taking all of this together, Kaplinski came to conclude that the regi songs express relationships in the "most loose," unobstructed, and inclusive way possible.[132] While retaining the focus on the concrete, they bind the distinct and the fuzzy.[133] Using philosophical language, called "concreteness and phenomenological nominalism in conceptional thinking,"[134] or "compound thinking,"[135] this way of perceiving and communicating addresses and expresses what seems at first impossible: an ideal where everything and everyone remains clearly visible – but unnoticed, as one might sum up Kaplinski's understanding of the regi song with the help of a paradox.[136] Echoing this sentiment, Kaplinski writes in his poem "Through the Forest": "We want to exist, but without bearing the burden of / existence, to be disembodied and carefree, / to see, but remain unseen, to hear, but remain unheard, to fly / with the wind and to pass through walls and rocks."[137]

Coinciding with the pivotal value of blandness for the regi song, the poet Kaplinski is drawn towards a "discreet" way of writing, an unadorned style that blends much of his poetry into speech, away from literary complexities, poetic conventions and techniques. Minimizing its crafted attributes,[138] he wants his art to be free from itself, one might say, to invent nothing and be as unremarkable as "washing hands in the evening / or a clean handkerchief that my late aunt / never forgot to put in my pocket."[139] Resonating with the regi songs, in a "frugal, doing-without kind of aesthetic," many of his poems then quietly "register what is around him":[140] "The snow's melting. Water's dripping. / The wind's blowing, gently. / Boughs sway. There's a fire in the stove. / The radiators are warm."[141] Characteristically for Kaplinski, the loosely connected images of this poem do not seek the symbolic. They point back to the tangible and boundless world to which they, too, belong. Early in life, this understanding of a reality rich in itself led Jaan Kaplinski to the regi song's magic. The ancient song's simple way with words and music has kept him spellbound to this day, on the move towards unforced flourishing.[142]

Notes

Jaan Kaplinski's diaries from 1989 and before are held at the Estonian Cultural History Archive of the Estonian Literary Museum in Tartu; those from 1990 to 1997 are part of his private archive.

Unless otherwise noted, all text messages referred to in the endnotes are from Jaan Kaplinski to the author or forwarded to the author.

Texts, written by Jaan Kaplinski, not available in English have been translated by Riina Tamm and the author.

PREFACE

1 Naess in Rothenberg, *Painful to Think*, 151.
2 Merton, *Thoughts on the East*, 52.

INTRODUCTION

1 Kaplinski, Diaries, 30 March 1987.
2 Kaplinski, *I Am Spring*, ix.
3 Kaplinski, *Isale*, 126.
4 Jerzy Kaplinski, "Interrogation Record." 1941–44, 1958. Jaan Kaplinski, Private Archive.
5 Kaplinski, *Isale*, 8.
6 Kaplinski, *Evening Brings Everything Back*, 55–6.
7 Jaan Kaplinski to Ilse Lehiste, 2 April 1969, in the author's possession.
8 Kaplinski, *Kust Tuli Öö*, 96–7.
9 Ibid., 99.
10 jaan.kaplinski.com, 18 January 2008.
11 Tiia Toomet to author, E-mail, 21 January 2008.

12 The telephone interview (15 July 2005) was conducted in confidentiality, and the name of the interviewee is withheld by mutual agreement.
13 Ain Kaalep, interviewed by author, 27 August, 2001, Tartu.
14 Grabbi, "Kolmnurk muutus nelinurgaks," 69–70; Kruus, "Meie luuleankeet," 3; Laht, "Kasseti katsikul," 789–90; Kalda, "Neli uut," 563–4.
15 Eilart, "Kaitsmas elu," 3.
16 Ibid.
17 Ivask, "*Tolmust ja värvidest*," 159–60.
18 Kaplinski, E-mail, 4 July 2003.
19 Jaan Kaplinski to Helmut Piirkop, 11 November 1973. Kaplinski Papers, Estonian Literary Museum, Tartu.
20 Jaan Kaplinski, interviewed by author, 2 October 2002, Mutiku (Estonia).
21 Ibid.
22 Kaplinski, E-mail, 26 June 2007.
23 Kaplinski, Diaries, 29 December 1990.
24 Krull, "Tagasi koju metafoori juurest," B12.
25 Jaan Kaplinski, lecture series (unpublished manuscript, Tartu University, 2000).
26 Salokannel, "Kaplinski ja modernism," 76–7.
27 Jaan Kaplinski to Ilse Lehiste, 17 April 1982. In the author's possession.
28 Jaan Kaplinski to Sam Hamill, 11 January 1985. Cage 700, Sam Hamill Papers. Manuscripts, Archives, and Special Collections, Washington State University Libraries, Pullman, WA.
29 Bloomsbury, "Same Sea."
30 Grumbach, "Review," 26.
31 Trevor Carolan, "Jaan Kaplinski, Calgary Olympics and Vancouver" (unpublished manuscript, November 2001).
32 Kaplinski, E-mail, 6 August 2012. Langemets, "Kaplinski kui Voltaire."
33 Kronberg, "Outlines of Books."
34 Sam Hamill to author, E-mail, 15 June 2005.

CHAPTER ONE

1 Kaplinski, *Same Sea*, 54. Reprinted by permission.
2 Kaplinski, *Isale*, 325.
3 Kaplinski, *Evening Brings Everything Back*, 38.
4 Kaplinski, Diaries, 16 November 1985.
5 O'Driscoll, "Count every dandelion," 25.
6 Tiia Toomet to author, E-mail, 20 April 2007.

7 Kaalep, "lapse naeratus," 1913.
8 Väljataga, "Literary perspectives."
9 Ivask, "Raske on kergeks saada," 81.
10 Jaan Kaplinski, untitled lecture (unpublished transcript, 20 January 1983, Tartu).
11 Godfrey, "reluctant prophet."
12 Elvi Pirk to Jaan Kaplinski, 12 April 1988. Kaplinski Papers, Estonian Literary Museum, Tartu.
13 Alan Golightly to Jaan Kaplinski, 31 October 1993. Kaplinski Papers, Estonian Literary Museum.
14 Niiniluoto, "My Generation."
15 Franks, "Estonian Nationalism."
16 Sam Hamill to author, E-mail, 15 June 2005.
17 Mare Lõhmus to author, E-mail, 25 January 2010.
18 Hamill, "Introduction," xiv.
19 Ivask, "Ma vaatasin päikese aknasse," 651.
20 Ivask, "Raske on kergeks saada," 135.
21 Martin, "Metaphor," 189.
22 Jaan Kaplinski to Gary Snyder, 18 May 1969. Gary Snyder Papers, Special Collections, University of California, Davis.
23 Gary Snyder to author, E-mail, 10 April 2002.
24 Jaan Kaplinski to Gary Snyder, 27 January 1971. Gary Snyder Papers, Special Collections, University of California, Davis.
25 Kaplinski, Diaries, 27 June 1981.
26 Norton, "Absence," 42.
27 Kaplinski, Diaries, 20 January 1985.
28 Kaplinski, *Same Sea*, 75.
29 Kaplinski, *Evening Brings Everything Back*, 40.
30 Joel Sang, *vastukarva*, 100.
31 Kaplinski, E-mail, 22 December 2003.
32 Kaplinski, *Isale*, 325.
33 Kaplinski, E-mail, 1 July 2005.
34 Tiia Toomet to Lia, 25 January 1986. Kaplinski Papers, Estonian Literary Museum, Tartu.
35 Kaplinski, "Estonia."
36 Jaan Kaplinski to Andres, 14 April 1985. Kaplinski Papers, Estonian Literary Museum, Tartu.
37 Jaan Kaplinski to Kaisa, 9 May 1982. Kaplinski Papers, Estonian Literary Museum, Tartu.
38 Kaplinski, E-mail, 15 July 2005.

39 Kaplinski, E-mail, 24 February 2005.
40 Kaplinski, E-mail, 14 September 2007; Kaplinski, E-mail, 12 September 2007.
41 Kaplinski, *Same River*, 227.
42 Ehin, "Pihtimus," 6.
43 E.g. Kesküla, "vastaline intellektuaal;" Beier, "lahkumine kultuurist;" Joel Sang, *vastukarva*.
44 Jullien, *Treatise on Efficacy*; Wenning, "Daoism as Critical Theory," 64–5.
45 Snyder, *Practice of the Wild*, 181.
46 Snyder, "Art of Poetry," 103.

CHAPTER TWO

1 Kaplinski, *Through the Forest*, 87. Reprinted by permission.
2 Kaplinski, *Selected Poems*, 211.
3 Kaplinski, *Paralleele ja parallelisme*, 55–6; Põlma, *Eesti Kirjakeele Seltussõnaraamat*, 186–7.
4 Buchloh, "Richter's Abstraction," 16.
5 Ibid., 11.
6 Ibid., 17.
7 Wilmes, "Gerhard Richter," 135–6.
8 Kaplinski, "Refleksid ja isiksused," 5.
9 Kaplinski, "Filosoofia ja vaikus," 5; Coupe 2000, 2.
10 Naess, "Heidegger, Postmodern Theory," 3, 5.
11 Kaplinski, "Tomas Tranströmer," 602.
12 Jaan Kaplinski to Francis L.K. Hsu, 14 May 1978. Kaplinski Papers, Estonian Literary Museum, Tartu.
13 E.g. Kaplinski, *Ööd valged*, 70–3.
14 Naess, "Simple in means," 26.
15 Kaplinski, "Hävitatud templid," B4.
16 Kaplinski, *Kevad Kahel Rannikul*, 279; Kaplinski, *Isale*, 41; Kaplinski, "tarku valitsejaid on harva."
17 Kaplinski, E-mail, 6 August 2012.
18 Edward Wilson, *Biophilia*, 1.
19 Kaplinski, *Jäljed Allikal*, 38.
20 Kaplinski, *Evening Brings Everything Back*, 72.
21 Kaplinski, *Through the Forest*, 28.
22 Kruus, "Meie luuleankeet," 3.
23 Kalda, "Neli uut," 563.
24 Eilart, "Kaitsmas elu," 3.
25 Grabbi, "For a New Heaven," 659.

26 Kaalep, "lapse naeratus," 1914.
27 Kaalep, "Avatud luule," 212.
28 Haug, "Pilk eesti luuleilma," 394.
29 Talvet, "Millennium Poetry," 206–7.
30 Talvet, "Transcendence," 7.
31 Kronberg, "Outlines of Books."
32 Salokannel, "Piirideta Kaplinski."
33 Zdeb, "Selected Poems."
34 Kaplinski, *Öölinnud*, 77.
35 Masing, *Mälestusi taimedest*, 53, 75–6.
36 Kaplinski, "Jaan Kaplinski maailm," 24.
37 Tiia Toomet to author, E-mail, 21 January 2008.
38 Kaplinski, *Kust Tuli Öö*, 43.
39 Jaan Kaplinski to Gary Snyder, 28 February 1972. Gary Snyder Papers, Special Collections, University of California, Davis.
40 Kaplinski, "Estonia: A Home," 140–7.
41 Kaplinski, "Jaan Kaplinski," 685.
42 Kaplinski, "Estonia: A Home," 147.
43 Jaan Kaplinski, interview by author, 25 August 2001, Võru county (Estonia).
44 Kaplinski, *Evening Brings Everything Back*, 49.
45 Tiia Toomet to author, E-mail, 21 January 2008.
46 Jaan Kaplinski to Gary Snyder, 28 February 1972. Gary Snyder Papers, Special Collections, University of California, Davis.
47 Tiia Toomet to author, E-mail, 21 January 2008.
48 Jaan Kaplinski in Raphaël Gianelli-Meriano, *The Kaplinski System* (transcript of documentary, 22 February 2012).
49 Kaplinski, *Evening Brings Everything Back*, 49.
50 Tiia Toomet to author, E-mail, 21 January 2008.
51 Kaplinski, *Isale*, 278.
52 jaankaplinski.blogspot.com, 27 April 2011.
53 Snyder, *Gary Snyder Reader*, 169.
54 Kaplinski, "Intervjuu Jaan Kaplinskiga."
55 Jaan Kaplinski to Ilse Lehiste, 15 September 1976. In the author's possession.
56 Kaplinski, *Isale*, 129.
57 Edward Wilson, *Biophilia*, 11.
58 Ibid., 121.
59 Kaplinski, *Usk on Uskmatus*, 298.
60 Ibid.

61 Kaplinski, "Pessimisti mõtteid," 4.
62 Kaplinski, "Mitte keskkond."
63 Kaplinski, "Jaan Kaplinski juubeliks Itaaliasse," 11.
64 Kaplinski, *see ja teine*, 132.
65 Ibid., 136.
66 jaan.kaplinski.com, 5 September, 2002.
67 Kaplinski, "Globalization."
68 Kaplinski, Diaries, 13 July 1992.
69 Ibid.
70 jaan.kaplinski.com, 5 September 2002.
71 Kaplinski, "Tarbimisűhiskond."
72 Kaplinski, *Kõik on ime,* 79–83.
73 Ibid., 82.
74 Jaan Kaplinski to Gary Snyder, 27 July 1972. Gary Snyder Papers. Special Collections, University of California, Davis.
75 Kaplinski, *Kust Tuli Öö*, 92.
76 Russell, *Not a Christian*, 7–8.
77 Cobb, *Protestant Theology,* 222.
78 Ibid., 227–8.
79 Kaplinski, "Ornitofilosoofia," 690.
80 Kaplinski, *Evening Brings Everything Back*, 59.
81 Cudworth, *Environment and Society*, 37–65.
82 Kaplinski, "Intervjuu Jaan Kaplinskiga."
83 Kaplinski, "Jaan Kaplinski Eesti talves."
84 Mack, "Politics of Species Arrogance," 279–87.
85 Naess, "Mountains and Mythology," 4.
86 Kaplinski, "Mõtisklusi inimkultuurist," 508.
87 jaankaplinski.blogspot.com, 10 March 2010.
88 Camus, *Sisyphus*, 119.
89 jaankaplinski.blogspot.com 27 April 2011.

CHAPTER THREE

1 Kaplinski, *Evening Brings Everything Back*, 58–9. Reprinted by permission.
2 Kaplinski, Diaries, 20 April 1981.
3 Kaplinski, *Paralleele ja parallelisme*.
4 Kaplinski, "Filosoofia ja vaikus," 5.
5 Zerzan, *Running on Emptiness.*
6 Ibid., 2.

7 Ibid., 204.
8 Jaan Kaplinski to Don, 17 November 1978. Kaplinski Papers, Estonian Literary Museum, Tartu.
9 Lendvai, *Hungarian Uprising*, 2008.
10 *Tuna*, 161.
11 *Rahva Hääl*, 30 October 1956, 3.
12 *Noorte Hääl*, 3 November 1956, 4.
13 *Rahva Hääl*, 6 November 1956, 1–4.
14 www.moritz.botany.ut.ee, 7 March 2000.
15 Kaplinski, *Same River*, 50.
16 Ibid., 45.
17 Jaan Kaplinski, interview by author, 25 August 2001, Võru county (Estonia).
18 Kaplinski, E-mail, 6 August 2012.
19 Kaplinski, "Jaan Kaplinski, Estonian Television."
20 Ibid.
21 Olesk, "Literary Life," 122–34.
22 Jaan Kaplinski, interview by author, 10 October 2002, Tartu.
23 Kaplinski and Grabbi, *Sõprade kirjad*.
24 Maurois, *Ariel*, 13.
25 Ibid.
26 Kaplinski, "Laulude sünnimailt," 109.
27 Kaplinski, *Isale*, 115.
28 Maurois, *Ariel*, 21.
29 Kaplinski, *Same River*, 14.
30 Kaplinski, "Jaan Kaplinski, Estonian Television."
31 Kaplinski, *Kust Tuli Öö*, 28.
32 Kaplinski, "Jaan Kaplinski, Estonian Television."
33 Ibid.
34 Kaplinski, *Same River*, 26.
35 Kaplinski, Diaries, 14 June 1995.
36 Maurois, *Ariel*, 15–16.
37 Powelstock, *Becoming Mikhail Lermontov*, 41, 102.
38 Jaan Kaplinski, lecture series, Tartu University, 2000.
39 jaan.kaplinski.com, 2 November 2006.
40 Kaplinski, "Jaan Kaplinski," 685.
41 Powelstock, *Becoming Mikhail Lermontov*, 3.
42 Webb, "Prometheus Unbound," 710.
43 Wright, "To make experience sing," 79.
44 Kaplinski, *Same River*, 117.

45 Ibid.
46 Kaplinski, "laulude sünnimailt," 109, 113.
47 Grabbi, "For a New Heaven," 660.
48 Kaplinski, E-mail, 27 August 2008.
49 Kaplinski, "Jaan Kaplinski," 684.
50 Lauris Kaplinski, interview by author, 24 August 2001, Tartu.
51 Kaplinski, E-mail, 27 August 2008.
52 Kaplinski, Diaries, 7 January 1995.
53 Kaplinski, *Isale*, 56–7.
54 Kaplinski, E-mail, 10 May 2005.
55 Kaplinski, "Jaan Kaplinski, Estonian Television."
56 Kaplinski, *Same Sea*, 5.
57 Küllike Kaplinski, interview by author, 13 August 2003, Tallinn.
58 Ain Kaalep, interview by author, 27 August 2001, Tartu.
59 Jaan Kaplinski to Kaisa, 18 December 1980. Kaplinski Papers, Estonian Literary Museum, Tartu.
60 Zerzan, *Against Civilization*, 263.
61 Grabbi, "For a New Heaven," 660.
62 Ibid., 661.
63 Ibid., 663.
64 Kaplinski, Diaries, 11 October 1981.
65 Kaplinski, Diaries, 21 March 1987.
66 Kaplinski, E-mail, 28 January 2013.
67 Kaplinski, "Semiootika suvekoolist," 764–5.
68 Lotman, "On the semiosphere," 205–29.
69 Mandelker, "Semiotizing the Sphere," 385.
70 Piatigorsky, "Lecture."
71 Ibid.
72 Kaplinski, *Paralleele ja parallelism*e, 80.
73 Kaplinski, *Same Sea*, 35.
74 Kaplinski, "Ain Kaalep," 14.
75 Annus, *Eesti Kirjanduslugu*, 435–7; Kaalep, *Kolm Lydiat*.
76 Kaplinski, E-mail, 10 August 2002.
77 Annus, *Eesti Kirjanduslugu,* 439-43.
78 Andres Ehin, interview by author, 26 June 2008, Rapla.
79 E.g. Misiunas and Taagepera, *Years of Dependence*, 145; Velsker, "Vaimuelu."
80 Solženitsõn, "Preface," 3.
81 Toomet, *Isamaa suvi*, 40.
82 Havel, "Second Wind," 209.
83 Kaplinski, *Same Sea,* 24.

84 Kaplinski, Diaries, 1962–64.
85 Ivar Ivask, "Eesti sõjajärgse luule arengusuunadest," (unpublished manuscript, Stockholm, 28 September1968).
86 Jaan Kaplinski, interviewed by author, 10 October 2002, Tartu; Merilai, "Estonian Poetic Surrealism."
87 Kaplinski, *Ööd valged*, 11.
88 Jaan Kaplinski to Gary Snyder, 27 July 1972. Gary Snyder Papers, Special Collections, University of California, Davis.
89 Kaplinski, *Ööd valged*, 10.
90 Derrida, *Monolingualism of the Other*, 39.
91 jaan.kaplinski.com, 2 November 2006.
92 Kaplinski, *Kõik on ime,* 293.
93 Kaplinski, Diaries, 1962–64.
94 Kaplinski, *Kirjutatud,* 706.
95 Kaplinski, *Through the Forest*, 16.
96 Jaan Kaplinski, interview by author, 15 August 2003, Mutiku (Estonia).
97 Tiia Toomet to author, E-mail, 20 May 2007.
98 Tiia Toomet, interview by author, 7 October 2002, Tartu.
99 Tiia Toomet to author, E-mail, 20 May 2007.
100 Kaplinski, Diaries, 5 April 1981.
101 Kaplinski, E-mail, 18 August 2008.
102 Kaplinski, "Sauna taga," B1.
103 Kaplinski, *Isale*, 34–5.
104 Kaplinski, "From Harem to Brothel."
105 Kaplinski, *Kõik on ime,* 293.
106 Kaplinski, *Kevad Kahel Rannikul*, 262.
107 Kaplinski, *Through the Forest*, 77.
108 Kaplinski, *Öölinnud*, 91.
109 Kaplinski, *Through the Forest*, 38.
110 Kaplinski, *Kõik on Ime*, 293.
111 Ibid., 295–6.
112 Kaplinski, E-mail, 18 August 2008.
113 Jaan Kaplinski to Sam Hamill, 9 April 1987. Cage 700, Sam Hamill Papers. Manuscripts, Archives, and Special Collections, Washington State University Libraries, Pullman, Washington.
114 Kaplinski, E-mail, 6 November 2007; Kaplinski, Diaries, 14 December 1980.

CHAPTER FOUR

1 Kaplinski, *Öölinnud*, 91. Reprinted by permission.
2 Kaplinski, *Same River,* 177.

3 Kaplinski, E-mail, 30 August 2008.
4 Kaplinski, E-mail, 2 August 2012.
5 Kaplinski, *Same River,* 157.
6 Ibid., 261.
7 Kaplinski, "olemise kummaline vaikus," 4.
8 Kaplinski, *Kust Tuli Öö*, 45.
9 Kaplinski, "Pessimisti mõtteid," 4–5.
10 Kaplinski, "Saateks," 99.
11 Kaplinski, *Same River,* 202.
12 Winnicott, *Human Nature,* 132.
13 Rodman, *Winnicott*, 301.
14 McDougall, *Theaters of the Body*, 33.
15 Kaplinski, *Same River,* 201.
16 Barrows, "Ecopsychology," 105.
17 Winnicott, *Playing and Reality*, 102–3.
18 Ibid., 109.
19 McDougall, *Theaters of the Mind*, 76.
20 Ibid., 77.
21 Winnicott, *Human Nature,* 101.
22 Mare Lõhmus to author, E-mail, 25 January 2010.
23 Kaplinski, E-mail, 6 August 2012.
24 Kaplinski, E-mail, 28 April 2005.
25 Kaplinski, *Same River,* 295.
26 Nussbaum, "People as Fictions," 237.
27 Young-Bruehl, "Where Do We Fall," 284.
28 Tallis, *Love Sick*.
29 Parisi, *Civilization*, 13.
30 jaan.kaplinski.com, 5 September 2002.
31 Kaplinski, "Paus," 33–4.
32 Jaan Kaplinski, "Liblikas ja Peegel" (unpublished manuscript, Estonian Drama Agency, Tallinn, 1980–81), 36.
33 McDougall, *Theaters of the Body*, 35.
34 Kaplinski, Diaries, 29 December 1994.
35 Kaplinski, *Evening Brings Everything Back*, 85.
36 Kaplinski, *I Am Spring*, 49.
37 Kaplinski, *Kalivägi*, #6.
38 Kaplinski, Diaries, 28 March 1982.
39 Lauris Kaplinski, interview by author, 24 August 2001, Tartu.
40 Tiia Toomet, interview by author, 22 August 2001, Tartu.
41 Kaplinski, E-mail, 18 August 2008.

42 The interview (telephone) was conducted in confidentiality, and the name of the interviewee is withheld by mutual consent. 15 July 2005.
43 Kaplinski, *Isale*, 34–5.
44 Kaplinski, E-mail, 8 March 2006.
45 Kaplinski, Diaries, 17 May 1996.
46 Kaplinski, Diaries, 23 January 1995.
47 Mare Lõhmus to author, E-mail, 25 January 2010.
48 Kaplinski, Diaries, 22 April 1994.
49 Kaplinski, E-mail, 29 November 2010.
50 Ibid.
51 Kaplinski, E-mail, 17 December 2001.
52 Ehin, "Pihtimus," 6.
53 Armula and Ants Järv, interview by author, 26 August 2001, Tartu.
54 Kaplinski, Diaries, 16 August 1988; Kaplinski, Diaries, 2 October 1986.
55 Kaplinski, Diaries, 12 April 1986.
56 Kaplinski, *Same River*, 34.
57 Ibid., 35.
58 Ibid., 72.
59 Kaplinski, *Ööd Valged*, 44.
60 Kaplinski, Diaries, 16 August 1988.
61 Kaplinski, *Same River*, 15.
62 Kaplinski, *Isale*, 113.
63 Kaplinski, E-mail, 16 December 2010.
64 Jaan Kaplinski, interview by author, 29 September 2002, Tartu.
65 Jaan Kaplinski, interview by author, 22 August 2003, Tartu.
66 Kaplinski, *Isale*, 124.
67 Jaan Kaplinski, interview by author, 22 August 2003, Mutiku (Estonia).
68 Tiia Toomet, interview by author, 22 August 2001, Tartu.
69 Kaplinski, Diaries, 27 June 1981.
70 Kaplinski, Diaries, 5 August 1981.
71 Kaplinski, *Isale*, 204.
72 Kaplinski, Diaries, 5 August 1981.
73 Winnicott, *Human Nature*, 100–21. McDougall, *Theaters of the Body*, 32–44.
74 McDougall, *Theaters of the Mind*, 66.
75 Ibid., 77.
76 Kaplinski, Diaries, 28 November 1992.
77 Kaplinski, Diaries, 28 September 1980.
78 Kaplinski, E-mail, 16 December 2010.
79 Ibid.

80 Kaplinski, *Same River,* 28.
81 Mare Lõhmus to author, E-mail, 25 January 2010.
82 Kaplinski, *Same River,* 36.
83 Kaplinski, E-mail, 8 March 2006.
84 Kaplinski, *Selected Poems*, 113.
85 Kaplinski, *Öölinnud*, 80.
86 Kaplinski, *Selected Poems*, 120.
87 Mare Lõhmus, E-mail, 25 January 2010.
88 Kaplinski, *Same River,* 90.
89 Tiia Toomet, interview by author, 20 August 2003, Mutiku (Estonia).
90 Kaplinski, *Same River,* 34, 232.
91 Kaplinski, *Evening Brings Everything Back*, 40.
92 Jaan Kaplinski, interview by author, 22 August 2003, Mutiku (Estonia).
93 Kaplinski, Diaries, 4 November 1996.
94 Lena Karlström, interview by author, 1 October 2001, Vancouver.
95 Ibid.
96 Kaplinski, E-mail, 6 August, 2012.
97 Kaplinski, Diaries, 9 November 1996; Kaplinski Diaries 18 November 1996.
98 Kaplinski, *Same River,* 232.
99 Tiia Toomet to author, E-mail, 20 April 2007.
100 Ibid.
101 Jaan Kaplinski, interview by author, 22 August 2003, Mutiku (Estonia).
102 Kaplinski, E-mail, 30 March 2006.
103 Kaplinski, E-mail, 28 April 2005.
104 Kaplinski, E-mail, 3 October 2006.
105 Kaplinski, E-mail, 2 October 2006.
106 Kaplinski, *Kust Tuli* Öö, 23.
107 Kaplinski, E-mail, 23 August 2008.
108 Kaplinski, Diaries, 9 November 1996; Kaplinski, E-mail, 23 August 2008; Kaplinski Diaries, 11 October 1992.
109 Jaan Kaplinski, "Liblikas ja Peegel" (unpublished manuscript, Estonian Drama Agency, Tallinn, 1980–81), 28.
110 Jaan Kaplinski, "Liblikas ja Peegel" (unpublished manuscript, Estonian Drama Agency, Tallinn, 1980–81), 38.
111 Kaplinski, *Isale*, 118.
112 Kaplinski, *Kevad Kahel Rannikul*, 41.
113 Kaplinski, *Same River,* 34, 70–1.
114 Ibid., 207.
115 Ibid., 177.
116 Kaplinski, *Kust Tuli* Öö, 61.
117 Kaplinski, Diaries, 8 April 1987.

118 Kaplinski, Diaries, 22 May 1984.
119 Kaplinski, Diaries, 5 January 1986.
120 Kaplinski, Diaries, 24 March 1985.
121 Kaplinski, Diaries, 1 March 1987; Kaplinski, Diaries, 21 March 1986.
122 Kaplinski, Diaries, 29 July 1981; Kaplinski, Diaries, 18 October 1984.
123 Jaan Kaplinski, interview by author, 10 October 2002, Tartu.
124 Kaplinski, *Isale*, 116.
125 Kaplinski, Diaries, 1 April 1987.
126 Kaplinski, "Avatusest ja armastusest," 6.
127 Kaplinski, *Same River*, 202.
128 Kaplinski, Diaries, 8 March 1982.
129 Watts, *Nature, Man and Woman*, 68.
130 Kaplinski, E-mail, 27 August 2008; Kaplinski, E-mail, 15 July 2005.
131 Kaplinski, E-mail, 1 May 2008.
132 Kaplinski, E-mail, 15 July 2005.
133 Kaplinski, E-mail, 14 November 2006.
134 Ibid.
135 Kaplinski, E-mail, 26 November, 2010.
136 Kaplinski, E-mail, 28 April 2005–17 October 2006.
137 Kaplinski, E-mail, 15 September 2007.
138 Kaplinski, E-mail, 14 September 2007.
139 Kaplinski, E-mail, 1 May 2008.
140 Kaplinski, E-mail, 12 September 2007.
141 Kaplinski, E-mail, 14 November 2006.
142 Kaplinski, E-mail, 26 November 2010.
143 Ibid.
144 Ibid.
145 Kaplinski, E-mail, 17 October 2006.
146 Kaplinski, E-mail, 2 April 2006.
147 Kaplinski, E-mail, 26 November 2010.
148 Kaplinski, E-mail, 6 August 2012.
149 Tiia Toomet to author, E-mail, 20 April 2007.
150 Kaplinski, Diaries, 7 April 1985.
151 Kaplinski, Diaries, 21 January 1981.
152 Kaplinski, Diaries, 22 May 1984.
153 Kaplinski, Diaries, 31 March 1985.
154 Kaplinski, Diaries, 5 September 1985.
155 Kaplinski, Diaries, 20 May 1986.
156 Kaplinski, *Same River*, 178.
157 Ibid.
158 Kaplinski, E-mail, 28 October 2007.

159 Ibid.
160 Kaplinski, E-mail, 5 August 2007.
161 Kaplinski, E-mail, 10 May 2005.
162 Ibid.
163 Rilke, *Rilke on Love*, 28; Rilke, *Briefe*, 166.
164 Jaan Kaplinski, "Liblikas ja Peegel" (unpublished manuscript, Estonian Drama Agency, Tallinn, 1980–81), 36.
165 Kaplinski, E-mail, 11 June 2007.
166 Kaplinski, Diaries, 28 September 1980.
167 Kaplinski, "Paus," 33–4.
168 Kaplinski, *Kust Tuli Öö*, 105.

CHAPTER FIVE

1 Kaplinski, *Wandering Border*, 105. Reprinted by permission.
2 Doi, *Anatomy of Self*, 160.
3 Vesilind, *Singing Revolution*, 114.
4 Freud, *Civilization and Its Discontents*, 69–70.
5 Ibid., 69.
6 Ibid., 82, 81, 51.
7 Warneken and Tomasello, "roots of human altruism."
8 Doi, *Understanding Amae*, 54.
9 Odin, *Social Self in Zen*, 353.
10 Doi, *Anatomy of Dependence*, 74, 168.
11 Kaplinski, E-mail, 22 September, 2009.
12 Young-Bruehl and Bethelard, *Cherishment*, 57.
13 Doi, *Anatomy of Self*, 138–9; Doi, *Understanding Amae*, 143.
14 Freud, *Civilization and Its Discontents*, 68.
15 Jullien, *Efficacy in China*, 265.
16 Jaan Kaplinski, interview by author, 15 August 2003, Mutiku (Estonia); Jaan Kaplinski, interview by Vallo Kepp, documentary *Masingu maastikud*, transcript, 22 November 2001; Kaplinski, *Same River*, 37.
17 Jaan Kaplinski, interview by Vallo Kepp, documentary *Masingu maastikud*, transcript, 22 November 2001; Kaplinski, E-mail, 24 January 2002; Kaplinski, "Uku Masing ja maailmarevolutsioon."
18 Kaplinski, E-mail, 24 January 2002.
19 Jaan Kaplinski, interview by Vallo Kepp, documentary *Masingu maastikud*, transcript, 22 November 2001.
20 Kaplinski, E-mail, 15 July 2005.
21 Kaplinski, E-mail, 6 August 2012.

22 August Sang, "Ühest varjujäänud luuletajast," 1275–6.
23 Kuusk, "Uku Masing."
24 Kaplinski, "Ütles Masing."
25 Kaplinski, "Ain Kaalep," 14.
26 Kaplinski, E-mail, 24 January 2002.
27 Kaplinski, *Same River,* 105–6.
28 Ibid., 79.
29 Jaan Kaplinski, interview by Vallo Kepp, documentary *Masingu maastikud,* transcript, 22 November 2001.
30 Kaplinski, E-mail, 15 July 2005.
31 Masing, *Mälestusi taimedest*, 131–50; Masing, *Pessimismi põhjendus*, 256–73; Kaplinski, E-mail 15 July 2005.
32 Kaplinski, E-mail, 6 August, 2012.
33 Kaplinski, E-mail, 22 September 2009.
34 Kaplinski, E-mail 17 May 2012; Kaplinski, E-mail, 15 July 2005.
35 E.g. Masing, *Keelest ja meelest.*
36 Arne Hiob, "Uku Masing teoloogia avaral maastikul," (unpublished manuscript, Tartu, 23 September 2009).
37 Merton, *Thoughts on the East*, 52.
38 Masing, *Haikud*, 40.
39 Masing, *Tankad*, 116–7.
40 Kaplinski, E-mail, 6 August 2012.
41 Ibid.
42 Kaplinski, "Filosoofia ja vaikus," 5.
43 Kaplinski, E-mail, 6 August 2012.
44 Sommer, "Geniaalne vanalaps," 98; Sommer, "Kujud ja tujud."
45 Vulf, "kõnelused Uku Masinguga," 397.
46 Arne Merilai to author, E-mail, 6 May 2009.
47 Vallo Kepp to author, E-mail, 30 October 2007.
48 Ivar Ivask, "Eesti sõjajärgse luule arengusuunadest," (unpublished manuscript, Stockholm, 28 September 1968).
49 Kaplinski, Diaries, 10 October 1993.
50 Jaan Kaplinski, interview by Vallo Kepp, documentary *Masingu maastikud,* transcript, 22 November 2001.
51 Kaplinski, "Ütles Masing."
52 Kaplinski, E-mail, 24 January 2002.
53 Kaplinski, E-mail, 15 July 2005.
54 Jullien, *Treatise on Efficacy*, 186.
55 Masing, *Meil on lootust*, 180.
56 Kaplinski, *Paralleele ja parallelisme*, 270.

57 Jaan Kaplinski, interview by Vallo Kepp, documentary *Masingu maastikud,* transcript, 22 November 2001.
58 Kaplinski, E-mail, 15 July 2005; Kaplinski, *Same River,* 24.
59 Kaplinski, *Same River,* 257.
60 Jaan Kaplinski, interview by Vallo Kepp, documentary *Masingu maastikud,* transcript, 22 November 2001.
61 Doi, *Understanding Amae*, 54, 183.
62 Odin, *Social Self in Zen*, 353.
63 Doi, *Anatomy of Dependence*, 74, 168.
64 Jaan Kaplinski to Uku Masing, 10 August 1979. Uku Masing archive, Tartu.
65 Johnson, *Dependency*, 28–37.
66 Young-Bruehl and Bethelard, *Cherishment*, 8.
67 Meri, *European Mind*, 39.
68 Ibid., 120–1.
69 Johnson, *Dependency*,15.
70 Kaplinski, E-mail, 15 July 2005.
71 Kaplinski, *Same River,* 258.
72 Kaplinski, "Ütles Masing."
73 Luhaäär, *Uku Masing*, 18, 36–8.
74 Jaan Kaplinski, interview by Vallo Kepp, documentary *Masingu maastikud,* transcript, 28 August 2001.
75 Kaplinski, *Kajakas Võltsmunal*, 185–8.
76 Kaplinski, E-mail, 17 December 2001.
77 E.g. Masing, *Pessimismi põhjendus*, 256–73; Kaplinski, "Vasakpoolne Uku Masing;" Kaplinski, "Uku Masing ja maailmarevolutsioon," Kaplinski, "Haige Geenius."
78 Kaplinski, "Haige Geenius."
79 Kaplinski, Diaries, 1 May1985.
80 Kaplinski, E-mail, 22 September 2009.

CHAPTER SIX

1 Kaplinski, *Selected Poems*, 196. Reprinted by permission.
2 Jaan Kaplinski in Raphaël Gianelli-Meriano, *The Kaplinski System* (transcript of documentary, 22 February 2012).
3 Jullien, *Blandness*, 62.
4 Kaplinski, E-mail, 19 October 2001; Jaan Kaplinski, lecture series, Tartu University, 2000.
5 Jaan Kaplinski to Don and Slava, 5 July 1980. Kaplinski Papers, Estonian Literary Museum, Tartu.

6 Jaan Kaplinski in Raphaël Gianelli-Meriano, *The Kaplinski System* (trailer 2009).
7 Kaplinski, *Evening Brings Everything Back*, 58–9.
8 Kaplinski, E-mail, 6 August 2012.
9 jaan.kaplinski.com, 10 June 2012.
10 Ibid.
11 Kaplinski, "Saateks," 93–125.
12 Jullien, *Treatise on Efficacy*, 103, 117; Wenning, "Daoism as Critical Theory," 65.
13 Wenning, "Daoism as Critical Theory," 67.
14 see Jullien, *Treatise on Efficacy*, 2004.
15 Wenning, "Daoism as Critical Theory," 50–71.
16 jaankaplinski.blogspot.com, 24 August 2010.
17 Kaplinski, "Mõttevahetus," 155.
18 Kaplinski, Diaries, 21 January 1981.
19 Kaplinski, Diaries, 5 April 1981.
20 Kaplinski, Diaries, 2 October 1980.
21 Kaplinski, Diaries, 22 June 1986; Kaplinski, Diaries, 20 May 1986.
22 Kaplinski, Diaries, 4 May 1986.
23 Kaplinski, *Poliitika Ja Antipoliitika*, 50.
24 Ibid., 34; Kaplinski, Diaries, 8 April 1985.
25 Kiin, Ruutsoo, Tarand, *40 kirja lugu*, 31.
26 Kaplinski, E-mail, 6 August 2012.
27 Ilves, "Estonia in 1984."
28 Kiin, Ruutsoo, Tarand, *40 kirja lugu*, 13.
29 Kukk, "Political Opposition," 370.
30 Jaan Kaplinski to Don and Slava, 5 July1980. Kaplinski Papers, Estonian Literary Museum, Tartu.
31 Jaan Kaplinski in Raphaël Gianelli-Meriano, *The Kaplinski System* (transcript of documentary, 22 February 2012).
32 Kiin, Ruutsoo, Tarand, *40 kirja lugu*, 32–3.
33 Raun, *Estonia and the Estonians*, 196.
34 Sileika, "mad dissident."
35 Kross, *The Czar's Madman*, 34–5.
36 Ibid., 9.
37 Jaanus, "Estonia and Pain," 312.
38 Kross, *The Czar's Madman*, 278–9.
39 Sileika, "mad dissident."
40 Tarand, *Kiri ei põle ära*, 70; Kiin, Ruutsoo, Tarand, *40 kirja lugu*, 67.
41 Vardys, "Open Letter," 292–6.

42 Ibid.
43 Kiin, Ruutsoo, Tarand, *40 kirja lugu*, 33.
44 Ibid., 58–62; Hando Runnel, interview by author, 10 October 2002, Tartu; Viivi Luik, interview by author, 14 October 2002, Tallinn.
45 Kaplinski, Diaries, 8 November 1980.
46 Ibid.
47 Ibid.
48 Kiin, Ruutso, Tarand, *40 kirja lugu*, 94.
49 Tiia Toomet, interview by author, 22 August 2001, Tartu.
50 Tiia Toomet, interview by author, 20 August 2003, Mutiku (Estonia); Kaplinski, Diaries, 8 November 1980.
51 Kaplinski, Diaries, 8 November 1980.
52 Ibid.
53 Kiin, Ruutso, Tarand, *40 kirja lugu*, 94.
54 Kaplinski, Diaries, 29 September 1980.
55 Kaplinski, Diaries, 13 December 1980.
56 Kaplinski, Diaries, 26 January 1982.
57 Kaplinski, *Same River*, 314.
58 Havel, "Power of the Powerless," 58.
59 Ibid., 56.
60 Falk, *Dilemmas of Dissidence*, 344, 346.
61 Havel, "Anti-Political Politics," 387.
62 Ibid., 396.
63 Ibid., 59.
64 Havel, "Anti-Political Politics," 395.
65 Havel, "Power of the Powerless," 29.
66 Kaplinski, Diaries, 13 November 1981.
67 Havel, "Power of the Powerless," 60.
68 Kaplinski, "Estonia Between Two Worlds," 14.
69 Falk, *Dilemmas of Dissidence*, 338.
70 Parfitt, "Piatigorsky Obituary."
71 Cohen, *Soviet Fates*.
72 Kaplinski, Diaries, 1 October 1980.
73 Kaplinski, Diaries, 2 October 1980.
74 Kaplinski, Diaries, 1 October 1980.
75 Oushakine, "Mimicry of Samizdat," 193.
76 Kaplinski, Diaries, 22 September 1980.
77 Kaplinski, Diaries, 5 September 1980; Kaplinski, Diaries, 22 October 1980; Kaplinski, Diaries, 3 October 1980.
78 Kaplinski, Diaries, 22 November 1980.

79 Kaplinski, Diaries, 15 December 1980.
80 Kaplinski, Diaries, 22 November 1980.
81 Kiin, Ristsoo, Tarand, *40 kirja lugu*, 34.
82 Kaplinski, Diaries, 2 October 1980.
83 Kapuściński, *Travels with Herodotus*, 68.
84 Ibid.
85 Kaplinski, E-mail, 18 August 2008.
86 Kull, "Jää pärast," 197.
87 Kaplinski, E-mail, 23 July 2008.
88 Kaplinski, "Definitions."
89 Naess, *Ecology*, 198.
90 Naess, "my philosophy," 225.
91 Jullien, *Blandness*, 59–60.
92 Misiunas and Taagepera, *Years of Dependence*, 38.
93 Goetz-Stankiewicz, *Good-bye, Samizdat*, 191.
94 Kaplinski, *Wandering Border*, 50.
95 Kaplinski, Diaries, 8 November 1980.
96 Kaplinski, Diaries, 19 January 1981.
97 Falk, "Resistance and Dissent," 339.
98 Sirje Kiin to author, E-mail, 25 September 2011.
99 Kiin, Ruutsoo, Tarand, *40 kirja lugu*, 35.
100 Ibid., 136.
101 Ibid., 56.
102 Ibid., 54.
103 Kaplinski, Diaries, 21 June 1981.
104 Taagepera, *Softening without Liberalization.*
105 Ibid., 1.
106 Kaplinski, Diaries, 29 March 1981.
107 Havel, "Power of the Powerless," 58–9.
108 *Estniska Dagbladet*, 10 December 1980: 2.
109 *Frankfurter Allgemeine Zeitung*, 15 January 1981: 6.
110 *The London Times*, 15 January 1981: 8.
111 *The Times of India*, 8 December 1980: 17.
112 Vardys, "Human Rights," 275–98.
113 Misiunas and Taagepera, *Years of Dependence*, 257.
114 Ilves, "Estonia in 1984."
115 Taagepera, *Return to Independence*, 115; Vahtre, *Eesti Ajalugu*, 313.
116 Kaplinski, Diaries, 19 January 1981.
117 Kaplinski, Diaries, 18 December 1980; see also Kaplinski and Grabbi, *Sõprade kirjad*, 259.

118 Kiin, Ruutsoo, Tarand, *40 kirja lugu*, 126.
119 Tarand, *Kiri ei põle ära*, 127-30.
120 Kiin, Ruutsoo, Tarand, *40 kirja lugu*, 41.
121 Constitution, 7 October 1977.
122 Kukk, "Political Opposition," 369.
123 Vahtre, *Eesti Ajalugu*, 313.
124 Kiin, Ruutsoo, Tarand, *40 kirja lugu*, 82.
125 Ohmann, "Gustav Naani kaebekiri,“ 99.
126 Kaplinski, Diaries, 22 March 1981; Kaplinski Diaries 6 May 1981.
127 Kaplinski, Diaries, 30 May 1981.
128 Kaplinski, Diaries, 22 November 1980.
129 Tarand, *Kiri ei põle ära*, 137.
130 Kiin, Ruutsoo, Tarand, *40 kirja lugu*, 89; Misiunas and Taagepera, *Years of Dependence*.
131 Misiunas and Taagepera, *Years of Dependence*, 93.
132 Kiin, Ruutsoo, Tarand, *40 kirja lugu*, 103, 159.
133 Ibid., 92.
134 Tarand, *Kiri ei põle ära*, 66.
135 Kaplinski, Diaries, 15 December 1980.
136 Kaplinski, Diaries, 18 January 1981.
137 Ohmann, "Gustav Naani kaebekiri," 102–4.
138 Tarand, *Kiri ei põle ära*, 145–6.
139 Naan, "Homo Mutans," 8, 13.
140 Ohmann, "Gustav Naani kaebekiri," 101.
141 Kiin, Ruutsoo, Tarand, *40 kirja lugu*, 100.
142 Ohmann, "Gustav Naani kaebekiri," 97–8.
143 Kaplinski, Diaries, 8 January 1992.
144 *The Washington Post*, 9 November 1980.
145 *The Christian Science Monitor*, 5 January 1981.
146 *The Washington Post*, 8 December 1980.
147 Pesti, *Dissidentlik Liikumine*, 33–7; Misiunas and Taagepera, *Years of Dependence*, 1983.
148 Pesti, *Dissidentlik Liikumine*, 24, 41.
149 Ohmann, "Gustav Naani kaebekiri," 99.
150 Kaplinski, Diaries, 8 May 1981.
151 Ohmann, "Gustav Naani kaebekiri," 98.
152 Ibid.
153 Anti Talur, interview by author, 18 August 2003, Tartu.
154 Kaplinski, Diaries, 16 June 1981; Kaplinski, Diaries, 21 June 1981.
155 Kaplinski, Diaries, 6 July 1981.

156 Kiin, Ruutsoo, Tarand, *40 kirja lugu*, 206.
157 Ibid., 208.
158 Ibid., 209.
159 Ibid., 207.
160 Rein Ruutsoo to Jaan Kaplinski, 25 August 1981. Kaplinski Papers, Estonian Literary Museum, Tartu.
161 Kaplinski, Diaries, 4 September 1981.
162 Ibid.
163 Ibid.
164 Kaplinski, Diaries, 26 September 1981.
165 Olev Utt to Jaan Kaplinski, 4 September 1981. Kaplinski Papers, Estonian Literary Museum, Tartu.
166 Sirje Kiin to author, E-mail, 23 September 2011.
167 Kaplinski, Diaries, 19 May 1986.
168 Jaan Kaplinski, interview by author, 18 August 2001, Mutiku (Estonia).
169 Kaplinski, Diaries, 20 February 1995.
170 Ibid.
171 Kaplinski, Diaries, 22 October 1980.
172 Sirje Kiin to author, E-mail, 23 September 2011.
173 Jaan Kaplinski, interview by author, 15 August 2003, Mutiku (Estonia); Ohmann 2005: 99; Anti Talur, interview by author, 18 August 2003, Tartu.
174 Ohmann, "Gustav Naani kaebekiri," 99.
175 Kaplinski, Diaries, 13 March 1981.
176 Ibid.
177 Ibid.
178 Kaplinski, Diaries, 25 May 1981.
179 Kaplinski, Diaries, 12 January 1985.
180 Kaplinski, Diaries, 8 February 1986; Kaplinski Diaries, 14 February 1986; Kaplinski Diaries, 21 February 1986; Kaplinski Diaries, 27 February 1986.
181 *Kodumaa*, 26 March 1986, 5–6.
182 Kaplinski, Diaries, 19 February 1985.
183 McDowell, "Oppression," C14.
184 Kaplinski, Diaries, 16 December 1980.
185 Kaplinski, Diaries, 21 December 1980.
186 Kaplinski, Diaries, 18 January 1981.
187 Kaplinski, Diaries, 22 January 1981.
188 Tarand, *Kiri ei põle ära*, 115.
189 Kaplinski, Diaries, 18 January 1985.
190 Kaplinski, Diaries, 28 December 1985.

191 Kaplinski, Diaries, 12 January 1985.
192 Kaplinski, Diaries, 17 December 1985.
193 Kaplinski, Diaries, 9 November 1982.
194 Jűrjo, *Pagulus*, 253–4.
195 Kaplinski, Diaries, 28 February 1987.
196 Ibid.
197 Kaplinski, Diaries, 3 March 1984.
198 Ohmann, "Gustav Naani kaebekiri," 97.
199 Kaplinski, Diaries, 9 April 1987.
200 Anti Talur, interview by author, 18 August 2003, Tartu.
201 Viivi Luik, interview by author, 14 October 2002, Tallinn.

CHAPTER SEVEN

1 Kaplinski, *Selected Poems*, 75. Reprinted by permission.
2 Kaplinski, "Olemise Kummaline Vaikus."
3 Kaplinski, *Paralleele ja parallelism*e, 241.
4 Elias, *Civilizing Process*.
5 Collins, *Violence*, 29.
6 Ibid., 24.
7 Tilly, *Coercion*, 1.
8 Freud, *Civilization and Its Discontents*, 68–9.
9 Kaplinski, *Kõik on ime*, 32–5; Kiossev, "The Self-Colonizing Metaphor"; Methis, *Special Issue* (2008).
10 Kaplinski, *Paralleele ja parallelism*, 94–144.
11 Parisi, *Civilization*, 45.
12 Kaplinski, "Vercingetorix kõneleb ordumeistriga."
13 Tilly, "War Making," 170.
14 Kaplinski, "Estonia."
15 Jaan Kaplinski, Neljakuningapäev (unpublished manuscript, Noorsooteater #2572/T7).
16 Tilly, *Coercion*, 187.
17 Kaplinski, *Kalivägi*, 10.
18 Kaplinski, "Vercingetorix kõneleb ordumeistriga."
19 Aarelaid-Tart, "Double Mental Standards."
20 Jirgens, "Carnival of Death," 270, 271.
21 Kaplinski, "Olla eurooplased."
22 Kaplinski, "Estonia."
23 Kundera, "Tragedy of Central Europe."
24 Kuus, "Puzzles from Central Europe," 95.

25 Ibid., 90-101.
26 Petersoo, "Constructing Estonian Identity," 124.
27 Aarelaid-Tart and Tart, "Development of Civil Society," 157.
28 Klima, *Spirit of Prague*, 114.
29 Vesilind, *Singing Revolution*, 169.
30 Tamm, "History as Cultural Memory," 511.
31 Meri, *A European Mind*, 143.
32 Kuus, "Intellectuals and geopolitics," 241–51.
33 Ibid., 244.
34 Talvet, *A Call for Cultural Symbiosis*, 17, 68.
35 Kaplinski, *Same River*, 299.
36 Ibid., 300.
37 Meri, *A European Mind*, 146.
38 Aarelaid-Tart and Tart, "Development of Civil Society," 155.
39 Veidemann, "Eesti Juhtum," 155–69.
40 Kaplinski, *Same Sea*, 5–6.
41 Kaplinski, *Tolmust Ja Värvidest*, 55.
42 Ibid., 21.
43 Taylor, *Malaise of Modernity*, 94.
44 Ehin, "Tolmust ja värvidest," 19; Rummo, "Vestlus," 3.
45 Jaan Kaplinski, untitled lecture (unpublished transcript, 20 January 1983, Tartu).
46 Kaalep, "lapse naeratus," 1914; Ehin, "Tolmust ja värvidest," 19.
47 Tormis, *Jonni pärast heliloojaks*, 154.
48 Ibid., 152–3.
49 Kaplinski, *Same Sea*, 10.
50 Ibid., 8–9.
51 McDowell, "Oppression," 1984.
52 Süvalepp, "Jaan Kaplinski," 163.
53 Kitching, "Jaan Kaplinski's *Vercingetorix*," 345.
54 Ibid., 335.
55 Ibid., 347.
56 Kaplinski, *Ööd valged*, 86.
57 Jaan Kaplinski, untitled lecture (unpublished transcript, 20 January 1983, Tartu).
58 Kiossev, "The Self-Colonizing Metaphor."
59 Jaan Kaplinski to Sam Hamill, 11 January 1985. Cage 700, Sam Hamill Papers. Manuscripts, Archives, and Special Collections, Washington State University Libraries, Pullman, Washington.
60 Jaan Kaplinski to Ilse Lehiste, 2 April 1969. In the author's possession.

61 Kaplinski, *Kevad Kahel Rannikul*, 58.
62 Racevskis, "Toward a Post-colonial Perspective," 168.
63 Petersoo, "Constructing Estonian Identity," 122.
64 Kaplinski, *Kõik on ime,* 175.
65 Viires, *Kultuur ja traditsioon*, 230; Lukas, "German literature in Estonia," 360; Undusk, "Eesti-saksa."
66 Viires, *Kultuur ja traditsioon*, 276.
67 Rähesoo, "Growing up in Modernity," 49.
68 Elias, *Civilizing Process*, 4.
69 Liulevičius, *German Myth*, 2009.
70 Elias, *Civilizing Process*, 5.
71 Kaplinski, *Paralleele ja parallelisme*, 94–144.
72 Kiossev, "The Self-Colonizing Metaphor."
73 Elias, *Civilizing Process.*
74 Loorits, *Meie, eestlased*, 217–21; see also Merilai, *Vokimeister*, 308–9.
75 Kaplinski, "Kultuurifilosoof Loorits."
76 Elias, *Civilizing Process*, 5.
77 Kaplinski, *see ja teine*, 142.
78 Kaplinski, *Kõik on ime,* 163.
79 Kaplinski, *Paralleele ja parallelism*e, 269.
80 Raun, *Estonia and the Estonians*, 74, 92.
81 Kaplinski, Diaries, 29 March 1984.
82 Rähesoo, "Growing up in Modernity," 49.
83 Hennoste, "Postkolonialism ja eesti," 88–9; Hennoste, "Eurooplaseks saamine," 2007.
84 Hennoste, "Eurooplaseks saamine," 2007.
85 Kaplinski, *see ja teine*, 34–5.
86 Raun, *Estonia and the Estonians*, 77; Lukas, "German literature in Estonia"; Kuldkepp, "Scandinavian Connection."
87 Lange, "Transnational Consciousness," 97.
88 Ibid., 100.
89 Kaplinski, "Mõeldes Noor-Eestile," 575.
90 Lauristin et al., *Return*, 29.
91 Ibid.
92 Kaplinski, *Kõik on ime,* 43–5.
93 Ibid., 32–8.
94 Ibid., 43.
95 Tormis, *Jonni Pärast Heliloojaks*, 153.
96 Klíma, *Spirit of Prague*, 114.
97 Kiossev, "The Self-Colonizing Metaphor."

98 Jaan Kaplinski, Neljakuningapäev (unpublished manuscript, Noorsooteater #2572/T7).
99 Jaan Kaplinski to "Dear Friends," 29 November 1980. Kaplinski Papers, Estonian Literary Museum, Tartu.
100 Kaplinski, *Teispool Sinist Taevast*, 8; Kaplinski and Grabbi, *Sõprade kirjad*, 279.
101 Snyder, "Language Goes Two Ways," 128.

CHAPTER EIGHT

1 Kaplinski, *Selected Poems*, 119-120. Reprinted by permission.
2 Jakob Hurt to Kaarle Krohn (1902). In Kalkun, "Rahvaluulekoguja kui looja," 73.
3 Jullien, *Treatise on Efficacy*, 87.
4 Bollas, "Normotic Illness," 319.
5 Ogden, "Playing, Dreaming," 257.
6 McDougall, *Many Faces of Eros*, 102.
7 Ogden, "Playing, Dreaming," 257.
8 Merton, *Thoughts on the East*, 35.
9 Ibid., 40.
10 Wilmes, "Gerhard Richter," 138.
11 Kaplinski, *Selected Poems*, 113.
12 Ibid., 78.
13 Sirr, "Jaan Kaplinski."
14 Snyder, *Gary Snyder Reader*, 169.
15 Talvet, "millennium poetry," 206.
16 Shenton, "Arvo Pärt," 116, 120-1.
17 Jullien, *Blandness*, 25.
18 See also Merilai, *Vokimeister*, 565-6.
19 Wilmes, "Gerhard Richter," 135-6. See also Meinhardt, "Illusionism in Painting," 135–51.
20 Berliner, *Thinking in Jazz*, 394, 492.
21 Ibid., 207.
22 Ibid., 492–8.
23 Kaplinski, *Kõik on Ime*, 158.
24 Kaplinski, "Tüdimusest ja rikkusest," 1425.
25 Kaplinski, *Isale*, 104.
26 Kaplinski, "Hinge Tagasi Kutsudes," 63.
27 Sarv, "Stichic and Stanzaic," 161–3.
28 Jaago, *Regilaulu poeetika*; Särg, "Melodic Accent."

29 Ross and Lehiste, *Temporal Structure*.
30 Kaplinski, "Hinge Tagasi Kutsudes."
31 Daitz, *Ancient Song Recovered*, 60.
32 Ibid., 43–5.
33 Kaplinski, *Kõik on ime,* 188.
34 Daitz, *Ancient Song Recovered*, 60.
35 Kaplinski, "Mõni sõna," 440.
36 Kaplinski, *Isale,* 104.
37 Kaplinski, *Kõik on ime,* 171.
38 Ibid., 171–2.
39 Kaplinski, E-mail, 6 August 2012.
40 Vesilind, *Singing Revolution*, 28; Laugaste, *Eesti Rahvaluule Ajalugu*, 60.
41 Weber, *Das veränderte Russland*, 70.
42 Lukas, "Estonian Folklore," 498.
43 Jannsen, "Tallinna laulo pidust," 111.
44 Kalkun, "Rahvaluulekoguja kui looja," 73.
45 Kaplinski, *Kõik on ime,* 187; Kaplinski, "Hinge Tagasi Kutsudes," 63.
46 Snyder, *Gary Snyder Reader*, 169.
47 Mürk, "Regi Song."
48 Daitz, *Ancient Song Recovered*, 57.
49 Ibid., 65.
50 Veidemann, "Laulev revolutsioon."
51 Raun, *Estonia and the Estonians*, 218.
52 Sarv, "Stichic and Stanzaic," 161.
53 Ibid., 168–9.
54 See also Salumets, *Baltic Postcolonialism*, 429–50.
55 Kaplinski, *Kõik on ime,* 159; Salumets, *Baltic Postcolonialism*, 429–50.
56 Daitz, *Ancient Song Recovered*, 60.
57 Ibid., 69.
58 Kaplinski, *Kõik on ime,* 173.
59 Ibid., 184.
60 Kaplinski, *Võimaluste Võimalikkus*, 228.
61 Daitz, *Ancient Song Recovered*, 60.
62 Kaplinski, *Kõik on ime,* 13.
63 Asu-Ôunas, "Introduction to Kaljo Põllo."
64 Kaplinski, *Kõik on ime,* 187–91.
65 Ibid., 190–1.
66 Kaplinski, "Vanu viise uuel kandlel," 43.
67 Kaplinski, *Kõik on ime,* 159.

68 Kaplinski, "Saateks," 104.
69 Jaan Kaplinski to Gary Snyder, 17 December 1969. Gary Snyder Papers, Special Collections, University of California, Davis.
70 Kaplinski and Grabbi, *Sõprade kirjad*, 212, 224; Kaplinski, *Isale,* 104.
71 Kaplinski, "Saateks," 114.
72 jaan.kaplinski.com, 20 March 2009.
73 Kaplinski, Diaries, 29 September 1980.
74 Jaan Kaplinski to Gary Snyder, 23 October 1978. Gary Snyder Papers, Special Collections, University of California, Davis.
75 Kaplinski, *Wandering Border*, 62.
76 Shunryu Suzuki, *Beginner's Mind*, 27, 108, 22, 47, 21.
77 Ibid., 49, 124, 58, 99.
78 Ibid., 78.
79 Kaplinski, "Hiina," 271.
80 Jullien, *Blandness*, 25, 62, 95, 72, 23.
81 Ibid., 132, 25.
82 Ibid., 116, 122.
83 Ibid., 143, 24.
84 Kaplinski, Introduction to *Täiskuutaeva All*, 7–15.
85 Kaplinski, *Through the Forest*, 40.
86 Kurrik, *Ilomaile*, 17–18.
87 Jaan Kaplinski, untitled lecture (unpublished transcript, 20 January 1983, Tartu).
88 Kaplinski, *Valge Joon Võrumaa Kohale*, 8.
89 Jullien, *Blandness*, 35–9.
90 Kaplinski, Diaries, 12 January 1985.
91 Krull, "Estonian Litrature."
92 Kaplinski, "Hinge Tagasi Kutsudes," 63.
93 Kaplinski, *Kajakas Võltsmunal*, 95.
94 Kaplinski, *Evening Brings Everything Back*, 20.
95 Daitz, *Ancient Song Recovered*, 60.
96 Tormis, *Jonni Pärast Heliloojaks*, 418.
97 Tormis, "Some problems with regilaul," Daitz, *Ancient Song Recovered*, 71, 76.
98 Daitz, *Ancient Song Recovered*, 48.
99 Ross and Lehiste, *Temporal Structure*, 15.
100 Kaplinski, "Jaan Kaplinski, Estonian Television."
101 Jullien, *Blandness*, 75.
102 Daitz, *Ancient Song Recovered*, 48.

103 Sarv, "Stichic and Stanzaic," 161–3.
104 Daitz, *Ancient Song Recovered*, 48.
105 Kaplinski, "Hinge Tagasi Kutsudes," 63.
106 Kõiv, "Nõnda lausus Jaan Kaplinski," 101.
107 Jaan Kaplinski in Raphaël Gianelli-Meriano, *The Kaplinski System* (trailer 2009).
108 Kaplinski, *Kõik on ime,* 219.
109 Kaplinski, *Paralleele ja parallelism*e, 20–2; Kaplinski, *Kõik on ime,* 219.
110 Ekelöf, *Songs of Something Else*, 71–4.
111 McCagney, *Nāgārjuna*, 29.
112 Snyder, "Language Goes Two Ways," 128.
113 Kaplinski, *Paralleele ja parallelism,* 22.
114 Kaplinski, *Kõik on ime,* 178.
115 Jaago, *Regilaulu poeetika*; Undusk, "Eesti regivärsi parallelism," 49.
116 Kaplinski, *Kõik on ime,* 203–7.
117 Kaplinski, "Tomas Tranströmerist."
118 Kaplinski, "*Paralleele ja parallelisme*, 63.
119 Kaplinski, *Ööd valged*, 13.
120 Kaplinski, *see ja teine*, 29.
121 Kaplinski and Grabbi, *Sõprade kirjad*, 224; Sarv, "Stichic and Stanzaic," 167–9.
122 Kaplinski, *Kõik on ime,* 419.
123 Ivar Ivask, "Eesti sõjajärgse luule arengusuunadest," (unpublished manuscript, Stockholm, 28 September 1968).
124 Kaplinski, "Olemise Kummaline Vaikus."
125 Kaplinski, *Paralleele ja parallelism*e, 63–4.
126 Kaplinski, "Soome-Ugri Keeled," 239.
127 Talvet, "millennium poetry," 206.
128 Kaplinski, *Paralleele ja parallelisme*; Kaplinski, "Paus"; "Ütles Masing."
129 Kaplinski, *Kõik on ime,* 128.
130 Jullien, *Detour and Access*, 332.
131 Ross and Lehiste, *Temporal Structure*, 13.
132 Kaplinski, *Kõik on ime,* 178.
133 Kaplinski, "Soome-Ugri Keeled," 238–9, Kaplinski, *Paralleele ja parallelism*e, 91.
134 Sallamaa, "Ethnofuturism."
135 Kádár, "Finno-Ugric Musicology."
136 Kaplinski, "Hinge Tagasi Kutsudes," 63; Kaplinski, *Paralleele ja parallelism*e, 91.
137 Kaplinski, *Through the Forest*, 38.

138 Krull, "Tagasi koju metafoori juurest." B12; Merilai, *Vokimeister*, 565–72.
139 Kaplinski, *Selected Poems*, 95. See also Meinhardt, "Illusionism in Painting," 135–51.
140 Sirr, "Jaan Kaplinski," 2012.
141 Kaplinski, *Selected Poems*, 145.
142 Kaplinski, *Isale*, 104; Kaplinski, "Võimaluste võimalikkus," 734.

Bibliography

Aarelaid-Tart, Aili and Tart, Indrek. "Culture and the Development of Civil Society." *Nationalities Papers* 23, no 1 (1995): 153–65.

Aarelaid-Tart, Aili. "Double Mental Standards in the Baltic Countries – Three Generations." In *The Baltic Countries Under Occupation: Soviet and Nazi Rule 1939–1991*, edited by Anu Mai Kõll, 215–28. Stockholm: Stockholm University Press, 2003.

Abram, Jan. *The Language of Winnicott: A Dictionary and Guide to Understanding His Work*. New Jersey: Jason Aronson Inc., 1997.

Allas, Tiia. "Kaplinski: eestlases elab edasi rahvuslik alaväärsustunne." *Koit* (4 November 1999): 6.

Alo, Ülo. "Tarud ja päike vanaisa aias." *Töörahva Elu,* 14 May 1973.

Annus, Epp et al. *Eesti Kirjanduslugu*. Tallinn: Koolibri, 2001.

Armstrong, Regis J., J.A. Wayne Hellmann and William J. Short, eds. *Francis of Assisi: The Saint*. New York: New City Press, 1999.

Asu-Ôunas, Ene. Introduction to *Kalivägi* by Kaljo Põllo. Oktoober: Tallinn, 1988.

Barnhill, David Landis and Roger S. Gottlieb, eds. *Deep Ecology and World Religions: New Essays on Sacred Ground*. New York: State University of New York Press, 2001.

Barrows, Anita. "The Ecopsychology of Child Development." In Roszak, *Ecopsychology,* 101–10.

Bartsch, Shadi and Thomas Bartscherer, eds. *Erotikon: Essays on Eros, Ancient, and Modern*. Chicago: University of Chicago Press, 2005.

Beier, Priidu. "J. Kaplinski lahkumine kultuurist." *Looming* 5 (1993): 700–3.

Berliner, Paul F. *Thinking in Jazz: The Infinite Art of Improvisation*. Chicago: University of Chicago Press, 2010.

Bertricau, A. (pseudonym), ed. *Eesti Identiteet ja Iseseisvus*. N.pl.: Avita, 2001.

Bloomsbury Review. "The Same Sea in Us All," 5 December 1985.

Bodian, Stephan. "Simple in Means, Rich in Ends. An Interview with Arne Naess." In *Deep Ecology for the Twenty-First Century*, edited by George Sessions, 26–36. Boston: Shambala, 1995.

Bollas, Christopher. "Normotic Illness." In *The Facilitating Environment: Clinical Applications of Winnicott's Theory*, edited by Gerard M. Fromm and Bruce L. Smith, 317–44. Madision: International University Press, 1989.

Buchloh, Benjamin H.D. "Richter's Abstraction: Gesture, Facture, Imprint." In *Gerhard Richter: Large Abstracts*, edited by Ulrich Wilmes, 9–17. Ostfildern: Hatje Cantz, 2008.

Buss, David M. *The Evolution of Desire: Strategies of Human Mating*. New York: Basic Books, 2003.

Caldwell, Lesley, ed. *Art, Creativity, Living*. New York: Karnac Books, 2000.

– *Sex and Sexuality, Winnicottian Perspectives*. New York: Karnac Books Ltd., 2005.

Campbell, Karen J. *German Mystical Writings*. New York: Continuum, 1991.

Camus, Albert. *The Myth of Sisyphus*. Translated by Justin O'Brien. London: Penguin, 2005.

Carson, Rachel. *Silent Spring: 40th Anniversary Edition*. New York: Mariner Books, 2002.

Chadwick, Charles. *Symbolism: The Critical Idioms*. London: Methuen & Co Ltd., 1971.

Ching-Yuen, Loy. *The Supreme Way: Inner Teachings of the Southern Mountain Tao*. Translated by Trevor Carolan and Du Liang. Berkeley: North Atlantic Books, 1997.

Claudel, Paul. *Knowing the East*. Trans. James Lawler. Princeton: Princeton University Press, 2004.

Cobb, John B. Jr. "Protestant Theology and Deep Ecology." In *Deep Ecology and World Religions,* edited by David Landis Barnhill and Roger S. Gottlieb, 213–28. Albany: State University of New York, 2001.

Cobley, Paul et al. eds. *Semiotics Continues to Astonish: Thomas A Sebeok and the Doctrine of Signs*. Berlin: De Gruyter Mouton, 2011.

Cohen, Stephen F. *Soviet Fates and Lost Alternatives: From Stalinism to the New Cold War*. New York: Columbia University Press, 2011.

Collins, Randall. *Violence. A Micro-sociological Theory*. Princeton: Princeton University Press, 2008.

"Constitution of the Union of Soviet Socialist Republics," 7 November 1977. http://departments.bucknell.edu/russian/const/77cons01.html#chap01. Accessed 23 May 2012.

Coupe, Laurence, ed. *The Green Studies Reader: From Romanticism to Ecocriticism*. New York: Routledge, 2000.

Cudworth, Erika. *Environment and Society*. Routledge Introductions to Environment Series. New York: Routledge, 2003.

Daitz, Mimi S. *Ancient Song Recovered: The Life and Music of Veljo Tormis*. Hillsdale: Pendragon Press, 2004.

Davies, Norman. *Rising '44: The Battle for Warsaw*. London: Macmillian, 2003.

Derrida, Jacques. *Monolingualism of the Other; or, The Prosthesis of Origin*. Stanford: Stanford University Press, 1998.

Devall, Bill and George Sessions. *Deep Ecology: Living as if Nature Mattered*. Salt Lake City: Peregrine Smith Books, 1985.

Dickens, Erik. "Ettevaatlik olemisest ja üle suure vee minemisest." *Sirp*, 22 March 1991: 1.

Doi, Takeo. *The Anatomy of Dependence: The Key Analysis of Japanese Behavior*. Translated by John Bester. New York: Kodansha International, 2001.

– *The Anatomy of Self: The Individual Versus Society*. New York: Kodansha International, 2001.

– *Understanding Amae: The Japanese Concept of Need–Love: Collected Papers of Twentieth-Century Japanese Writers on Japan*. Vol. 1. Folkestone: Global Oriental, 2005.

Drengson, Alan and Yuichi Inoue, eds. *The Deep Ecology Movement: An Introductory Anthology*. Berkeley: North Atlantic Books, 1995.

Drikkit, Ivi. "Jaan Kaplinski: mul on anne ebameeldivad asjad unustada." *Postimees Extra*, 26 February 1994: 2–3.

– "Jaan Kaplinski: tegemata asjade koorem ei anna mulle rahu" *Postimees Extra*, 8 April 1995: 3–4.

Ehin, Andres. " Eestlus mahub eurooplusse küll." *Postimees*, 3 July 1999: 7.

– "Kuuekümnendate aastate põlvkond eesti luules." *Mana* 50 (1982): 73–8.

– "Pihtimus: Mõtteid Jaan Kaplinski uut teost lugedes." *Nädaline* 13, 13 March 2004: 6–7.

– "Tolmust ja värvidest kõnelev luulemaailm." *Noorus*, 4 (1968): 18–19.

Ehrenfeld, David. *The Arrogance of Humanism*. Oxford: Oxford University Press, 1981.

Eilart, Jaan. "Eestlased Jüriöö radadel." *Järva Teataja*, 22 October 1991: 3.

– "Kaitsmas elu." *Edasi*, 6 May 1968: 3.

Eintalu, Jüri. "Ainetu mõtleja voi mõttetu ainleja." *Akadeemia* 9 (1993): 1996–2004.

Ekelöf, Gunnar. *Songs of Something Else: Selected Poems of Gunnar Ekelöf*. Translated by Leonard Nathan and James Larson. New Jersey: Princeton University Press, 1982.

Eliade, Mircea. *Shamanism: Archaic Techniques of Ecstasy*. Translated by Willard R. Trask. New Jersey: Princeton University Press, 1974.

Elias, Norbert. *The Civilizing Process: The History of Manners and State Formation and Civilization*. Translated by Edmund Jephcott. Oxford: Blackwell Publishers, 1994.

Estniska Dagbladet 93, Stockholm, 10 December 1980: 2.

Falk, Barbara J. *The Dilemmas of Dissidence in East-Central Europe: Citizen Intellectuals and Philosopher Kings*. Budapest: Central European University Press, 2003.

– "Resistance and Dissent in Central and Eastern Europe. An Emerging Historiography." *East European Politics & Society* 25, no 2 (2011): 318–60.

Ferber, Michael, ed. *The Poetry of Shelley*. London: Penguin Books, 1993.

Franks, Alan. "London Hearing for Poet of Estonian Nationalism." *The Times*, 12 April 1990.

Freud, Sigmund. *Civilization and Its Discontents*, second edition. New York: Norton, 1989.

Fromm, Gerard M. and Bruce L. Smith. *The Facilitating Environment: Clinical Applications of Winnicott's Theory*. Madison: International Universities Press, 1989.

Frye, Northrop. *The Educated Imagination*. Toronto: House of Anansi Press, 1993.

Funk, Karlo. "Erapooletuse poolt." *Looming* 11 (1998): 1757–60.

Garrard, Greg. *Ecocriticism: The New Critical Idiom*. New York: Routledge, 2005.

Gianelli-Meriano, Raphaël. *The Kaplinski System*. France: Eaux Vives Productions and Estonia: Allfilm, 2012.

Gill, Jo and Melanie Waters. "Poetry and Autobiography." *Life Writing* 6, vol 1 (2009): 1–9.

Givens, David. *Love Signals: A Practical Field Guide to the Body Language of Courtship*. New York: St. Martin's Press, 2005.

Glotfelty, Cheryll and Harold Fromm, eds. *The Ecocriticism Reader: Landmarks in Literary Ecology.* Athens: University of Georgia Press, 1996.

Godfrey, Stephen. "Celebrated Estonian poet a reluctant prophet." *Globe and Mail*, 4 February 1988.

Goetz-Stankiewicz, Marketa. *Good-bye, Samizdat: Twenty Years of Czechoslovak Underground Writing.* Evanston: Northwestern University Press, 1992.

Grabbi, Hellar. "Eesti esindusluulest." In *Tulgu uus taevas: Mõtteid viiekümnest kirjanikust*, 240–2. Tallinn: Virgela, 1999.

– "For a New Heaven and a New Earth: Comments on the Poetry of Jaan Kaplinski." *Books Abroad* 47, no 4 (1973): 658–63.

– "Jaan Kaplinski 'Neljakuningapäev.'" *Mana* 53 (1984): 50–5.

– "Kolmnurk muutus nelinurgaks." *Mana* 1–2 (1965): 69–70.

Gross, Toomas. "Jaan Kaplinski 'see ja teine:' antropoloogilisi tähelepanekuid." *Vikerkaar* 4/5 (1997): 154–65.

Grumbach, Doris. "The Review." *Small Press* 3, no 3 (1986): 23–6.

Grünthal, Ivar. "Sähvatavad pinnad." *Mana* 1 (1968): 123–5.

Guenther, Herbert V. *Treasures on the Tibetan Middle Way.* The Clear Light Series. Berkeley: Shambala Publications Inc., 1971.

Gurian, Jay P., and Julia M. Gurian. *The Dependency Tendency: Returning to Each Other in Modern America.* New York: University Press of America, 1983.

Hallamish, Moshe. *An Introduction to the Kabbalah.* Translated by Ruth Bar-Ilan and Ora Wiskind-Elper. New York: State University of New York Press, 1999.

Hamill, Sam. Introduction to *Jaan Kaplinski: The Same Sea in Us All.* Portland: Breitenbush, 1985. xiii–xv.

– "Sisyphus." http://www.best-poems.net/sam_hamill/sisyphus.html. Accessed 10 May 2012.

Hamilton, Paul. *Percy Bysshe Shelley.* Horndon, England: Northcote House Publishers, 2000.

Hanson, Allan F. *The Trouble with Culture: How Computers are Calming the Culture Wars.* Albany: State University of New York Press, 2007.

Harner, Michael. *The Way of the Shaman.* San Francisco: Harper, 1990.

Harvey, Peter. *An Introduction to Buddhist Ethics.* Cambridge: Cambridge University Press, 2000.

Haug, Toomas. "Eesti prosa 1999. Väike teejuht." *Looming* 3 (2000): 430.

– "Jaan Kaplinski koht eesti mõttekultuuris." 2 August 2000. n.pl.

– "Kaplinski, ökoloogia- ja dualismikurat." *Eesti Ekspress (Areen)*, 30 May 1997: B2.
– "Pilk eesti luuleilma 1984." *Looming* 3 (1985): 394–5.
Havel, Václav. "Anti-Political Politics." In *Civil Society and the State. New European Perspectives,* edited by John Keane, 381–98. London: Verso, 1988.
– "Second Wind." In *Good-bye, Samizdat. Twenty Years of Czechoslovak Underground Writing,* edited by Marketa Goetz-Stankiewicz, 205–10. Evanston: Northwestern University Press, 1992.
– "The Power of the Powerless." In *The Power of the Powerless. Citizens against the state in central-eastern Europe*, edited by John Keane, 23–96. Armonk: M. E. Sharpe, 1985.
Hellat, Henn-Kaarel. "Etüüd rikkast tundeihnurist." *Sirp ja Vasar,* 19 January 1973: 3.
– "Kes tajub tõeluse puudutust ..." *Keel ja Kirjandus* 11 (1973): 684–6.
– "Kõigel on kõigega seos." *Kirjanduse jaosmaa '85*, edited by Endel Mallene, 123–7. Tallinn: Eesti Raamat. 1987.
Hellerma, Kärt. "Ärkamine inimese mõõtmest." *Keel ja Kirjandus* 11 (1998): 776–8.
Hennoste, Märt. *Väike eesti kirjanduslugu: IX klassi õpik-lugemik.* Tallinn: Koolibri, 1997: 385–7.
– "Eurooplaseks saamine ja kolonialismi vaim." *Eesti Ekspress,* 28 June 2007. http://www.ekspress.ee. Accessed 10 March 2007.
Hennoste, Tiit. "Postkolonialism ja eesti. Väga väike leksikon." *Vikerkaar* 4–5 (2003): 85–100.
Hinrikus, Rutt and Kronberg, Janika. "Short Outlines of Books by Estonian Authors." *Estonian Literary Magazine* 8 (Spring) (1999): 29–30.
Hint, Mati. "Õnnetus läks napilt mööda." *Eesti Päevaleht,* 23 October 1996: 7.
Holmes, Richard, ed. *Shelley on Love, An Anthology.* Berkeley: University of California Press, 1980.
Honko, Lauri, Senni Timonen, Michael Branch and Keith Bosley eds. *The Great Bear: A Thematic Anthology of Oral Poetry in the Finno-Ugrian Languages*. Pieksämäki: The Raamattutalo Press, 1993.
Ilves, Thomas. "Estonia in 1984." 17 December 1984. Open Society Archives 300-8-3: 89-1-7. http://www.osaarchivum.org/files/holdings/300/8/3/text/89-1-7.shtml. Accessed 21 January 2012.
Ingerman, Sandra. *Soul Retrieval: Mending the Fragmented Self.* San Francisco: Harper Collins Publishers, 1991.

Ivask, Ivar. "Jaan Kaplinski. Raske on kergeks saada." *Mana* 53 (1984): 81.
– "Jaan Kaplinski. *Ma vaatasin päikese aknasse.*" *World Literature Today* 51, no 4 (1977): 651–2.
– "Jaan Kaplinski. Raske on kergeks saada." *World Literature Today* 58, no 1 (1984): 134–5.
– "Jaan Kaplinski. Tolmust ja värvidest." *Books Abroad* 42, no 1 (1968): 159–60.

Jaago, Tiiu and Ülo Valk, eds. *Kust tulid lood minule ....* Tartu: Tartu Ülikooli Kirjastus, 2000.

Jaago, Tiiu. *Regilaulu poeetika.* Tartu 1998. http://haldjas.folklore.ee/UTfolkl/loengud/poeetika. Accessed 7 January 2002.

Jaago, Tiu and Mari Sarv. *Regilaul – keel, muusika, poeetika.* Tartu: Kirjandusmuuseum, 2001.

Jaaksoo, Andres. "Kaplinski, Jaan." In *Kes on kes ja mis on mis eesti lastekirjanduses,* edited by Andres Jaaksoo, 83. Tallinn: Eesti Raamat, 1987.

Jaanus, Maire. "Estonia and Pain: Jaan Kross' The Czar's Madman." In *Baltic Postcolonialism*, edited by Violeta Kelertas, 309–29. Rodopi: Amsterdam, 2006.

Jaks, Ilmar. "Teisitimõtleja Jaan Kaplinski." *Looming* 7 (1998): 1132–4.

James, Judi. *Sex Signals: Decode Them and Send Them.* London: Judy Piatkus Publishers Ltd., 2003.

Jannsen, Johann Woldemar. "Veel natuke Tallinna laulo pidust." *Perno Postimees* 14, 2 October 1857: 109–11.

Järg, Tiia. "Veljo Tormise ja Jaan Kaplinski kantaat-kollaazist 'Sünnisõnad'" *Teater. Muusika. Kino.* 12 (1999): 66–7.

Jensen, Derrick. *How Shall I Live My Life? On Liberating the Earth from Civilization.* Oakland: PM Press, 2008.

Jirgens, Karl E. "Carnival of Death: Writing in Latvia Since Independence." *World Literature Today* 72, no 2 (1998): 269–81.

Jõerüüt, Jaak. "Luuleaasta tunnetusi." *Looming* 3 (1977): 493–4, 502.

Jõgi, Mall. "Tagasivaateid veebruarikuisesse Calgarysse." *Sirp ja Vasar,* 22 April 1988: 10.

Johnson, Frank A. *Dependency and Japanese Socialization, Psychoanalytic and Anthropological Investigations into Amae.* New York: New York University Press, 1993.

Jullien, François. *A Treatise on Efficacy. Between Western and Chinese Thinking.* Translated by Janet Lloyd. Honolulu: University of Hawai'i Press, 2004.
– *Detour and Access. Strategies of Meaning in China and Greece.* Translated by Sophie Hawkes. New York: Zone Books, 2000.

– *In Praise of Blandness. Proceeding from Chinese Thought and Aesthetics*. Translated by Paula M. Varanso. New York: Zone Books, 2008.
– *The Propensity of Things. Toward a History of Efficacy in China*. Translated by Janet Lloyd. New York: Zone Books, 1999.
Jürisson, Helvi. "Valgest joonest Võrumaa kohal." *Looming* 3 (1973): 515–17.
Jűrjo, Indrek. *Pagulus ja Nõukogude Eesti*. Tallinn: Umara, 1996.
Kaagjärv, Leo. "Emakeelt peab kaitsma." *Sõnumileht*, 21 June 1996: 15.
Kaalep, Ain. "Avatud luule." In *Kirjanduse jaosmaa '76* edited by Endel Mallene, 211–13. Tallinn: Eesti Raamat. 1978.
– "Kust eksib lapse naeratus kuningakotta?" *Looming* 12 (1967): 1912–15.
– *Kolm Lydiat*. Tartu: Ilmamaa, 1997.
Kádár, György. "Is There a Reason for the Existence of an Independent Finno-Ugric Musicology? A Cognitive Approach to the Compound Nature of Finno-Ugric Music Cultures." http://www.folklore.ee/folklore/vol23/compound.pdf. Accessed 2 February 2011.
Kala, Martin, ed. *Eesti müütoloogiad*. Arvamusring Tänase Eesti Teemadel.Tallinn: Tallinna Raamatutrükikoda, 2008.
Kalda, Maie. "Neli uut." *Keel ja Kirjandus* 9 (1965): 562–5.
Kalkun, Andreas. "Rahvaluulekoguja kui looja. Seto pärimuse representeerimisest Jakob Hurda 'Setukeste lauludes.'" In *Regilaul – esitus ja tõlgendus: Eesti Rahvaluule Arhiivi Toimetused*, edited by Aado Lintrop, 67–84. Eesti Kirjandusmuuseum: Tartu, 2006.
Kaplinski, Jaan. "Ain Kaalep ja alternatiivne ülikool." *Sõnumileht*, 4 June 1996: 14.
– "Alistumise ja leppimise aeg." *Postimees*, 12 September 1998: 7.
– "Aukartus elu ees." *In Teooria ja mudelid eluteaduses*. Tartu: ENSV TA, 1984. 235–9.
– "Avatusest ja armastusest." *Sirp ja Vasar* 26, 27 June 1980: 6–7.
– "Definitions. Estonian poet Jaan Kaplinski refuses to be categorized." *The Guardian*, 1 May 2004. http://.www.guardian.co.uk/books/2004/may/01/featuresreviews.guardianreview27. Accessed 26 May 2012.
– "Eesti on kaugenenud oma juurtest ja maailmast." Valle-Sten Maiste, *Sirp* 3, 20 January 2011. http://www.sirp.ee. Accessed 22 January 2011.
– "Estonia Between Two Worlds – Geopolitics and Culture." In *The Baltic States as New Actors in the Nearby Environment*, edited by R. Grönick, L. Koskinen and I. Fjuk, 12–17. Tallinn: Tallinna Raamatutrükikoda, 1994.

– "Estonia: A home named Tammiku." *Index on Censorship* 33, no 3 (2004): 140–7.
– "Estonia." *The Guardian*, 26 May 2004. http://www.guardian.co.uk/world/2004/apr/26/eu.politics6. Accessed 29 May 2012.
– *Evening Brings Everything Back*. Tarset: Bloodaxe Books, 2004.
– "Filosoofia ja vaikus." *Sirp*, 19 September 1997: 5.
– "From Harem to Brothel." *Eurozine*, 30 June 2007. http://www.eurozine.com/articles/2007-06-30-kaplinski-en.html. Accessed 28 May 2012.
– "Globalization: for nature or against nature." Eurozine, 2 November 2003. http://www.eurozine.com/articles/2003-02-11-kaplinski-en.html. Accessed 21 March 2012.
– "Haige Geenius." *Maaleht*, 5 August 1999: 8.
– "Hävitatud templid." *Eesti Ekspress*, 7 September 2000: B4.
– "Hiina vastupandamata võlu." *Keel ja Kirjandus* 4 (1995): 271–2.
– "Hinge Tagasi Kutsudes." *Teater. Muusika. Kino.* 12 (1999): 62–5. ["Birth charms," jaan.kaplinski.com/philosophy/Spells of Birth.html].
– "*Hinge Tagasitulek. Poeem.* Tallinn: Eesti Raamat, 1990.
– *I Am the Spring in Tartu and Other Poems Written in English.* Vancouver: Laurel Press, 1991.
– "Intervjuu Jaan Kaplinskiga." *Loodus.* (November 2000). http://www.loodusajakiri.ee. Accessed 20 March 2012.
– "Introduction." In *Täiskuutaeva All. Valimik hiina ja jaapani luulet,* 7–15. Tallinn: Perioodika, 1985.
– *Isale*. Tallinn: Varrak, 2003.
– "Jää ja Kanarbik." *Looming* 11 (1989): 1443–57.
– *Jää…* n.pl.: Võluri Tagasitulek n.d. [2009].
– "Jaan Kaplinski Hiina puhvaika ja Vene viltidega Eesti talves." Margus Mikomägi. *Maaleht,* 1 October 2010. http:// www.maaleht.ee. Accessed 28 March 2012.
– "Jaan Kaplinski maailm algab Mutikult." Rein Veidemann, *Arter*, 17 August 2002: 24.
– "Jaan Kaplinski pageb Eesti riigi eest metsa." Andrus Esko. *SL Õhtuleht,* 21 October 2001: 16–17.
– "Jaan Kaplinski pages juubeliks Itaaliasse." *SL Õhtuleht*, 22 January 2001: 11.
– "Jaan Kaplinski." *ETV* [Estonian Television] (1991).
– "Jaan Kaplinski." *Keel ja Kirjandus* 11 (1973): 684–86.
– *Jäljed Allikal.* Tallinn: Eesti Raamat, 1965.
– *Kajakas Võltsmunal.* Tallinn: Vagabund, 2000.

– *Kalad Punuvad Pesi*. Tallinn: Kunstiinstituut, 1966.
– *Kalivägi*. In Põllo.
– *Käoraamat: Luulet 1956–1980*. Tallinn: Eesti Raamat, 1986.
– "*Kevad Kahel Rannikul: ehk tundeline teekond Ameerikasse*. Tallinn: Vagabund, 2000.
– *Kirjutatud. Valitud luuletused*. Tallinn: Varrak, 2000.
– "Kirves ja puu." *Edasi*, 15 December 1972: 1.
– *Kõik on ime*. Edited by Thomas Salumets. Tartu: Ilmamaa, 2004.
– "Kultuurifilosoof Loorits ja tema sõnum." *Eesti Ekspress*, 16 November 2000: B8–9.
– "Kultuurimõjud ja kultuurimured." *Keel ja Kirjandus* 3 (1983): 149–51.
– *Kust Tuli Öö*. Tallinn: Eesti Raamat, 1990.
– *Lahkujad*. Tallinn: Tänapäev, 2009.
– "Laulude sünnimailt." In *Teose sünd*, edited by Endel Priidel. 108–17. Tallinn: Eesti Raamat. 1976.
– *Ma vaatasin päikese aknasse: Luulet*. Tallinn: Eesti Raamat, 1976.
– "Mitte keskkond, vaid loodus." *Maaleht*, 3 January 2003. http://www.maaleht.ee. Accessed 8 March 2003.
– *Mitu suve ja kevadet*. Tallinn: Vagabund, 1995.
– "Mõeldes Noor-Eestile." *Keel ja Kirjandus* 7 (2005): 574–5.
– "Mõni sõna ühest isemoodi antoloogiast." *Keel ja Kirjandus* 7 (1970): 438–40.
– "Mõtisklusi inimkultuurist ja ökosüsteemidest." Eesti *Loodus* 7 (1973): 443–7; 8 (1973): 502–8; 9 (1973): 569–74.
– "Mõttevahetus." In A. Bertricau. *Eesti Identiteet ja Iseseisvus*, 152–64.
– *Õhtu toob tagasi kõik*. Tallinn: Eesti Raamat, 1985.
– "Ökoloogia ja ökonoomika." In *See ja teine*, 46–73.
– "Olemise Avar ja Kummaline Vaikus: Essee Lao-Zist." *Sirp ja Vasar*, 29 February 1980, 7 March 1980, 14 March 1980.
– "Olla eurooplased, saada indiaanlasteks." *Eesti Ekspress*, 3 August 2000: B5.
– *Ööd Valged Ja Mustad*. With Johannes Salminen. Tallinn: Perioodika, 2003.
– *Öölinnud, Öömõtted. Yölintuja, Yöajatuksia. Night Birds, Night Thoughts*. Luuletusi 1995–1997. Tallinn: Vagabund, 1998.
– "Ornitofilosoofia: Ronk Nestori märkmeid." *Looming* 4 (2004): 491–508. *Looming* 5 (2004): 683–700.
– *Paralleele ja parallelisme*. Tartu: Tartu Ülikooli Kirjastus, 2009.
– "Parallelismist Lingvisti Pilguga." In *Kõik on Ime*, 125–46.

– "Pärandus ja pärijad." *Sirp ja Vasar*, 28 February 1969: 3. In Daitz, *Ancient Song Recovered*, 60–2.
– "Paus." *Looming* 1 (2011): 10–38.
– "Pessmisti mõtteid kultuuritõkestamisest." *Eesti Päevaleht. Arkaadia*, 5 November 2005: 4–5.
– *Poliitika Ja Antipoliitika*. Tallinn: Olion, 1992.
– "Putukad ja inimesed." In *See ja teine*, 118–32.
– "Rahvalaulu juurde jõudmine" (1970–72). In *Kõik on Ime*, 158–91.
– *Raske on kergeks saada*. Tallinn: Eesti Raamat, 1982.
– "Refleksid ja isiksused." *Sirp ja Vasar*, 6 February 1970: 5.
– "Roheline Buddha." In *Kajakas Võltsmunal*, 152–5.
– "Saateks." *Laozi Daodejing*, 93–125.Tallinn: Vagabund, 2001.
– "Sauna taga tiigi ääres." *Eesti Ekspress (Areen)*, 30 May 1997: B1.
– *See ja teine*. Tartu: Tartu Ülikooli Kirjastus, 1996.
– *Seesama Jõgi*. Tallinn: Vagabund, 2007.
– *Selected Poems*. Translated by Jaan Kaplinski with Sam Hamill, Hildi Hawkins, Fiona Sampson. Tarset: Bloodaxe Books, 2011.
– "Semiootika suvekoolist Käärikul." *Keel ja Kirjandus* 12 (1964): 764–5.
– *Sõnad Sõnatusse*. Tallinn: Vagabund, 2005.
– "Soome-Ugri Keeled ja Filosoofia." *Looming* 2 (2002): 231–48.
– *Sõprade kirjad on su poole teel*. With Hellar Grabbi. *Jaan Kaplinski ja Hellar Grabbi kirjavahetus: 1965–1991*. Edited by Sirje Olesk. Litteraria. Tartu: Eesti Kirjandusmuuseum, 2013.
– "Tarbimisühiskond tarbimisühiskonna vastu." *Eesti Päevaleht*, 1 March 2005. http://www.epl.ee. Accessed 3 April 2012.
– "Tarku valitsejaid on harva." *Maaleht*, 29 June 2012. http://www.maaleht.ee/news/uudised/elu/jaan-kaplinski-tarku-valitsejaid-on-harva.d?id=64601900. Accessed 29 June 2012.
– *Teekond Ayia Triadasse*. Tartu: Greif, 1993.
– *Teiselpool järve*. Tallinn: Tänapäev, 2008.
– *Teispool Sinist Taevast*. Tallinn: Ajakirjade Kirjastus, 2009.
– Texts to reproductions by Kaljo Põllo. In *Kalivägi*. Tallinn: Kunst, 1988
– *The Same River*. Translated by Susan Wilson. London: Peter Owen, 2009.
– *The Same Sea in Us All*. Translated by Jaan Kaplinski with Sam Hamill. Portland: Breitenbush Books, 1985.
– *The Wandering Border*. Translated by Jaan Kaplinski with Sam Hamill and Riina Tamm. Port Townsend: Copper Canyon Press, 1987.
– *Through The Forest*. Translated by Hildi Hawkins. London: Harvill, 1996.

– *Tolmust Ja Värvidest*. Loomingu Raamatukogu 24. Tallinn: Perioodika, 1967.
– "Tomas Tranströmer and the Mach Principle." *World Literature Today* 64, no 4 (1990): 601–4.
– "Tomas Tranströmerist." *Sirp*, 13 October 2011. http:// www.sirp.ee. Accessed 29 November 2011.
– "Tüdimusest ja rikkusest." *Looming* 9 (1968): 1425–6.
– *Tükk Elatud Elu. Tekste 1986–1989*. Tartu: Kostabi, 1991.
– *Tule tagasi helmemänd*. Tallinn: Eesti Raamat, 1984.
– "Uku Masing ja maailmarevolutsioon." *Eesti Ekspress*, 12 August 1999: B12–13.
– *Usk on Uskmatus*. Tallinn: Vagabund, 1998.
– "Ütles Masing." *Vikerkaar* 1–2 (2012): 74–98.
– *Uute Kivide Kasvamine*. Tallinn: Eesti Raamat, 1977.
– *Vaikus Saab Värvideks*. Tallinn: Tänapäev, 2006.
– *Valge Joon Võrumaa Kohale. 54 luuletust 1967–1968*. Tallinn: Eesti Raamat, 1972.
– "Vanu viise uuel kandlel." *Noorus* 2 (1972): 43.
– "Vasakpoolne Uku Masing." *Maaleht*, 26 August 1994.
– "Vercingetorix kõneleb ordumeistriga." *Kultuurimaa* (11 September 1996): 3.
– "Võimaluste võimalikkus, keel." *Looming* 5 (1969): 734–41.
– *Võimaluste Võimalikkus*. Tallinn: Vagabund, 1997.
Kapuściński, Ryszard. *Travels with Herodotus*. New York: Vintage, 2007.
Kelertas, Violeta, ed. *Baltic Postcolonialism*. Amsterdam: Rodopi, 2006.
Kern, Robert. "Silence in Prosody: The Poem as Silent Form." In *Critical Essays on Gary Snyder*, edited by Patrick D. Murphy, 105–22. Boston: G.K. Hall, 1991.
Kesküla, Kalev. "Avalik ja vastaline intellektuaal." *Eesti Ekspress*, 16 February 2004. http://Paber.ekspress.ee. Accessed 24 March 2008.
– "Kaplinski ja viinakurat." *Eesti Ekspress*, 30 May 1997: B3.
Kiin, Sirje and Rein Ruutsoo, Andres Tarand. *40 kirja lugu*. Tallinn: Olion, 1990.
Kiin, Sirje. "All you need is love." *Looming* 8 (1983): 1138–41.
Kiis, Jüri. "Tulevalgus või uinutav palderjanitilk? Veel kord uuemast luulest." *Sirp ja Vasar*, 17 January 1986: 5.
Kiossev, Alexander. "The Self-Colonizing Metaphor." In *Atlas of Transformation* (2011). http://monumenttotransformation.org/atlas-of-transformation/html/s/self-colonization/the-self-colonizing-metaphor-alexander-kiossev.html. Accessed 6 March 2013.

Kirby, David. *The Baltic World 1772–1993: Europe's Northern Periphery in an Age of Change*. London: Longman Group Limited, 1995.
Kirss, Tiina, Ene Kõresaar and Marju Lauristin, eds. *She Who Remembers Survives. Interpreting Estonian Women's Post-Soviet Life Stories*. Tartu: Tartu University Press, 2004.
Kitching, Laurence P.A. "In the spirit of independence: Jaan Kaplinski's *Vercingetorix ütles* – Classical sources and metaphorical interpretations." *Journal of Baltic Studies* 19, no 4 (1988): 335–50.
Kivisildnik, Sven. "Aukartus ees, maaharimine järel." *Postimees*, 16 January 1997: 19.
Klíma, Ivan. *The Spirit of Prague*. London: Penguin Books, 1994.
Kodumaa, 26 March 1986: 5–6.
Kõiv, Madis. "Nõnda lausus Jaan Kaplinski." *Keel ja Kirjandus* 1 (2000): 73–101.
Kõll, Anu Mai. *The Baltic Countries Under Occupation. Soviet and Nazi Rule 1939–1991*. Stockholm: Acta Universitatis Stockholmiensis, 2003.
Krikmann, Arvo and Sirje Olesk, eds. *Võim & Kultuur*. Tartu: Kirjandusmuuseum, 2003.
Kronberg, Janika. "Jaan Kaplinski eksootikat ületamas." *Postimees*, 4 November 1995: 13.
– "Kas Jaan Kaplinski on olemas?" *Keel ja Kirjandus* 6 (1992): 376–7.
– "Short Outlines of Books by Estonian Authors." *Estonian Literary Magazine* 12 Spring (2001). http://www.einst.ee. Accessed 10 April 2008.
Kross, Jaan. *The Czar's Madman*. Translated by Anselm Hollo. New York: Pantheon, 1993.
Krull, Hasso. "All you need is kõlblus." *Katkestuse kultuur*. Tallinn: Vagabund, 1996. 104–6.
– "Estonian Literature 1990–1995." *Estonian Literary Magazine* 4 (1997). http://old.estinst.ee/historic/literary/spring97/. Accessed 14 June 2012.
– "Jaan Kaplinski: teine ja pööratav aeg: 1." *Vikerkaar* 1 (1991): 49–52.
– "Jaan Kaplinski: teine ja pööratav aeg: 2." *Vikerkaar* 2 (1991): 81–3.
– "Kaplinski liikumine." *Vikerkaar* 7 (1996): 78–82.
– "Mic contract of a crazy motherfucker: Kaplinski räppimas." *Vikerkaar* 7 (1992): 82–7.
– "Tagasi koju metafoori juurest." *Eesti Ekspress (Areen)*, 4 March 1999: B12.
Kruus, Oskar. "Meie luuleankeet" *Sirp ja Vasar*, 2 April 1965: 3.
– *Eesti kirjarahva leksikon*. Tallinn: Eesti Raamat, 1995. 181–3.

Kukk, Mare. "Political Opposition in Soviet Estonia 1940–1987." *Journal of Baltic Studies* 24, no 4 (1993): 369–84.

Kuldkepp, Mart. "The Scandinavian Connection in Early Estonian Nationalism." *Journal of Baltic Studies* 44, no 3 (2013): 313–38.

Kull, Kalevi. "Jää pärast." In Jaan Kaplinski. *Jää…*, 197–213. n.pl.: Võluri Tagasitulek n.d. [2009].

– "Mõistuse ökoloogia." *Vikerkaar* 4/5 (1997): 165–8.

Kulmar, Tarmo. ""Liblikas ja peegel" Pärnus." *Pärnu Kommunist*, 31 March 1982: 3.

Kundera, Milan. "The Tragedy of Central Europe." *New York Review of Books* 31, no 7 (26 April 1984).

– *The Curtain. Essays in Seven Parts*. New York: Harper, 2008.

Kurrik, Juhan. Ilomaile. *Anthology of Estonian Folksongs with Translations and Commentary*. Scarborough: Maarjamaa, 1985.

Kuus, Merje. "Intellectuals and geopolitics: The 'cultural' politicians of Central Europe," *Geoforum* 38 (2007): 241–51.

– "Ubiquitous Identities and Elusive Subjects: Puzzles from Central Europe." *Transactions of the Institute of British Geographers* 32 (2007): 90–101.

Kuusk, Külliki. "Uku Masing: Stretching the Borders," *Elm Magazine* 28 (2009). http://elm.estinst.ee/issue/28/. Accessed 4 August 2013.

Laar, Mart, ed. *14. Juuni 1941*. Stockholm: Välis Eesti, 1990.

Labi, Kanni. "Isamaalaulud ja okupatsioonirežiim – nostalgia, utoopia ja reaalsus." *Methis* 7 (2011): 109–121.

Laht, Uno. "Kasseti katsikul." *Looming* 5 (1965): 785–91.

– "Miks tasub armastada Kaplinskit." *Looming* 1 (1991): 110–12.

Lange, Anne. "Transnational Consciousness and National Identity: A Case Study of Ants Oras." *Thresholds of Interpretation. Crossing the Boundaries of Literary Criticism*, edited by Markku Lehtimäki and Julia Tofantsuk, 89–103. TLÜ Kirjastus: Tallinn, 2006.

Langemets, Andres. "Kaheksanda kümnendi esimese poole eesti luulest." *Looming* 6 (1986): 813.

– "Kai Pu Lini luulepäevik." *Looming* 2 (1996): 273–4.

– "Kaplinski kui Voltaire või vana kreeklane." *Eesti Päevaleht*, 4 June 2004. epl.delfi.ee/news/kultuur/kaplinski-kui-voltaire-voi-vana-kreeklane.d?id=50985684. Accessed 20. November 2013.

– "Neli kuningat näitejuhtimise meelevallas." *Teater. Muusika. Kino.* 10 (1987): 32–6.

– "Tule tagasi, tõelus!" *Sirp ja Vasar* (5 April 1985): 4–5.

Laugaste, Eduard, ed. *Eesti Rahvaluuleteaduse Ajalugu*. Valitud Tekste ja Pilte. I–II. Tallinn: Eesti Riiklik Kirjastus, 1963–1980.

Laulik, Heino. "See maailm sind peab kandma ja sina pead kandma maailma." *Kodumaa*, 26 March 1986: 5–6.

Laur, Mati, *et al. History of Estonia*. Tallinn: Avita, 1997.

Lauristin, Marju and Peeter Vihalemm, et al., eds. *Return to the Western World: Cultural and Political Perspectives on the Estonian Post-Communist Transition*. Tartu: Tartu University Press, 1997.

Lehiste, Ilse. "Kahe uue luuletuskogu vormist ja sisust." *Mana* 1 (1968): 95–9.

– *Keel Kirjanduses*. Tartu: Ilmamaa, 2000.

Lehtimäki, Markku and Julia Tofantšuk. *Thresholds of Interpretation. Crossing the Boundaries in Literary Criticism*. Tallinn: TLÜ, 2006.

Lendvai, Paul. *One Day that Shook the Communist World. The 1956 Hungarian Uprising and its Legacy*. Princeton: Princeton University Press, 2008.

Lermontov, Mikhail. *Major Poetical Works*. Translated by Anatoly Liberman. Minneapolis: University of Minneapolis Press, 1983.

Lias, Pärt. *Eesti kirjandus. Õpik XII klassile*. Tallinn: Koolibri, 1996. 57–9.

– "'Looming' linnulennult" *Sirp ja Vasar*, 4 August 1972: 3.

Liiv, Toomas. "Kaplinski: filoloogi võimalused ja võimalikkus." *Looming* 5 (1998): 802–3.

Lintrop, Aado, ed. *Regilaul – esitus ja tõlgendus*. Tartu: Kirjandusmuuseum, 2006.

Liulevičius, Vejas Gabriel. *The German Myth of the East. 1800 to the Present*. Oxford: Oxford University Press, 2009.

Lõhmus, Aivo. "Jaan Kaplinski 'Tule tagasi helmemänd.'" *Edasi* 16, no 3 (1985): 5.

– "Kaks Kaplinskit." *Hommikuleht* (12 March 1993): 10.

Lõhmus, Ele. "Jaan Kaplinski (sünd. 1941)" *Eesti kirjandus XII klassile*. Tallinn: Valgus, 1989. 56–7. *London Times*, 15 January 1981: 8.

Loorits, Oskar. *Meie, eestlased*. Tartu: Ilmamaa, 2000.

Lotman, Juri. "On the semiosphere." Translated by Wilma Clark. *Sign Systems Studies* 33, no 1 (2005): 205–29.

Luhaäär, Ingvar. *Nii õpetas Uku Masing*. Intuitiivteaduste Kool: Tallinn, 2003.

Luik, Viivi. *Seitsmes Rahukevad*. Tallinn: Eesti Raamat, 1985.

Lukas, Liina. "Estonian Folklore as a Source of German-Baltic Poetry." *Journal of Baltic Studies* 42, no 4 (2011): 491–510.

– "The shifting position of German literature in Estonia: from adapted literature to translated literature." *Forum for World Literature Studies* 4, no 3 (2012): 358–69.

MacIntyre, Carlyle Ferren, ed. *French Symbolist Poetry*. Translated by Carlyle Ferren MacIntyre. Berkeley: University of California Press, 1964.

Mack, John E. "The Politics of Species Arrogance." *Ecopsychology*, edited by Theodore Roszak, Mary Gomes, Allen Kanner. 279–87. Sierra Club: San Francisco, 1995.

Mäger, Mart. "Luule ja maailm ühes luuletuses." *Keel ja Kirjandus* 4 (1985): 201–8.

Maiste, Valle-Sten. "Õhtumaise vaimu enesekriitika." *Postimees (Arter),* 18 March 2000.

Mallene, Endel. "Jaan Kaplinskit lugedes." *Noorte Hääl*, 4 April 1965: 2.

– "Kaks intellektuaali omavahel ja endamisi." *Looming* 3 (1991): 425–46.

Mandelker, Amy. "Semiotizing the Sphere: Organicist Theory in Lotman, Bakhtin, and Vernadsky." *PMLA* 109, no 3 (1994): 385–96.

Martin, Julia. "The Pattern which Connects: Metaphor in Gary Snyder's Later Poetry." In *Critical essays on Gary Snyder*, edited by Patrick D. Murphy, 188–210. Boston: G.K. Hall, 1991.

Masing, Uku. *Eesti usund*. Tartu: Ilmamaa, 1998.

– *Haikud*. Jaapani luulet Uku Masingu tõlkes. Tartu: Ilmamaa, 1997.

– *Keelest ja meelest*. Tartu: Ilmamaa, 2004.

– *Mälestusi taimedest*. Tartu: Ilmamaa, 1996.

– *Meil on lootust*. Tartu: Ilmamaa, 1998.

– *Pessimismi põhjendus*. Tartu: Ilmamaa, 1995.

– *Tankad*. Jaapani luulet Uku Masingu tõlkes. Tartu: Ilmamaa, 1997.

Mattheus, Ülo. "Ärge uskuge Jaan Kaplinskit." *Sirp*, 6 March 1992: 2.

Maurois, André. *Ariel, A Shelley Romance*. Translated by Ella D'Arcy. London: Penguin Books, 1936.

McCagney, Nancy. *Nāgārjuna and the Philosophy of Openness*. Oxford: Rowman & Littlefield, 1997.

McDougall, Joyce. *The Many Faces of Eros, A Psychoanalytic Exploration of Human Sexuality*. New York: W.W. Norton & Co., 1995.

– *Theaters of the Body. A Psychoanalytic Approach to Psychosomatic Illness*. New York: W.W. Norton & Co., 1989.

– *Theaters of the Mind. Illusion and Truth on the Psychoanalytic Stage*. New York: Brunner/ Mazel, 1991.

McDowell, Edwin. "Oppression Hasn't Stilled Estonian Literature." *New York Times*, 12 July 1984: C14.

Meinhardt, Johannes. "Illusionism in Painting and the *Punctum* of Photography." In *Gerhard Richter*, edited by Benjamin H.D. Buchloh. 135–51. Cambridge: MIT Press, 2009.

Meri, Lennart. 1970–97. *Five Documentaries*. Tallinn: Tallinnfilm, 2009.

– *A European Mind. Selected Speeches by Lennart Meri, the Late President of Estonia*. Tallinn: Lennart Meri European Foundation, 2009.

Merilai, Arne. "Estonian Poetic Surrealism: Laaban and Ehin." *Interlitteraria* (2012): 167–79.

– "Kreutzwald ja Kaplinski ehk hinge tagasitulek." *Postimees*, 20 November 1992: 6.

– *Õnne Tähendus*. Tartu: Tartu Ülikooli Kirjastus, 2011.

– *Vokimeister*. Tartu: Tartu Ülikooli Kirjastus, 2011.

Merton, Thomas. *Thoughts on the East*. Introduction by George Woodcock. New York: New Directions, 1995.

Methis. "Noor-Eesti kümme aastat: esteetika ja tähendus." Special Issue 1, no 1–2 (2008).

Mihkelson, Ene. "Vastandumine." *Keel ja Kirjandus* 5 (1973): 304–5.

Miłosz, Czesław. *The Captive Mind*. New York: Vintage, 1981.

Mirov, Ruth. "Regilauluelementidest nüüdisluules." *Keel ja Kirjandus* 4/5 (1976): 208/265–6.

Misiunas, Romuald J. and Rein Taagepera. *The Baltic States: Years of Dependence. 1940–1980*. Berkeley: University of California Press, 1983.

Mitchell, Stephen A. *Relational Concepts in Psychoanalysis, An Integration*. Cambridge Mass.: Harvard University Press, 1988.

Mitchell, Stephen, ed. *Gilgamesh. A New English Version*. New York: Free Press, 2004.

Mürk, Harri. "Regi Song." *Estonian Literary Magazine* 26 (2008). http://www.estinst.ee/eng/estonian-literary-magazine-eng/. Accessed 6 July 2008.

Muru, Karl. "Lõuna Eesti murdeliste luuletuste võistlus." *Edasi*, 2 November 1969: 2.

– "Luuleaasta 1977 ehk nii palju värsse." *Looming* 3 (1978): 480–1.

– "Ääremärkusi "Käoraamatu" juurde" *Sirp ja Vasar*, 27 March 1987: 5.

Must, Ann. "Kaplinski kollokvium." *Sirp*, 22 March 1991: 3.

Mutt, Mihkel. "Kosmopoliitiline euroskeptitsism." *Eesti Ekspress*, 27 May 1999: B7.

– "Ühest algupärandist" *Teatrimärkmik 1976/77*. Tallinn: 1979. 200–3.

Naan, Gustav. "Homo Mutans." *Sirp ja Vasar*, 27 February 1981: 8, 13.

Naess, Arne and Per Ingvar Haukeland. *Life's Philosophy. Reason and Feeling in a Deeper World*. Translated by Roland Huntford. Athens: The University of Georgia Press, 2002.

Naess, Arne. "Heidegger, Postmodern Theory and Deep Ecology." *Trumpeter* 4 (1997): 2–7.

– "How my philosophy seemed to develop." In *Philosophers on Their Own Work*. Vol. 9, 207–26. Frankfurt/Bern: Peter Lang, 1982.

– "Mountains and Mythology." *Trumpeter* 12 (1995): 4.

– *Ecology, Community and Lifestyle: Outline of an Ecosophy*. Translated and edited by David Rothenberg. Cambridge: Cambridge University Press, 2001.

Nagelmaa, Silvia. "Jaan Kaplinski." In *Eesti kirjanduse ajalugu* V, no 2, edited by Maie Kalda, 499–506. Tallinn: Eesti Raamat, 1991.

Nagelmaa, Silvia. "Kahest raamatust ja rohkemgi." *Looming* 9 (1977): 1570–3.

– "Läinud aasta luulest." *Edasi,* 4 February 1968: 2.

– "Meestelaulude aasta" *Looming* 4 (1973): 675–8.

Nair, P.G.R. "The Wandering Border: The Poetry of Jaan Kaplinski." http://www.boloji.com/index.cfm?md=Content&sd=PoemArticle&PoemArticleID=95#sthash.Aoxvfoj2.dpuf. Accessed 3 March 2013.

Neidhart, Christoph. "Kas on olemas *homo estonicus*?" *Vikerkaar* 6 (1991): 89–91.

Nelissen, Nico, Jan van der Straaten and Leon Klinkers, eds. *Classics in Environmental Studies: An Overview of Classic Texts in Environmental Studies*. Utrecht: International Books, 1997.

Nigols, Helju and Rebane, Merike. *Väike eesti kirjanike leksikon*. Tallinn: Virgela. 1998. 37.

Niiniluoto, Maarit. "The Dream of My Generation." *Universitas Helsingiensis* 4 (2001) http://www.helsinki.fi/lehdet/uh/401l.htm. Accessed 5 May 2012.

Nirk, Endel and Sõgel, Endel, eds. *Eesti kirjanduse biograafiline leksikon*. Tallinn: Eesti Raamat. 1975.

– *Eesti kirjandus: arengulooline ülevaade*. Tallinn: Perioodika, 1983.

Norton, Jody. "The Importance of Nothing: Absence and its Origins in the Poetry of Gary Snyder." *Contemporary Literature* 28, no 1 (1987): 41–66.

Nussbaum, Martha C. "People as Fictions: Proust and the Ladder of Love." In *Erotikon. Essays on Eros, Ancient and Modern,* edited by

Shadi Bartsch and Thomas Bartscherer, 223–40. Chicago: University of Chicago Press, 2005.

O'Driscoll, Dennis. "Count every dandelion." *Times Literary Supplement*, 18 October 1996: 25.

Odin, Steve. *The Social Self in Zen and American Pragmatism*. New York: State University of New York Press, 1996.

Ogden, Thomas H. "Playing, Dreaming, and Interpreting Experience: Comments on Potential Space." In *The Facilitating Environment: Clinical Applications of Winnicott's Theory*, edited by M. Gerard Fromm and Bruce L. Smith, 255–78. Madison: International University Press, 1989.

– *The Matrix of the Mind: Object Relations and the Psychoanalytic Dialogue*. Northvale, NJ: Jason Aronson Inc., 1986.

Ohmann, Valdur. "Gustav Naani kaebekiri EKP Keskkomiteele." *Tuna* 3 (2005): 96–104.

Oja, Arno. "Kaplinski kui Saatan." *Eesti Aeg*, 9 August 1995: 12.

Olesk, Sirje. "Kaplinski mediteerib kolmes keeles." *Eesti Päevaleht*, 27 January 1999: 10.

– "Luuleaasta 1982 Tartu poolt vaadatuna." *Edasi*, 2 February 1983: 4.

– "On the Literary Life in the Soviet Estonia," *Colloquia* 17 (2006): 122–34.

Õnnepalu, Tõnu. "Kaplinski (Pealekaebus ja ülestunnistus)." *Sirp*, 24 December 1991: 10.

– "Kirjandus on surnud, elagu..." *Vikerkaar* 4 (1990): 91–6.

– "Setud, Narkissos ja midagi muud." *Eesti Ekspress*, 12 March 1993: 21.

Oras, Ants, ed. Arbujad. *Valimik Eesti Lüürikat*. Tallinn: Tänapäev, 2001.

Oushakine, Serguei Alex. "The Terrifying Mimicry of Samizdat." *Public Culture* 13, no 2 (2001): 191–214.

Pala, Evald. "Juhan Liivi luuleauhind Jaan Kaplinskile." *Edasi*, 6 May 1968: 3.

Palli, Ilmar. "Ôpetajast lahti." Maaleht, 31 May 2007. http:// www.maaleht.ee. Accessed 9 April 2007.

Parfitt, Tudor. "Alexander Piatigorsky Obituary." www.guardian.co.uk/world/2010/jan/05/alexander-piatigorsky-obituary. Accessed 19 February 2013.

Parhomenko, Eduard. "Eksitused. Visand nostalgiast ja sokolaadist." *Vikerkaar* 1 (1994): 61–9.

Parisi, Thomas. *Civilization and Its Discontents: An Anthropology for the Future?* New York: Twayne, 1999.

Pentikäinen, Juha, ed. *Shamanism and Northern Ecology*. New York: Mouton de Gruyter, 1996.

– et al., eds. *Shamans*. Tampere: ST-Print, 1998.

– *Kalevala Mythology*, Expanded Edition. Translated. and edited by Ritva Poom. Bloomington: Indiana, University Press, 1999.

– *Shamanism and Culture*, 2nd ed. Helsinki: Etnika Co., 1998.

Pesti, Arvo. *Dissidentlik Liikumine Eestis Aastatel 1972–1987*. Tallinn: Riigiarhiiv, 2009.

Petersoo, Pille. "Reconsidering Otherness: Constructing Estonian Identity." *Nations and Nationalism* 13, no 1 (2007): 117–33.

Phillips, Adam. *Winnicott: Fontana Modern Masters*. London: Fontana Press, 1988.

Piatigorsky, Alexander. Lecture at Yuri Lotman Memorial Conference, Tallinn 2001 http://www.youtube.com/watch?v=KWE6Bl3n2Oo. Accessed 18 February 2013.

Pilvre, Parbi. "Kirjutamine kui loomulik vajadus." *Vikerkaar* 8 (1992): 88–9. Point Press, 1990.

Põldmäe, Jaak. "Eesti nõukogude luule piirjooni 1970ndail aastail." *Looming* 4 (1979): 561.

Põldmäe, Paavo. "Kirjad Ida-Euroopast." *Keel ja Kirjandus* 9 (1995): 636–8.

Põllo, Kaljo. *Kalivägi*. Tallinn: Kunst, 1988.

– *Kodalased*. Tallinn: Kunst, 1978.

Põlma, V. ed. *Eesti Kirjakeele Seletussõnaraamat*. III.1. Tallinn: Eesti Teaduste Akadeemia Keele ja Kirjanduse Instituut, 1992.

Powelstock, David. *Becoming Mikhail Lermontov: The Ironies of Romantic Individualism in Nicholas I's Russia*. Illinois: Northwestern University Press, 2005.

Priimägi, Linnar. "Mütoloogiast ajalooni." *Vikerkaar* 8 (1989): 90–1.

Pruul, Kajar. "Lõunapoolse Eesti luuleraamatud 1984." *Edasi*, 16 March 1985: 4.

Pullerits, Heivi, ed. *Tartu. Ajalugu ja Kultuurilugu*. Tartu: Ilmamaa, 2005.

Racevskis, Karlis. "Toward a Post-colonial Perspective on the Baltic States." *Baltic Postcolonialism*, edited by Violeta Kelertas, 165–86. Rodopi: Amsterdam, 2006.

Rähesoo, Jaak. "Growing up in Modernity: The Comparative Place of Estonian Culture." In *Comparative Literature Today: Theory and Practice*, 47–55. Vilnius Pedagogical University: Vilnius, 2000.

Raud, Rein. "Diamat ja Tiamat." *Vikerkaar* 10/11 (1998): 169–73.

Raudvassar, Valdur. "Jaan Kaplinski ja nõukogude inimesed." *Sirp*, 26 March 1999: 18.
Raun, Toivo U. *Estonia and the Estonians*. Studies of Nationalities in the USSR Series. Stanford: Hoover Institution Press, 2001.
Rebas, Hain. "Aeg mõtteid ja seisukohti tuulutada." *Sõnumileht*, 30 January 1996: 2.
Reiman, Donald A., and Neil Fraistat. *The Norton Critical Edition, Shelley's Poetry and Prose*. New York: W.W. Norton & Co., 2002.
Remmel, Maie. "Meie kiisul kriimud silmad." *Reede*, 21 December 1990: 12–13.
Rilke, Rainer Maria. *Briefe aus den Jahren 1892 bis 1904*, edited by Ruth Sieber-Rilke and Carl Sieber. Leipzig: Insel, 1939.
– *Rilke on Love and Other Difficulties*. Translated by John J.L. Mood. New York: W.W. Norton & Co., 1975.
– *Rilke's Late Poetry: Duino Elegies, The Sonnets to Orpheus, Selected Last Poems*. Translated and edited by Graham Good. Vancouver: Ronsdale Press, 2004.
– *Sonnets to Orpheus with Letters to a Young Poet*. Translated by Stephen Cohn. Manchester: Carcanet Press Ltd., 2000.
Rink, Marika. "Ühemehemäng. Jaan Kaplinski 'Põgenik' Noorsooteatris." *Noorte Hääl*, 27 February 1977: 3.
Rodman, F. Robert. *Winnicott, Life and Work*. Cambridge Mass.: Perseus Publishing, 2003.
Rorty, Richard. *Philosophy and the Mirror of Nature*. New Jersey: Princeton University Press, 1980.
Rosenberger, Nancy R., ed. *Japanese Sense of Self*. Cambridge: Cambridge University Press, 1999.
Rosendale, Steven, ed. *The Greening of Literary Scholarship: Literature, Theory, and the Environment*. Iowa City: University of Iowa Press, 2002.
Ross, Jaan and Ilse Lehiste. *The Temporal Structure of Estonian Runic Songs*. Berlin: Mouton de Gruyter, 2001.
Ross, Kristiina. "Joonast ja valaskalast." *Keel ja Kirjandus* 10 (1988): 577–84.
Roszak, Theodore, Mary E. Gomes, and Allen D. Kanner, eds. *Ecopsychology, Restoring the Earth, Healing the Mind*. San Francisco: Sierra Club Books, 1995.
Rothenberg, David. *Is It Painful to Think? Conversations with Arne Naess*. Minneapolis: University of Minneapolis Press, 1993.

Rucker, Rudy. *Infinity and the Mind: The Science and Philosophy of the Infinite*. Boston: Birkhäuser, 1982.
Rudnytsky, Peter L., ed. *Transitional Objects and Potential Spaces, Literary Uses of of D.W. Winnicott*. New York: Columbia University Press, 1993.
Rummo, Paul. "Ääremärkusi jäämäe serval." *Looming* 5 (1995): 710–11.
– "Armas Janka Plinski!" *Sirp* (18 January 1991): 2–3.
– "Luule 67" *Looming* 4 (1968): 627.
– "Pilk eesti luulesse 1976–80 ja veidi ka 1981. Aastal." *Looming* 5 (1981): 713–14.
– "Vestlus Jaan Kaplinski 'Tolmust ja värvidest.'" *Sirp ja Vasar,* 6 October 1967: 3.
– *Eesti luule. Antoloogia aastaist 1637–1956*. Tallinn: Eesti Raamat, 1967.
Russell, Bertrand. *Why I Am Not A Christian and Other Essays on Religion and Related Subjects*. Edited by Paul Edwards. New York: Touchstone, 1957.
Rysdyk, Evelyn C. *Modern Shamanic Living: New Explorations of an Ancient Path*. Boston: Weiser Books, 1999.
Saar, Johannes. "Vaimuvangerdused kirjandusteadvuses." *Postimees (Arter),* 15 January 2000: 11.
Ṣallamaa, Kari. "Ethnofuturism and Cosmofuturism. About the forth-developing of our philosophy." Ethnofutu 4 conference (2001). http://www.suri.ee/etnofutu4/cosmo-en.html. Accessed 5 August 2003.
Salminen, Johannes. "Kas Tartus laulab veel ööbik?" *Sirp,* 18 January 1991: 2–3.
Salokannel, Juhani. "Piirideta Kaplinski." *Eesti Päevaleht,* 19 January 2001. http://www.epl.ee/news/kultuur/piirideta-kaplinski.d?id=50797486. Accessed 9 May 2012.
– "Kaplinski ja modernism. Kuidas mõistetakse Kaplinski lüürikat Soomes." *Vikerkaar* 8 (1991): 76–7.
Saluäär, Anu. "Maailmaklassi eestlane." *Looming* 10 (1999): 1594–6.
Salumets, Thomas. "Conflicted Consciousness: Jaan Kaplinski and the Legacy of Intra-European Postcolonialism in Estonia." In *Baltic Postcolonialism*, edited by Violeta Kelertas, 429–50. Amsterdam: Rodopi, 2006.
– "Jaan Kaplinski Uku Masing." *Keel ja Kirjandus* 53, no 1 (2010): 37–44.
– "Jaan Kross: rahvuse rajajoontest." In *Võim ja Kultuur,* 437–50. Tartu: Eesti Kirjandusmuuseum, 2003.

– ed. *Norbert Elias and Human Interdependencies*. Montreal: McGill-Queen's University Press, 2001.

Salupere, Malle. *Millenary Tartu. The City of Youth and Good Ideas*. Tartu: Tartu University Press, 2006.

Sang, August. "Tänavune Juhan Liivi auhind." *Sirp ja Vasar,* 5 May 1968: 6.

– "Ühest varjujäänud luuletajast." *Looming* 8 (1969): 1275–6.

Sang, Joel. "Kummardus dissidendile." *Looming* 4 (1991): 572–3.

– "Luuleaasta pildistusi" *Looming* 3 (1983): 383–4.

– "Tõelisem ja vabam?" *Sirp ja Vasar,* 15 October 1982: 6–7.

– *Päripidi vastukarva, kirjatöid aastaist 1976–1986*. Tallinn: Eesti Raamat, 1987.

Särg, Taive. "Does Melodic Accent Shape the Melody Contour in Estonian Folk Songs?" *ICMPC* (2006): 1304–8.

Sarv, Mari. "Stichic and Stanzaic Poetic Form in Estonian Tradition and in Europe." *Traditiones* 38, no 1 (2009): 161–71.

Schmuul, Aivi. "Isetud sõnad." *Looming* 6 (1977): 1046–8.

Schweitzer, Albert. "The Ethics of Reverence for Life." http://www.chapman.edu/schweitzer/sch.reading4html. Accessed 30 August 2002.

Sells, Michael. *Mystical Languages of Unsaying*. Chicago: University of Chicago Press, 1994.

Seppel, Ly. "Algupärane lastekirjandus 1986/87." *Looming* 4 (1988): 546.

Sessions, George, ed. *Deep Ecology for the 21st Century: Readings on the Philosophy and Practice of the New Environmentalism*. Boston: Shambhala, 1995.

Shenton, Andrew. "Arvo Pärt: in his own words." In *The Cambridge Companion to Arvo Pärt*, edited by Andrew Shenton. 111–27. Cambridge: Cambridge University Press, 2012.

Sileika, Antanas. "The Mad Dissident Is a Splendid Guide to Europe's New Literature." *Globe and Mail*, 20 March 1993.

Singer, Isaac Bashevis. *The Collected Stories of Isaac Bashevis Singer*. New York: Farrar Straus Giroux, 1996.

Sirr, Peter. "Jaan Kaplinski: A Particular Sort of Ignorance." http://petersirr.blogspot.ca/2012/04/jaan-kaplinski-particular-sort-of.html. Accessed 3 March 2013.

Skinner, Burrhus Frederic. *Walden Two*. Indianapolis: Hackett, 2005.

Slingerland, Edward. *Effortless Action: Wu-Wei as Conceptual Metaphor and Spiritual Ideal in Early China*. Oxford: Oxford University Press, 2003.

Smidchens, Guntis. "National Heroic Narratives in the Baltics as a Source for Nonviolent Political Action." *Slavic Review* 66, no 3 (2007): 484–508.

Smith, Graham, ed. *The Baltic States: The National Self-Determination of Estonia, Latvia and Lithuania*. London: The MacMillan Press Ltd., 1994.

Smith, Sidonie and Julia Watson. *Reading Autobiography: A Guide for Interpreting Life Narratives*. Minneapolis: University of Minnesota Press, 2001.

Snyder, Gary. "Language Goes Two Ways." In *The Green Studies Reader: From Romanticism to Ecocriticism*, edited by Laurence Coupe, 127–31. Routledge: New York, 2000.

– "The Art of Poetry LXXXIV." *The Paris Review* 141 (1996): 89–118.

– *The Gary Snyder Reader: Prose, Poetry, and Translations: 1952–1998*. Washington: Counterpoint, 1999.

– *The Practice of the Wild: Essays by Gary Snyder*. San Francisco: North Point Press, 1990.

– *Turtle Island*. New York: New Directions Publishing, 1974.

Solženitsõn, Aleksander. *Üks päev Ivan Denissovitši elus*. Tallinn: Loomingu Raamatukogu 11, 1963.,

Sommer, Lauri. "Janka ja Uku: vinjett kahest tõrkujast. Ettekanne konverentsil 'Janka 60 – Kaplinskist Kaplinskita' *Tartus*." Sirp, 26 January 2001. http://www.sirp.ee/2001/26.01.01/Kirjand/kirjand1-1.html.

– "Kujud ja tujud. Romantilise luule jätkuvusest Eestis. Veste mõne jõnksuga." *Looming* 6 (2012): 848–58.

– "Pyydlikkuse tont." *Sirp*, 3 December 1999: 6–7.

– "Geniaalne vanalaps ja vaimu Jäädvustamine." (2005). http://www.temuki.ee/arhiiv/2005/06/lugu12.pdf.

Soosaar, Enn. "Olla oma saatusest suurem." *Sõnumileht*, 5 August 1996: 2.

– "Vaja on oma ajalooga kokkuleppele jõuda." *Rahva Hääl*, 25 May 1995: 2.

– *Vikerkaar* 4 (1991): 86–91.

Soovik, Ene-Reet. "Crossing the Sea: Tomas Tranströmer and Jaan Kaplinski." *Interlitteraria* 4 (1999): 236–46.

Suislepp, Harald. "Reisikiri Jaan Kaplinski luuleriigist" *Looming* 8 (1973): 1377–92; 9 (1973): 1558–68.

Sulbi, Raul. "Eesti ulmeautorite lühiproosa: 1998" *Mardus* 3 (1999): 81–6.

Susi, Rannar. "Kaplinskit on vaja näha." *Võru Teataja*, 7 March 1991: 3.

Sutrop, Urmas. "Nietzsche, Kaplinski ja eesti filosoofia" *Akadeemia* 6 (1996): 1146–1162.

Süvalep, Ele. "Jaan Kaplinski." In *Twentieth-Century Eastern European Writers*. Third Series. Volume 232, edited by Steven Serafin, 163–72. Detroit: Layman, 2001.

Suzuki, Daisetz Teitaro. *Mysticism: Christian and Buddhist, The Eastern and Western* Way. New York, Collier Books, 1962.

– *The Essence of Buddhism*. Newport, England: R.H. Johns Ltd., 1957.

– *Zen and the Japanese Culture*. New York: MJF Books, 1959.

Suzuki, David and Amanda McConnell. *The Sacred Balance: Rediscovering Our Place in Nature*. Vancouver: Greystone Books, 2002.

Suzuki, Shunryu. *Not Always So: Practicing the True Spirit of Zen*. Edited by Edward Espe Brown. New York: First Quill, 2003.

– *Zen Mind, Beginner's Mind: Informal Talks on Zen Meditation and Practice*. New York: Weatherhill Inc., 1996.

Taagepera, Rein. *Estonia: Return to Independence*. San Francisco: Westview Press, 1993.

– *Softening without Liberalization in the Soviet Union: The Case of Jüri Kukk*. Lanham: University Press of America, 1984.

Tallis, Frank. *Love Sick: Love as a Mental Illness*. New York: Thunder's Mouth Press, 2005.

Talve, Juhan. "Jaan Kaplinski ja müüdid." *Reede*, 23 February 1990: 12.

Talvet, Jüri. "Aastatuhandelõpu poeetilised diskursused: vaatlusi Jaan Kaplinski ja Hando Runneli luulest." *Looming* 11 (1998): 1738–47.

– *A Call for Cultural Symbiosis: Meditations from U*. Toronto: Guernica, 2005.

– "End-of-the-millennium Poetry: Discourses and Resources (with notes on the poetry of Jaan Kaplinski and Hando Runnel)." *Interlitteraria* 4 (1999): 196–214.

– "The Transcendence of Jaan Kaplinski's Poetry." *Estonian Literary Magazine* Spring (1998): 7.

Tamm, Marek. "History as Cultural Memory: Mnemohistory and the Construction of the Estonian Nation." *Journal of Baltic Studies* 39, no 4 (2008): 499–516.

Tammeveski, Agu. "Lugeja eelised." *Sirp*, 22 January 1993: 5.

– "Proosa ohutustehnika." *Reede*, 25 May 1990: 4–5.

Tarand, Andres. *Kiri ei põle ära. Päevaraamat 1980*. Tallinn: Eesti Päevaleht, 2005.

Taylor, Charles. *The Malaise of Modernity*. Toronto: Anansi, 1991.

Tedre, Ülo and Veljo Tormis. *Uus Regilaulik*. Tallinn: SO Muusika, n.d.

Tilly, Charles. "War Making and State Making as Organized Crime." In *Bringing the State Back*, edited by Peter B. Evans, Dietrich Rueschemeyer and Theda Skocpol, 169–91. Cambridge: Cambridge University Press, 1985.

– *Coercion, Capital, and European States, AD 990–1992*. Blackwell: Cambridge and Oxford, 2001.

Times of India, 8 December1980: 17.

Tinn, Eduard. "Neli kuningat ja suhtumine ajaloosse." *Sirp ja Vasar*, 8 April 1977: 6–7.

Tode, Emil. "Sõnadest ja asjadest." *Vikerkaar* 5/6 (1995): 165–9.

Tonts, Ülo. "Stabiilsus või seisak?" *Teatrielu 1982*. Tallinn: Eesti Raamat, 1985. 15–22.

Toomet, Tiia. *Argipäeva Õhtu*. Tallinn: Eesti Raamat, 1987.

– *Isamaa Suvi*. Tartu: Ilmamaa, 1997.

Tootmaa, Rein. "Tõlkija päevaraamat." *Maaleht*, 18 April 1996: 29.

Tormis, Veljo "Some problems with that regilaul." Presentation at the Viljandi Culture Academy for the international conference RING 2007. Translated by Ülle Leis.

– *Lauldud Sõna*. Tartu: Tartu Ülikooli Kirjastus, 2000.

– *Jonni Pärast Heliloojaks*. Tallinn: Prisma, 2000.

– *Personaalnimestik*. Tallinn: Eesti Rahvusraamatukogu, 1990.

– *Tähemõrsja/Star Bride*. CD. Tartu: TÜAN, 1999.

Tranströmer, Tomas. *New Collected Poems*. Translated by Robin Fulton. Newcastle upon Tyne: Bloodaxe Books, 1997.

– *Truth Barriers*. Poems by Tomas Tranströmer. Translated by Robert Bly. San Francisco: Sierra Club, 1980.

Trubon, Terje. "Ida peegeldusi Jaan Kaplinski luules." *Keel ja Kirjandus* 5 (1991): 272–82.

Tuna 3 (2006): 161 (reproduction of a 1956 flyer: ERAF 129, S. 25850 2. Kd. 1. 106).

Tuulik, Ülo. "Teine teisel pool tanumat." *Looming* 7 (2000): 1104–09.

Tuumalu, Tiit. "Jaan Kaplinski – resideeriv kirjanik Walesis." *Postimees*, 22 October 1997: 2.

Tüür, Kadri. "Öö nagu ökoloogia." *Vikerkaar* 5–6 (1999): 180–2.

Udam, Haljand. "Õpetaja Kaplinski." *Looming* 10 (1991): 1408–11.

Uibo, Udo. "Pigem arutlus kui arvustus." *Keel ja Kirjandus* 9 (1985): 554–5.

– "Rahvustervikluse radadel tasakaalu taotlemas." *Looming* 12 (1993): 1706–7.

Ülenurme, Ave. "Augustis, õhtutaeva all." *Edasi*, 14 September 1985: 5.
– "Jaan Kaplinski 'Õhtu toob tagasi kõik.'" *Edasi*, 14 September 1985: 5.
Undusk, Jaan. "Eesti regivärsi parallelism ja maagilise elutunde taandumine." http://www.folklore.ee/tagused/nr24/undusk.pdf. 2004. Accessed 18 February 2013.
– "Eesti-saksa kirjandussuhete tüpoloogia." *Keel ja Kirjandus* 10–12 (1995): 577–87, 669–79, 746–56.
Unt, Mati. "Ükskõik!" *Looming* 6 (1992): 842.
Ürt, Julius. "Raske on kergeks saada." *Edasi*, 16 July 1983: 5.
Vähi, Peeter. "... ja Buddhast ja Dalailaamast ja Kaplinskist." *Sirp*, 10 January 1992: 13.
Vahtre, Lauri. "Kuuekümnendate kustumatu kuma." *Päevaleht*, 14 January 1993: 6.
– "Õnnetustel kipub olema põhjuseid." *Eesti Päevaleht*, 25 October 1996: 7.
Vahtre, Sulev ed. *Eesti Ajalugu VI*. Tartu: Õpetatud Eesti Selts, 2005.
Valgemäe, Mardi. "Ingli(s)keelne Kaplinski." *Tulimuld* 4 (1985): 221–2.
– "Tolmu ja värvide Kaplinski." *Mana* 55 (1986): 30–8.
Väljataga, Märt. "Järjekindlalt haaramatu." *Looming* 10 (1997): 1423–8.
– "Kes on parempoolsed?" *Sirp*, 4 September 1992: 12–13.
– "Kõigest eimidagi: intervjuu Jaan Kaplinskiga." *Keel ja Kirjandus* 1 (1991): 39–41.
– "Literary perspectives: Estonia. Waiting for the Great Estonian Novel." *Eurozine*, 30 June 2007. http:// www.eurozine.com/articles/2007-06-30-valjataga-en.html. Accessed 5 June 2012.
– "Milleks meile konnasööjad kärbsed?" *Eesti Ekspress*, 22 April 1999: B14.
– "Mina juurest rahvalaulu juurde." *Eesti Ekspress (Areen)*, 5 December 1997: B2.
Valton, Arvo. "Ma ei ole tige Kaplinski peale." *Sirp*. 10 January 1992: 13.
– "Mina vajan Eestimaad." *Sirp*, 15 November 1993: 3.
Vananurm, Ilmar. "Augustis, õhtutaeva all." *Edasi*, 14 September 1985: 5.
Vardys, Stanley V. Appendix "Open Letter from the Estonian SSR." *Journal of Baltic Studies* 12, no 3 (1981): 275–98 (English translation of letter 292–6).
– "Human Rights Issues in Estonia, Latvia, and Lithuania." *Journal of Baltic Studies* 12, no 3 (1981): 275–98.
Vaska, Lauri. "Väliseestlased." *Kultuurileht*, 17 May 1996: 5.
Veidemann, Rein. "60ndate põlvkond ikka veel vormis." *Eesti Päevaleht*, 10 March 2000: 11.

– "Kirjandus Sotstsiaalse Sidususe Tergurina. Eesti Juhtum." In *Võim ja Kultuur*, edited by Arva Krikmann and Sirje Olesk, 155–69. Eesti Kirjandusmuuseum: Tartu, 2003.

– "Laulev revolutsioon." *Postimees,* 7 June 2008. http://www.postimees.ee/070608/esileht/ak/335521.php. Accessed 23 April 2011.

– "Masing nagu mõtlev mägi." *Eesti Päevaleht,* 11 August 1999: 7.

– "Triptühhon." *Vikerkaar* 6 (1991): 56–8.

Velsker, Mart. "Mis On Kuuekümnendad Eesti Kirjanduses?" *Looming* 8 (1999): 1210–16.

– "Teekond tekstini." *Looming* 6 (2000): 938–43.

– "Vaimuelu all kannatava inimese mõtisklused." In *VVV: Veljesto IX koguteos*, edited by Aare Pilv, 99–106. Tartu: Eesti Üliõpilaste Selts "Veljesto," 1999.

Vene, Ilmar. "Kultuur kui kohustus." *Postimees,* 12 March 1993: 18.

– "Piiritlemisest." *Postimees,* 5 January 1994: 15.

– "Poliitika valgustaja esituses." *Eesti Elu,* 27 August 1993: 2–3.

Vesilind, Priit. *The Singing Revolution. How Culture Saved a Nation.* Tallinn: Varrak, 2008.

Veskimägi, Kaljo-Olev. *Kuidas valitseti Eesti NSV-d.* Tallinn: Varrak, 2005.

– *Nõukogude unelaadne elu. Tsensuur Eesti NSV-s ja tema peremehed.* Tallinn: n.p. 1996.

Vessar, Kristiina. "Kirjandusaasta 1978 läbi mitme pilgu." *Sirp ja Vasar,* 16 March 1979: 4.

Vetemaa, Enn. "Dramaturgiast kahe kongressi vahel." *Looming* 4 (1981): 569.

– "Kiri Jaan Kaplinskile." *Looming* 7 (2000): 1100–4.

Viiding, Ine."Lp. Sirje Kiin!" *Rahva Hääl*, 6 February 1966: 2.

Viires, Ants. *Kultuur ja traditsioon.* Tartu: Ilmamaa, 2001.

– *Puud Ja Inimesed: Puude Osast Eesti Rahvakultuuris.* Tallinn: Valgus, 1975.

Vulf, Küllike. "Eesti kirjanduskriitika kõnelused Uku Masinguga. Monoloog või dialoog?" *Keel ja Kirjandus* 6 (2002): 385–400.

Warneken, Felix and Michael Tomasello. "The roots of human altruism." *British Journal of Psychology* (2009): 455–71.

Washington Post, 9 November 1980.

Watts, Alan W. *Nature, Man and Woman.* New York: Pantheon Books, 1958.

– *Tao: The Watercourse Way.* New York: Pantheon Books, 1975.

– *The Spirit of Zen: A Way of Life, Work, and Art in the Far East.* New York: Grove Press, 1958.

– *The Way of Zen*. New York: Pantheon Books, 1958.
– *This Is It and Other Essays on Zen and Spiritual Experience*. Toronto: Collier Books, 1967.
Webb, Timothy. "The Unascended Heaven. Negatives in Prometheus Unbound." *Shelley's Poetry and Prose*. Edited by Donald H. Reiman and Neil Fraistat, 694–711. Norton: New York, 2002.
Weber, Friedrich Christian. *Das veränderte Russland*. Frankfurt: N. Förster, 1721.
Wenning, Mario. "Daoism as Critical Theory." *Comparative Philosophy* 2, no 2 (2011): 50–71.
Williams, Paul. *Mahayana Buddhism. The Doctrinal Foundations*. London: Routledge, 2007.
Wilmes, Ulrich. "Gerhard Richter: One Moment in Time. On the Documentation of the Conditions in which Abstract Paintings are Made." In *Gerhard Richter: Large Abstracts*, edited by Ulrich Wilmes, 135–53. Ostfildern: Hatje Cantz, 2008.
Wilson, Edward O. *Biophilia*. Cambridge: Harvard University Press, 1984.
– *The Future of Life*. New York: Vintage Books, 2002.
Wilson, Peter. "Letter to Gorbachev got results." *The Vancouver Sun*, 2 February 1988: D4.
Winnicott, D.W. *Babies and Their Mothers*. Edited by Clare Winnicott, Ray Shepherd, and Madeleine Davis. Reading, MA: Addison-Wesley Publishing Company, 1986.
– *Deprivation and Delinquency*. Edited by Clare Winnicott, Ray Shepherd, and Madeleine David. New York: Brunner-Routledge, 2000.
– *Holding and Interpretation, Fragment of an Analysis*. New York: Grove Press, 1986.
– *Human Nature*. New York: Schocken Books, 1988.
– *On the Child*. Cambridge, MA: Perseus Publishing, 2002.
– *Playing and Reality*. New York: Brunner-Routledge, 2001.
– *Psycho-Analytic Explorations*. Edited by Clare Winnicott, Ray Shepherd, and Madeleine Davis. Cambridge, MA: Harvard University Press, 1989.
– *The Child, the Family, and the Outside World*. Harmondsworth, England: Penguin Books Ltd., 1973.
– *The Maturational Processes and the Facilitating Environment*. London: Karnac Books Ltd., 1990.
Wright, Ken. "To make experience sing." In *Art, Creativity, Living*, edited by Lesley Caldwell, 75–96. London: Karnac Books, 2000.

Young-Bruehl, Elisabeth and Faith Bethelard. *Cherishment, A Psychology of the Heart*. New York: The Free Press, 2000.

– "Where Do We Fall When We Fall in Love?" *Journal for the Psychoanalysis of Culture and Society* 8, no 2 (2003): 279–88.

Zdeb, Nicole. "Selected Poems by Jaan Kaplinski." 5 December 2011. http://quarterlyconversation.com/selected-poems-by-jaan-kaplinski. Accessed 20 March 2012.

Zerzan, John. *Running on Emptiness. The Pathology of Civilization*. Los Angeles: Feral House, 2002.

– ed. *Against Civilization. Readings and Reflections*. Los Angeles: Feral House, 2005.

Zimmermann, Michael E. and J. Baird Callicot, Karen J. Warren, Irene J. Klaver, John Clark, eds. *Environmental Philosophy. From Animal Rights to Radical Ecology*. Upper Saddler River: Prentice Hall, 2005.

Index

Alliksaar, Artur, 59, 62
Amae: Hsu, Francis, 88; craving for closeness, 97; critical attitude towards, 97–8; dependency need, 87; Freud, 88–97; pre-verbal, 89; unfulfilled, 99–100
"Anti-Political Politics," 110–11
Ariste, Paul, 161
"Ashes," 15
"Avatusest ja armastusest" (Of Openness and Love), 82

"Ballad of Mary's Own Land" (Maarjamaa ballaad), 140
Bashō, Matsuo, 93–4
Baudelaire, Charles, 51, 62
"Birth Spells" (Sünnisõnad), 154, 161
blandness, 158, 164, 167, 171. *See also* Jullien, François
Budapest 1956, 43–4
Buddhism and Zen: awareness of, 55; character without character, 101–2; *The Butterfly and the Mirror* (Liblikas ja Peegel), 72, 81, 86; and Finno-Ugric culture, 143; general interest of Kaplinski in, 163; Lao-Tse, 67–8; and Masing, 93–4; mystical non-action, 102–3; poetry aligned with, 8, 18, 19; renouncing the game, 114; unremarkable as positive quality, 162–3; yun-shui, 115. *See also* Chinese culture; Guenther, H.V.; Suzuki, D.T.; Suzuki, Shunryu; Watts, Alan
Bukovsky, Vladimir, 113

Calgary, 11
Camus, Albert, 38–9
"Carillon," 27
Carolan, Trevor, 11
Carpelan, Bo, 16
character without character, 68–70, 95–6, 101–3, 115, 125–6
Chinese culture, 8, 10, 16, 31, 88, 114–15, 150, 162–7. *See also* Buddhism and Jullien, François
Clinton, Bill, 81
colonialism, 134–6. *See also* Germans, Baltic
Coltrane, John, 54, 57, 152
communicative mode, 41, 70, 94, 134, 143, 150; symbolic order,

42, 51–2, 55–6, 133, 136, 168, 171; verbal signs, 26, 58, 71, 78, 88–9, 163
consciousness, ecological: impact of, 37–8; language, 20; poetry, 19. *See also* Buddhism and Zen; flourishing, unforced; Naess, Arne; nature; Richter, Gerhard; Schweitzer, Albert; Snyder, Gary; Tranströmer, Tomas; Wilson, Edward
contrarian views, 22–4, 40, 56, 65–6, 71, 98, 131, 150
"Correspondences," 51
creativity, 26, 38, 51, 58, 70, 149–52, 171. *See also* looma
crisis, personal, 9, 16, 20–3, 53
culture: capital as, 138; critique of, 52, 54–7, 63, 134; Eurocentric, 61–2, 145–6; and innate aggression, 133; literary, 63–5; and nation, 136–9; ontologization of, 58; oppressive, 60–1; (over-)-dependence on, 70, 133; and propaganda, 60–1; and resistance, 136–9; revival of, 59–60; and symbols, 41–2; transitional phenomena, 69–71; understanding of, 55; unintended consequences, 147; and violence, 144–5; Western, 63; writers' festivals, 64
"Curse Upon Iron," 161
Czar's Madman, The, 105–6

Daitz, Mimi, 157–8
Daodejing, 68, 114, 163
Day of the Four Kings, The, 135, 147–8
dissent: Bukovsky, Vladimir, 113; Cold War, 112, 116–17, 130; consoling effect of, 112–13; crackdown, 123; critique, 112–13; dualism inherent in, 115–16, 125, 130; Havel, Václav, 110–11; Kukk, Jüri, 118; reprisals, 126–9; third way, 110–14, 116. *See also* Letter of 40; Piatigorsky, Alexander
Doi, Takeo. *See* amae

ecological crisis, 34–5, 40
Ehin, Andres, 62
Ekelöf, Gunnar. *See* "Gymnosophist, The"
Elias, Norbert, 95, 132, 143, 163
Elva, 21–2, 53
Evening Brings Everything Back, 5, 9, 29, 37, 165–6

Father, To (Isale), 14, 20–3, 48, 76, 81
Faust, 51, 140
"Filosoofia ja vaikus" (Philosophy and Silence), 94
Finno-Ugric, 93, 142–3, 156, 159, 161, 169. *See also* regi song
flourishing, unforced: challenging Winnicott, 70; and contingency, 26; core concept, 23–4; diminished human control, 26; elementary humanism, 65–6; hardwired for peace, 132–6; and identity, 101, 114, 115, 125–6, 129; maturity, 67–70, 95, 97–8; the unsayable, 26, 27; the untamed, 24, 26; wu-wei, 102–3. *See*

also amae; blandness; ecological consciousness; nature; regi song
folklore, 153. *See also* regi song
Forest Brothers, 45
Franks, Alan, 17
Freud, Sigmund 72, 88–9, 97, 132–3, 151

Germans, Baltic, 134–5, 142–3, 145–8, 157, 159. *See also* Elias, Norbert
"Ghost Ship, The." *See* Lermontov
Gianelli-Meriano, Raphaël, 167. *See also Kaplinski System, The*
Gilgamesh, 57
Godfrey, Stephen, 17
Gorbachev, Mikhail, 11, 120, 130
Grabbi, Hellar, 47, 56
grey zone, the, 126–9
Grumbach, Doris, 10
Guenther, H.V., 163
Gulag, 5, 45, 60. *See also* Kaplinski, Jerzy; *Ivan Denisovich, One Day in the Life of*
"Gymnosophist, The," 168

"Haige Geenius" (Sick Genius), 99
Hamill, Sam, 10, 17–18, 39, 141
Havel, Václav, 61, 110–11, 118, 126. *See also* dissent
Hennoste, Tiit, 144
"Heritage and Heirs" (Pärandus ja pärijad), 155
heroic mode, 50–1, 103, 129, 145, 147, 169–70. *See also Kalevipoeg*; *Faust*
Hinge tagasitulek (Soul's Returning), 9
Hsu, Francis L. K., 27, 88
Hurt, Jakob, 137, 157

"Ice and Heather," 33
"I Don't Take Refuge in Poetry," 67.
"I Have No Principles," 25
"I Opened the Russian-Chinese Dictionary," 101
infancy, 55, 68–71, 73, 76–7, 133
Ivan Denisovich, One Day in the Life of, 60
Ivask, Ivar, 8, 17–18, 47, 63, 94, 170

Jäljed allikal (Tracks at the Wellspring), 7, 28–9
"Jälle kisub kevad," 58
Jannsen, Johann Voldemar, 157
Järve, Neeme, 128
jazz, 54, 152
Jirgens, Karl, 136
Juhan Liiv prize, 7–8, 12
Jullien, François, 96, 115, 151, 164

Kaalep, Ain, 7, 16, 29, 36, 59, 109
Kalad punuvad pesi (Fish Weave Their Nests), 7, 56–7
Kalevipoeg, 145, 169
"Kalivägi" (Power of the Kalevs), 161
Kaljuste, Tõnu, 117
Kangro, Bernhard, 47
Käoraamat (The Cuckoo's Book), 10
Kaplinski, Jaan: adolescence, 42–52; autobiographical texts, 14; awards, 7–8, 11–12; botanical interests, 32–3; branding of, 108, 119, 120–2; children's books, 13; Communist rule, 43–7, 59–61,

102, 102–5; contacts abroad, 47, 59; craving for beauty of, 47–51; essays, 13; family, 9; human growth, 103, 132–3; international recognition, 8, 10, 16–18; memories of war, 3, 5–6; newspaper articles by, 14; persona, 16–18; publications in English by, 13, 14; rising star, 7–14; Tallinn, 9, 64; Tartu University, 6, 9–10, 16; travel, 10–11, 17, 28, 128–9, 164. *See also* Kaplinski, Nora (mother); Kolk, Küllike (first wife); Toomet, Tiia (second wife)

Kaplinski, Jerzy Bonifacy Edward (father): arrest and deportation, 4–5, 45; life of, 3; marriage, 4; music, 152; Tartu, 3

Kaplinski, Maarja (first daughter), 53

Kaplinski, Nora (mother): dancing, 4; high culture, 52; marriage, 4; maternal care, 73, 75–6; relationship with son (Jaan Kaplinski), 52–3, 76; reprisals against, 46; trauma 6. *See also* Kaplinski, Jerzy.

Kaplinski System, The, 19, 33, 102

Kapuściński, Ryszard, 114

Kevad kahel rannikul (Spring on Two Shores), 81

KGB, 8, 20, 47, 60, 107–10, 116, 119–130, 138

Khrushchev, Nikita, 44–45, 47, 60–1, 104, 138, 161

Kirjutatud: Valitud luuletused (What Is Written: Selected Poems), 13, 30n31

"Kodalased" (Ancient Dwellers), 161

Kodumaa (Homeland), 124, 127

Koidula, Lydia, 147

Kõik on ime (Everything is a Miracle), 13

Kolk, Küllike, 53–4

Kross, Jaan, 106–7. *See also Czar's Madman, The*

Krull, Hasso, 165

Kukk, Jüri, 121–2. *See also* dissent

Kull, Kalevi, 114–15

Kundera, Milan, 136

Kust tuli öö (Where the Night Came From), 14, 68

Laaban, Ilmar, 47, 62–3

Lauristin, Marju, 117

Lehiste, Ilse, 5, 33, 47, 141

Lepik, Kalju, 47

Lermontov, Mikhail, 49–52

Letter of 40, 20, 105–8; censorship of, 119–20; condemnation of Kaplinski, 124–6; Kaplinski recants, 123–4; main author and initiator of, 121; popularity of, 120; reform from within 117–18; Western response to, 118–19

Lill, Märt-Matis, 152

looma (to bring and to come about), 25–6, 68. *See also* creativity

Loorits, Oskar, 143. *See also* Finno-Ugric

love: artless, 82–3, 86; flirting, 75, 77; homosexual, 98; intensity of, 71, 78–9, 80, 81; poetry masking passion, 79; sublimated, 71–2; tragic, 81; unrequited, 79, 88,

100; wordless, 78. *See also* amae; silence
Lõhmus, Mare, 18
Lotman, Yuri, 58
Luiga, Juhan, 143. *See also* Finno-Ugric
Luik, Viivi, 46, 98, 130

Maa vaatasin päikese aknasse (I Looked into the Sun's Window), 9
Maarjamaa. *See* Mary's Land
Mägi, Arvo, 47
Mary's Land (Maarjamaa), 140, 146–8
Masing, Uku: anthropological and philosophical inclinations, 95–6; biographical facts about, 90, 92–3, 99–100; Kaplinski's bond to, 91–3; character of, 98–9; charisma and erudition of, 89; as counter-cultural figure, 59, 91; desire for dependence, 94–6; critics, 94; double-bind, 95; foster parent, 89; Lutheran theologian, 94; as mentor, 14, 90, 99; and nature, 93, 96; persona non grata, 90–1, 99; *Same River, The*, 91–2, 96, 98; as soul mate, 96; wordless communication, 92–4, 94. *See also* amae
Maurois, André, 47–9
Meri, Lennart, 98, 137–8, 146, 161
Merton, Thomas, 93, 150
Miłosz, Czesław, 11
Mitu suve ja kevadet (Several Summers and Springs), 11–12
"Mother's Grave, At," 154, 168. *See also* regi song
Mutiku, 30–3. *See also* nature
"muu meel unus mägede taha," 50

Naan, Gustav, 121–2
Naess, Arne, 26, 38, 115
Nagy, Imre, 43
Napoleon Bonaparte, 50–1, 57
National Awakening, 144, 145, 147, 159
nature: biophilia, 28–30; and consumerism, 34, 35; critics mention of, 29–30; equality of, 27–8, 34–6; Kaplinski's essays about, 35; lack of closeness to, 34; and poetry, 30; receptivity towards, 27, 40; richness of, 27; sacredness of, 35, 38; and symbols 42, 51–2. *See also* Mutiku; Naess, Arne; Tammiku
Nibelungenlied, the, 145, 169
Night Birds, Night Thoughts, 65
Niiniluoto, Maarit, 17
Niklus, Mart, 122. *See also* dissent
Nisonen, Pertti, 18
Nobel Prize, 11
"Nurmekund," 135

O'Driscoll, Dennis, 16
Ööd valged ja mustad (White and Black Nights), 63
Oras, Ants, 145

parallelism, 168, 170. *See also* regi song
Parallels and Parallelisms (paralleele ja parallelisme), 41, 94
Paris, Ilse, 47
Pärt, Arvo, 60, 128, 151
"Peace conquers everything," 29

Piatigorsky, Alexander, 58, 111
Põllu, Kaljo, 135. *See also* Finno-Ugric
"Power of the Powerless, The," 110–11. *See also* dissent; Havel, Václav
Prague Spring, 61
Pravda, 105
prostitution, literary, 64.

Radio Free Europe, 43, 104, 119, 127
Radio Liberty, 120
Rähesoo, Jaak, 142–3
Raske on kergeks saada (It Is Difficult to Become Light), 9, 20
Raudsepp, Jaan (grandfather), 4
Raudsepp, Marie (grandmother), 4
Raudsepp, Nora (mother). *See* Kaplinski, Nora
Raun, Toivo, 158
regi song (regilaul): compound thinking, 168–71; features of, 154–5, 166–7; monotony as strength, 166; performance in Tartu, 152–3; lost art of, 153–6; resisting the abstract, 164–5. *See also* blandness, song festival
religion, 22, 35–6, 40, 65, 85–6
Richter, Gerhard, 26, 151
Rilke, Rainer Maria, 86
Rimbaud, Jean Nicolas Arthur, 51–2
Russell, Bertrand, 36
Russification, 61, 103–5, 124, 137, 142

sacred, 17, 22, 35, 38–9, 62, 165
Salminen, Johannes, 63, 169
salon, the, 59
Same River, The, 44, 51, 75–6, 138; bliss of infancy, 69; Masing, 91, 92, 96, 98; mood swings, 23; mystical dimension, 67, 82, 86; power of literature, 138; sexual desire, 78–9, 81–2; truth, 110
Same Sea in Us All, The, 10, 14, 18
school, 49, 74–5
Schweitzer, Albert, 30, 35–6
Selected Poems, 14
self-colonization, 131–48; and independence, 134; civilized for coercion, 132–6; Cross of Terra Mariana, 146–8; Europe as master signifier, 141; retreat into culture, 133–4. *See also* Germans, Baltic
shamanism, 9, 17–19, 22, 85, 93, 139
silence, 151; endless song and text, 167; escape from art, 62–6; meditative mode, 17, 41–2, 150, 164; unmediated closeness, 78; wordless communication, 94. *See also* amae
Šiklová, Jiřina, 115
Singer, Isaac Bashevis, 72
Singing Revolution. *See* song festival
Sisyphus. *See* Camus, Albert
Snyder, Gary, 18–19, 30, 36, 63, 148, 150–1
Solzhenitsyn, Alexander, 45, 60
song festival, 137, 156–60
Soul's Returning (Hinge tagasitulek), 9
Stalinism, 44–6, 53, 60, 75, 107
sublimation, 88–9, 150. *See also* Freud
Suzuki, Daisetz Teitaro, 163
Suzuki, Shunryu 87, 114, 163–4

Taagepera, Rein, 118, 121

Tallinn, 60, 105, 106
Tallis, Frank, 72, 86
Talur, Anti, 122, 124, 128. *See also* KGB
Talvet, Jüri, 29–30, 138
Tamm, Marek, 137
Tammiku, 32. *See also* nature
Tartu, 3–6, 17, 31, 49, 53–4, 89, 126, 151–2
Thaw, the, 44
Through the Forest, 13, 65, 78, 171
Toomet, Tiia (wife), 22; and Nora Kaplinski, 6; betrayal, 85; effect of Jaan Kaplinski's poems on, 16; Jaan Kaplinski's antisocial disposition, 73; Jaan Kaplinski's childhood, 76; Mutiku, 31; telling moments about Jaan Kaplinski, 80; Tallinn, 3, 9, 64
Tolmust ja värvidest (Of Dust and Colors), 7–8, 53–4, 139–42
Tormis, Veljo, 60, 107, 140, 147; choir piece and cantata, 161; regi song, 154–5, 158–9, 166
Toronto, 17
transitional space, transitional phenomena, and transitional objects. *See* Winnicott, Donald Woods
Tranströmer, Tomas, 26–7, 30, 169
Tule tagasi helmemänd (Come Back Amber-Pine), 9

Undusk, Jaan. *See* Germans, Baltic
university, alternative to, 59
Uute kivide kasvamine (New Stones Growing), 9, 50

Valge Joon Võrumaa Kohale (A White Line over Võrumaa), 8, 165
Vancouver, 11, 12–13, 79
"Vercingetorix Said," 139–42
Vesilind, Priit. *See* song festival
Viiding, Juhan, 74
Voice of America, 109, 118, 120
Volkslied, 159. *See also* Baltic Germans; regi song; song festival
Vyatka, 4–5. *See also* Gulag

Wandering Border, The, 13, 18
"washing never gets done, The," 131
Watts, Alan, 83
Western mind, 63. *See also* culture and communicative mode
"What, After All, Can I Write?," 149
Whorf, Benjamin Lee, 55
Wiesel, Elie, 12
wild, wildness. *See* Snyder, Gary; flourishing, unforced
Wilson, Edward, 28, 33–4
Winnicott, Donald Woods, 55–6, 69–71, 77, 151
women: affairs, 79, 83–4; conflicted view of, 76–7; gender roles, 82–3; inhibitions, 75, 77; Masing, 92. *See also* love
Wright, Georg Henrik von, 102

Young Estonia, 145–6

Zen Mind, Beginner's Mind. *See* Suzuki, Shunryu
Zerzan, John, 42